MEET ME
IN VENICE

MEET ME IN VENICE

A Chinese Immigrant's Journey from the Far East to the Faraway West

Suzanne Ma

ROWMAN & LITTLEFIELD
Lanham • Boulder • New York • London

Published by Rowman & Littlefield
A wholly owned subsidiary of The Rowman & Littlefield Publishing Group, Inc.
4501 Forbes Boulevard, Suite 200, Lanham, Maryland 20706
www.rowman.com

Unit A, Whitacre Mews, 26-34 Stannary Street, London SE11 4AB, United Kingdom

Distributed by NATIONAL BOOK NETWORK

British Library Cataloguing in Publication Information Available

Library of Congress Cataloging-in-Publication Data

Ma, Suzanne.
  Meet me in Venice : a Chinese immigrant's journey from the far East to the faraway
West / Suzanne Ma.
    pages cm
  Includes bibliographical references.
  ISBN 978-1-4422-3936-4 (cloth : alk. paper) — ISBN 978-1-4422-3937-1
(electronic) 1. Chinese—Italy—Venice—Case studies. 2. Venice (Italy)—Emigration
and immigration—Case studies. 3. China (Italy)—Emigration and immigration—Case
studies. I. Title.
  DG457.C47M3 2015
  305.48'8951045311092—dc23
  [B]
                                                            2014027473

∞™ The paper used in this publication meets the minimum requirements of
American National Standard for Information Sciences—Permanence of Paper
for Printed Library Materials, ANSI/NISO Z39.48-1992.

Printed in the United States of America

To Mom and Dad, for all the opportunities,
and to Marc, for all the possibilities.

少小离家老大回
乡音无改鬓毛衰
儿童相见不相识
笑问客从何处来

I left home as a youth and as an old man returned
My accent unchanged but my temples turned grey
The children see me but don't know who I am
Smiling, they ask: "Stranger, where do you come from?"

"Returning Home"
Tang Dynasty poet Zhang Zhi
44 CE

CONTENTS

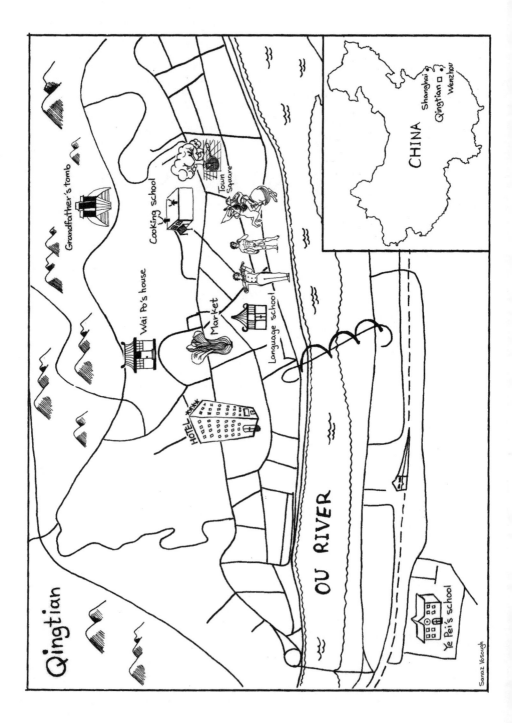

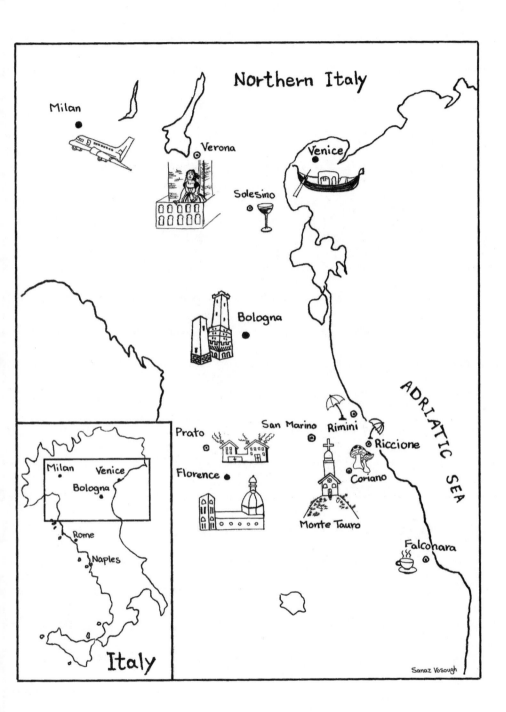

A NOTE ABOUT PRONUNCIATIONS AND SPELLINGS

China's standard romanization system—*hanyu pinyin*—uses the letter "X" for words that make a "sh" sound and "Q" for words that sound like "ch" in English. Thus, Qingtian is pronounced Ching' ti-enne.

PROLOGUE

When my husband's grandfather died, we returned to his ancestral home in eastern China and burned spirit money at his grave. The saffron flames devoured pastel fake euros. Faux American greenbacks were consumed whole. And gold paper ingots glowed like a sunset before they turned black and crumbled to ash. It was important for Grandfather to have foreign currency in the afterlife. For even in death, the dream of making it rich overseas was still very much alive.

In Zhejiang province, not far from the East China Sea, there is a county shaped by the collective belief that emigration brings wealth and prosperity. Emigration is so common that locals often say: "If you are born in Qingtian, you are destined to leave." People started leaving Qingtian in the seventeenth century when, according to local lore, some of the earliest globe-trotters trekked across Siberia to get to Europe. Today, this is a story that continues to inspire generations to leave. In the beginning people were desperate to escape. Qingtian literally means "green fields," but the county's name was betrayed by a barren, mountainous landscape. With so little fertile land in the region, people were starving and isolated with no roads and little infrastructure. Rugged cliffs carved lines into the horizon, closing in on towns and villages like an army of unmovable stone warriors. The migrants first made their way to other regions in China. Some traveled to Japan and other parts of Southeast Asia. Eventually, they boarded ships and then planes bound for every corner of the globe. The habit of migration spread to surrounding regions. Soon, hundreds of thousands were leaving Zhejiang province, fanning out to more than 120 countries around the world. But they were particularly drawn to Europe.

Qingtian is not the kind of place the average tourist visits. It's a small and isolated county, three hundred miles south of Shanghai and nearly forty miles from the coast, and so seemingly unimportant that it wasn't even visible on Google Maps until a few years ago. But this is my husband's ancestral home—a place with a long history of emigration to the outside world. What inspired so many people to leave this landlocked county? How did my husband's family end up spread out across Europe, in Holland, Germany, Austria, Italy, Spain, and Portugal; and why would people from Qingtian continue to leave, as China booms and Europe grapples with a debilitating debt crisis and rising unemployment? I moved to Qingtian in January of 2011 to find the answers to these questions.

My husband, Marc, came with me, and together we discovered a place where people were obsessed with the dream of a life in Europe. To prepare, people enroll in English, French, Dutch, Italian, Spanish, and Portuguese lessons. Jewelers melt down 50-cent euro coins to make lucky pendants and bracelets. Grandmothers gather outside banks and pass the time watching digits on the giant electronic boards rise and fall as exchange rates fluctuate day to day. On the streets, they swap euros for yuan and discuss the latest unemployment figures in Spain as if the news was just another tidbit of small-town gossip. I encounter the children of emigrants, born in Europe but sent back to Qingtian to be raised by relatives while their parents work long hours overseas. They run around town shouting, "*Hola!*" and "*Buongiorno!*" Aged grandparents chase after them, greeting others on the street with the familiar Chinese salutation: *Ni chi le ma?* Have you eaten yet?

Marc's grandmother, whom we call Waipo, still lives in Qingtian. She is more than eighty years old, and every morning before dawn, she climbs the mountain behind the family home, stopping near the top to do her morning exercises. She punches her fists in the air, kicks her legs high until her knees almost touch her forehead. Then, just as the sun peeks out from between the verdant hills, she heads back down, stopping at home to fetch her shopping bags. When Marc and I moved to Qingtian, we lived in the empty apartment above Waipo's place. A decade ago, the family built a seven-story concrete apartment building, tall enough to accommodate Waipo and all six of her children and their families. But with most of the family living overseas, many of the floors remain empty. Other homes in Qingtian were like that, too. When I peered through the windows of such homes, I saw no people, just dry kitchen sinks, flat-screen TVs sealed in plastic wrap, and furniture draped in faded bedsheets. Qingtian was not always this way. For most of her life, Waipo lived in a rustic, two-story adobe house. As her children migrated one by one to Europe, they sent money back home to help build the seven-story concrete apartment, a home for each son and daughter who had left to Europe and who would probably never return.

After her morning hike, Waipo walks downhill toward the center of town and crosses a narrow intersection to get to the market where she buys slabs of fatty pork, leafy greens, and long noodles hand-pulled by a man covered head to toe in flour. The road outside the central market was once a dusty trail lined with hawkers and bicycle pedicabs. Today the hawkers and pedicabs are still there, but they must negotiate the space with luxury sedans, trucks, and motorcycles that honk their horns and stir up dirt and dust. Crossing the narrow intersection can be dangerous, but Waipo, with her sharp brown eyes and her short gray hair curled tight, remains bold and perhaps a little stubborn. "Fear what? This road has and always will be for the people," she declares, remembering a time when she never had to look both ways before crossing the street. Without hesitation, she traipses between the symphony of horns and rumbling engines and emerges on the other side of the road unscathed. I could never do what she did. I once witnessed a car knock a young woman to the ground at that very intersection. She crumbled like tissue paper on the pavement, and when a police officer came to her aid, he took a look at the driver, gave him a smile and a wave, and then told the young woman to get up. She stood up slowly, bare legs shaking with dust, and limped up the hill past an old man who slaughtered white-feathered pigeons in the shadow of an idling Mercedes Benz.

Whenever Marc and I are in Qingtian, one of the first places we visit is the rugged mountain behind his family home. There, we line up for our three ritual kowtows before massive stone tombs carved out of the rock; watching threads of ash swirl around my feet, I think about my in-laws' migration story: how my husband's great-grandfather traveled to Holland by boat and sold peanut candy on the street. The Dutch called such men *pindaman*—peanut men. But in China, he would have been called a rich man. With the Dutch guilders he earned, he returned home to Qingtian to build his family a new house: a two-story structure with an open-air courtyard and several bedrooms held up by strong wooden beams. This house, which still stands today, was built more than seventy years ago. Listening to the old stories can be inspiring and heart wrenching at the same time. I imagine how Great-grandfather must have braved the rough seas for months before finally arriving at the port in Marseilles. I think about how he survived in a foreign land, where people spoke a language he did not understand, ate food he had never tasted before, and looked oddly extraterrestrial with their green and blue eyes and blond hair. It is a tale of first contact and first encounters—a narrative shared by immigrants all around the world, even today. There are now more than 214 million international migrants worldwide. That means one out of every thirty-three persons in the world today is a migrant. If all the migrants gathered in one place, they would form the fifth most populous country in the world. Nearly half of all international migrants are women.

In America we understand, perhaps better than anyone, what it is like to leave your home and start someplace new. Why do people migrate? What attracts or repels migrants? Who wins and who loses with migration? Is it true that immigrants steal jobs away from local workers? Or do they provide fresh labor and talent for ailing economies? What happens to the home countries emigrants leave behind? Immigration is one of the most talked about issues in the world, a testy subject that is taking on an increasingly negative tone in light of the global economic downturn. European governments have only recently started to take multiculturalism and minorities seriously. And with the arrival of so many newcomers, far-right political parties are gaining momentum in immigrant-receiving nations. More than two dozen parties across the European continent have denounced immigrants as invaders, a drain on finite resources, and a threat to already scarce jobs in the workplace. This rhetoric is also heard in America, despite our continent's heritage of immigration, where laws deny undocumented immigrants basic human rights. Still, migrants today will continue to seek opportunities in places they aren't always welcome. Why?

I have always liked writing stories about people on the move. I am drawn to characters who seem a little out of place, and I like talking to people who are searching for something. But getting them to talk is not always easy. The Chinese tend to be wary of strangers, and though I am of Chinese heritage and my husband's family is from southern Zhejiang, I was a stranger in Qingtian. To make things even more difficult, I found many Chinese people shied away from telling their own stories. It can take months and even years to get a person to talk freely, often because they are intensely private and deeply modest. Many of them asked: "Why me? You should interview a famous migrant, someone who has already made it." But I remembered the words of author Peter Hessler who has written extensively about China: "The everyday matters just as much as the exceptional." Eventually, I found those who loved telling their own stories. But they often had an agenda to push and an ego to stroke. During my talks with migrants, I discovered many of them withheld important details—but not always on purpose. After so many years, they had simply forgotten what had happened. And so, asking Chinese migrants to recall their stories of going abroad was like talking to someone with selective amnesia. I realized nothing could replace firsthand observation. I wanted to witness emigration myself. What would it be like to watch a migrant's tale unfold? To see someone prepare to leave home for the first time and travel to a faraway land? What kind of life awaits a Chinese emigrant on a continent that was once the major source of emigration to the

Americas? When she finally arrives, what surprises await her? I hoped to be an emigrant's shadow, to experience the fear, the loneliness, and the courage needed to leave home and go someplace new. But could I meet someone who was willing to share her story with me? Days before the 2011 Lunar New Year, I arrived in Qingtian to find out.

The first time I met Ye Pei she was sixteen years old and was still in high school. I remember she had the face of a doll, pale and round with a set of gleeful eyes shaped like sunflower seeds, her chubby cheeks and rosy complexion framed by a black, boyish bob. While her face radiated innocence, she dressed like a hipster in a white T-shirt and black vest. And like all teenage girls around the world, she spoke fast. Like, very fast. Pei had a tendency to say a lot, all in one breath, jumping from story to story and topic to topic without pausing in between. Sometimes I had trouble keeping up and I would ask her to slow down. I told Pei it was so I could get everything down in my notepad, but most of the time it was because I couldn't understand her. It didn't take long for her to see through my lie. "Your Chinese isn't very good, is it?" Pei said to me not long after we met. Sheepishly, I explained to her that I was born and raised in Canada and had gone to school in the United States. I had only recently come to China to brush up on my Mandarin.

Chinese is a difficult language to learn. When I was a child, my parents enrolled me in Chinese school hoping I could pick up some Mandarin. I resented having to wake up early on a Saturday morning (while my non-Chinese friends could sleep in), and I loathed drawing out characters that didn't make sense to me and sitting through a class where I barely understood the teacher. Both my parents immigrated to North America as students, graduated with degrees from a Canadian university, and found good professional jobs. My mother was a nurse for many years before retiring, and my father continues to work as a financial advisor for a large Canadian bank. For as long as I can remember, my mom and dad spoke English fluently, so as a child I wondered: why is it so important for me to be "Chinese"?

I grew up in a rather "Chinese" household. During the Chinese New Year, I received red pockets stuffed with money; I ate moon cakes during the Mid-Autumn Festival; I went to dim sum on the weekend with my grandparents; and I shopped for groceries in Toronto's satellite Chinatowns. My mother is an excellent cook, and I was lucky to grow up with the tantalizing flavors of a Cantonese kitchen. I have always relished Mom's home-style dishes like soya sauce chicken, steamed whole fish with gingers and scallions, and minced pork patty with salted fish. However, while I had a great interest in Chinese food as a child, I did not have the same passion for the Chinese language.

I was enrolled in a local Chinese school in Toronto that taught us Mandarin, which has been the official language of mainland China since 1913. There is so much diversity when it comes to the Chinese language, which is composed of four main regional language varieties—Mandarin, Wu, Yue, and Min. Some linguists refer to these varieties as separate languages, but because they share a common written form, most Chinese speakers and Chinese linguists refer to them as dialects. These dialects are not mutually intelligible, and within each dialect are hundreds of non-mutually-intelligible subvarieties. My Mom speaks Cantonese, a Yue dialect that is primarily used in southern China. A distinguishing feature of the Chinese language is tonal: Mandarin has four tones and Cantonese has seven.

It was only in my midtwenties when I began to realize how important it was for me to learn Chinese. There was much of Chinese culture, especially the food and the festivals, that I loved. But without a good command of the Chinese language, I felt incomplete in my understanding and appreciation. A desire to better understand my roots began to take hold. I also hoped learning Chinese would give me a professional advantage. Speaking a second language would make me a more versatile journalist, and as China's extraordinary growth dominated the headlines, learning my mother tongue became a bit of an obsession, even prompting me to take a year off work to enroll in an intensive Chinese-language program at Beijing's Tsinghua University in 2007.

In Qingtian people traditionally spoke a form of Wu dialect, which was completely unintelligible to me. The older people in town, like Marc's Waipo, spoke Qingtian dialect exclusively, but people like Pei's parents and Pei herself learned Mandarin in school. Pei looked at me with a sideways glance, curious to meet a Chinese-looking person who didn't speak Chinese very well. What was life like in America? In China, did I consider myself a foreigner? Could I teach her English? And did I know how to speak Italian? Her mother had already been in Italy for five years. Soon, Pei said, she would be joining her. "I'm not sure exactly where Mama lives," Pei said. "But when she first went to Italy, she told me she was in Venice." Then she pressed the palm of her hand into her chubby, pink cheek and spoke dreamily of bridges shaped like crescent moons and a beautiful city of stone, floating atop a glittering lagoon. In Chinese, she referred to Venice as *shui cheng*, "the water city." "When you open the door, there's water everywhere. The water comes right up to your doorstep," she explained in rapid-fire Chinese. "I read about the *shui cheng* in a book once. In my mind, Venice *is* Italy and Italy *is* Venice." I told Pei to stay in touch. Three months later, she left China for Italy. But when I traveled to meet her, she was not in Venice and she was not with her mother.

THE BAR

Never in her life had she been so determined to accomplish something. Anything, really. In China, things were easy. But here in Italy, nothing was.

She had been working at the bar for less than a week when the skin on her hands started to peel. Little bits of skin, translucent and pink, flaked off like Parmesan cheese. Then the cracks appeared. Tiny fissures ruptured at the joints and split her knuckles open. She started to bleed. Everyone told Ye Pei it was normal.

"We all go through this when we first start," her boss said.

"You're just not used to the work," her mother reassured. "It will get better over time."

Pei calculated out of the twelve hours she worked each day, her hands spent six of those hours waterlogged in soapy water. Her tasks at the bar were simple but exhausting—sweep the floors, wipe the counters and tables, wash the dishes, polish the glassware, and scrub the toilets. If the orders were simple enough, sometimes she could mix drinks and serve coffee. But she was never allowed to make cappuccinos. The boss was a Chinese woman with a belly, ruddy cheeks, and dark penciled-in eyebrows, the kind that made her look angry all the time. She insisted the cappuccino was a perfect science, one that a foolish young girl like Pei couldn't even begin to understand. After all, the country's "national breakfast," drunk on an empty stomach before 11 a.m., was an art form, a ritual so ingrained in Italian culture that it would be a sin to get it wrong.

One-third espresso, one-third steamed milk, and one-third foamed milk. You could lose a customer over the slightest imprecision.

"You don't want to mess up an order," the boss told a disheartened Pei. But to work in an Italian bar without learning how to make a cappuccino would be like working in an ice cream shop and never learning to scoop, or working at McDonald's and never learning how to fry. Pei believed she wasn't allowed near the cappuccino machine because once she had mastered the cappuccino, it meant that she was more employable. She could find a job elsewhere, maybe in a city or perhaps somewhere closer to her family. But as it stood, no other bar owner would hire someone incapable of brewing a proper cup. Over time, seventeen-year-old Pei came to realize that learning the art of the cappuccino was the key to her freedom.

In the bar where Pei worked, most of the customers were old men. Some liked to sip their drinks while reading the daily newspaper from Milan, peering over thick-framed glasses perched on the bridge of their big noses. Others preferred the back room where they could sit on high stools that brought them face to face with the bewitching glare of the digital slot machines. Most liked to gather around in groups, flinging down narrow playing cards on the bar's square wooden tables in an intense game of Briscola—their spirited interjections drowned out by the constant grinding of coffee beans, punctuated by the swooshing sound of hot, pressurized water. All of the customers seemed amused to find a Chinese woman behind the bar.

"*Ni hao!*" they'd holler, sauntering up to the bar.

"*Ciao, ciao,*" Pei often replied with a smile. Her short, pageboy bob had grown into dark locks she now piled into a bun atop her head. Her bangs, trimmed neatly above her brow, framed her full face.

"*Bella,*" one old man loved to say, pointing directly at the girl, his finger coming dangerously close to her button nose.

"*Ge-lazie,*" she'd say, blushing.

And that's when the banter came to an awkward halt, for Pei had been in Italy for all but three months. Her vocabulary was extremely limited, though she had picked up a few key words. *Ti Amo*, a phrase Pei liked to write in her diary every night, starting each entry as if she were penning a love letter to her boyfriend back home in China. *Spritz*, because customers often asked for this popular wine-based cocktail. *Gelato*, because it was the only Italian delicacy that Pei truly enjoyed eating. *Grazie*, because it was polite to say this to customers, though Chinese speakers often have difficulty pronouncing "r" and end up making an "l" sound instead. Thus, *Grazie* sounds like *Ge-lazie* and *Roma* comes out *Luo-ma*. And *domani*, because some customers liked to ask whether she would be at work the next day.

The answer to that question was always *sì*, because Pei worked seven days a week. Her shift started at 10:30 every morning and was supposed to end around 3 p.m., although she usually got off closer to 3:30. She had a few hours rest in between before starting work again at 7 p.m., her night shift ending at one or two in the morning or when the final straggler threw up his hands and abandoned the slots for the night. During her shift, Pei was always on her feet but she rarely stood still. When there weren't many customers to tend to, she swept and reswept the floors. She polished the glassware. Then, she took all the liquor bottles down one by one so she could dust the shelves. She took note of the numerous shapes and sizes. There was the green, pear-shaped one with a large, rounded belly; the square and wide-bodied one that always held just a trickle of bronze fluid; and the slender-bodied one filled with what could be mistaken for water, if not for the smell of rubbing alcohol that hit Pei's nostrils the minute she twisted off its cap. It reminded her of the potent Chinese rice liquor, *baijiu*. If you stood close enough to Pei while she worked, sometimes you could hear the sound of her tongue flicking the roof of her mouth: "Tttttttrrrrrrrr. Tttttttttrrrrr." She was practicing how to roll her Rs. Within days her hands had become swollen and blistered, but it was after her first day when her feet trembled with fatigue. Her heels ached and her toes grew tender. Pei watched in awe as her body adapted and grew accustomed to the strain. The soles on her feet hardened and her calves bulged. For her labor, she was paid 500 euros a month (about $690 USD at the time) and the boss let Pei stay in a spare bedroom in her second-floor apartment just a few minutes walk from the bar.

"Can I come up and see your room?" I asked Pei one night.

"No, I don't think Ayi would like that," she replied, looking sorry. "I feel terrible I cannot invite you in. It's just that . . . it's not my home."

"Tell me what your room looks like."

"It's small, but I have a bed, a desk and a dresser. It's not bad at all," she said. "It just isn't home."

When Pei wasn't in her room, she was at work. When she wasn't at work, she could be found in her room, where she tenderly rubbed lotion into her swollen hands. She spent late nights writing in her diary and thumbing through her Chinese-Italian dictionary, placing the thick hardcover book on her lap until her thighs turned numb. Her parents called every day to check in on her, but she could never tell them how she truly felt. She whispered through the receiver and assured them she was fine. She didn't dare to say anything else, for the walls were thin and Ayi and her family would certainly overhear her. This wasn't the life Pei envisioned for herself in Italy. But for a girl who came from a small mountain town in eastern China, working at this bar was a painful yet valuable opportunity she could not refuse. "I will work very hard to learn Italian and to acquire the skills necessary for running a bar. This way, Mama and Baba can have an early retirement," Pei wrote in her diary one night. "This bar has been open for four years and now they are millionaires. How accomplished they are! I am not jealous of them because I know one day our family will be even better off. I firmly believe it!"

Never in her life had she been so determined to accomplish something. Anything, really. In China, things were easy. But here in Italy, nothing was. Pei was determined to change her family's circumstances—to work hard, send her earnings back to her parents, and help them save enough money to one day open their own cappuccino bar. Every Chinese migrant went abroad with a similar plan in mind. Working for others was a stepping stone to becoming your own *lao ban*—your own boss. Pei's resolve started in her gut, stirring her awake every morning. It propelled her out of bed and to the bar, pumping adrenaline through her veins and into her calves. It fueled her through the long days until she finally returned to her room, where the urgency remained, keeping her awake as she pored over the Chinese-Italian dictionary until her eyelids grew heavy and finally drooped to a close. "I am no longer in a country where everything is simple and straightforward," she told me. "In China, I was never under any real pressure. Now I am forced to make plans for myself, to make things right for me and my family." At seventeen years of age, Pei had taken it upon herself to earn enough money so her parents could soon retire.

Three months earlier, her priorities couldn't have been more different. She was a high school student in China whose major preoccupation was hanging out with her new boyfriend, a quiet and gangly boy named Li Jie. He was at least a head taller than she, and Pei loved pressing her toes in the ground as she raised her face upward to see his. Though they saw each other every day in school, their time together spilled into the evenings when they roamed through town, snacking on skewers and soupy wontons and hanging out at the Internet café. Pei spent hours uploading photos to her blog, chatting online with friends, and feeding her virtual fish. She had become a cyber-entrepreneur, operating a virtual hair salon and restaurant. Li Jie preferred racing sports cars around a virtual track in online tournaments that lasted through the night. Now that Ye Pei was in Italy, she had left Li Jie and that virtual world behind in China. The town of Solesino was her bleak reality.

There are no canals here. There are no crescent-shaped bridges. No sleek, black gondolas. No glittering lagoon. Venice, the water city, is more than two hours away by train, and to catch it, you have to get on a bus and head for the next town because there is no train station in Solesino. The road into town is flanked by long parcels of land, some pea green and some wheat gold, giving way to two-story pale yellow homes topped with earthy red tiles. A tall, blue steeple marks the center of town, where there is one church, one cemetery, one nursery school, one elementary school, one junior high, one police station, one sports hall, and more than a dozen bars. At least two of the bars in town are run by Chinese families, and their presence is a sign that immigrants are here to stay. Locals say they first started noticing Chinese immigrants in Solesino about ten years ago at the weekly Sunday market. They all seemed more like nomads then, traveling in a caravan of big white vans that rumbled past the fields, sending slight tremors across the terra-cotta rooftops. Once in town, their vans fold open like a Transformer gearing up for battle: white shelves stretch out like arms and the wiry ribs of a canopy unravel over a display of colorful football jerseys, chiffon blouses, knit sweaters, and fake leather jackets. Bins overflow with polka dot socks, lacy bras, and spandex underwear, and the Chinese haggle with their customers, their dialogue limited to *uno, due, tre* and a lot of sign language.

"The entire street will be lined with stalls!" Pei told me one fall evening in Solesino. "There are numerous vendors, even Chinese vendors! And there are many, many things for sale." She looked forward to the commotion and chaos every Sunday. During the week, Solesino was far too quiet and too clean for her liking. Back home in China, hawkers lined the streets, their knickknacks scattered across tattered tarps and their wicker baskets piled full of pears and *yangmei*—crimson, dimpled bayberries the size of a ping pong ball. But what Pei missed most was the street food. Vendors roasted sweet potatoes and chestnuts in smoldering charcoal, minced pork was tucked inside thin wonton wrappers dusted in flour, and lamb kebabs flecked with cumin and chili pepper sizzled over a smoking barbecue. Every night, smoke and steam threaded its way through Qingtian's streets. The Sunday market in Solesino didn't have roasted chestnuts or wonton soup or lamb kebabs, but tomatoes and artichokes were piled into pyramids and crispy French fries were scooped into paper cones. Of course, Pei would not see any of this for herself. Sundays were one of the busiest days at the bar, and she could never steal away, not even for a few minutes, to visit the market. Instead, from behind the bar, she watched the vendors drive into town and set up their stalls, and eventually her hungry eyes would follow the children who clutched oil-stained cones overflowing with fries as golden as corn.

While Pei was at work, I shopped around the market without her. One day, I found myself in front of a mobile food van selling seafood. I watched a young Italian woman pour fried fish into a tray bathed in the red glare of a heat lamp, and I noticed that the tip of her nose was kissed pink by the sun. "I just got back from Kenya," Laura Cavaliere explained in fluent English. Laura was a globe-trotter who made every effort to learn about the outside world, either by going to those far-flung destinations herself or hosting international students at her home in Solesino. Laura and her parents recently took in a student from China, who stayed with them for ten months. Laura had a master's degree in psychology from an Italian university. But like many young and educated Italians, she could not find a job, so she helped her parents dole out seafood at the market. Just meters away from where her van was parked, Chinese merchants were busy selling winter sweaters. I asked her what the townspeople thought of the migrants in their midst. "The Chinese are a mystery to most Italians," Laura said. "They stay in their circles. When they go out, they never walk alone. They are always with other Chinese." It was especially rare for the migrants to engage in long or meaningful conversations with others, Laura observed. "We have brief exchanges, but it never goes deeper than that. I think integrating is very hard for them." For as long as Laura could remember, Bar Girasole had been owned by Italians. When the Chinese family moved in five years ago, locals worried the bar would change. It wasn't just happening in Solesino. The Chinese seemed to be everywhere. The migrants were drawn to Italy's textile and manufacturing industries, which provided ample employment opportunities for unskilled workers, and to the country's frequent amnesties that gave undocumented migrants a chance to gain lawful residency. In the early 2000s, undocumented Chinese residents were estimated to represent 10 to 15 percent of the total Chinese migrant population in Italy. Experts believe that number has since dropped due to amnesties. Since 2000, the number of registered Chinese residents in Italy has swelled from approximately sixty thousand to nearly three hundred thousand in 2014.

If Pei could read the newspapers, she would have learned that the press liked to describe this influx in terrifying yet poetic ways: immigrants from the Far East are "an invading army of dragons." Pei's illiteracy shielded her from xenophobic headlines and editorials. For her, thumbing through her Chinese-Italian dictionary every night was already causing her head to spin. If Italian was supposed to be a romantic language, well, it certainly came with all the headaches and complexities of a true romance.

"It is so much simpler to just read and write in Chinese," Pei muttered.

"But learning a Roman alphabet has its advantages," I countered. "Once you know your ABCs, you can learn to read and write pretty quickly."

"That's not the case for me," Pei said. "Chinese words are not just words. They are symbols. Every wisp and every stroke *means* something." Tenses and conjugations were especially hard for her to grasp. In Chinese, there is no plural and verbs don't change even if an action takes place in the past, present, or future. And Pei couldn't help but wonder: why did objects have to be either masculine or feminine? Was it *il cappuccino* or *lo cappuccino*? Everything seemed so needlessly complicated. If Pei could read the papers, she would have learned that Italian reporters liked to call Chinatown an ethnic ghetto where workers hide in the shadows. And no doubt, she would have seen the word *clandestini*—a word that means illegal or undocumented, but comes loaded with so many other connotations. Criminal, terrorist, drug dealer, pimp, thief. The immigrants seldom respond to such allegations. And the journalists have fun with this, too. Speaking with the Chinese is like "having a dialogue with ghosts." A reporter's questions are met with "a wall of silence." Was there a point to responding? Would it help dispel some of the rumors? The Chinese are silent for more practical reasons. Immigrants like Pei don't have the ability to respond, and many others don't have the time to engage in any kind of dialogue because they are all too busy working. And so everyone agrees that the Macedonians, the Albanians, and even the Moroccans and Romanians have an easier time integrating. The Chinese don't even try: "Few know Italian—despite having Italian residency for years. Many will soon have the right to vote, having received full Italian citizenship, making decisions for us," a newspaper in the northern city of Brescia writes. "It doesn't matter that they can only communicate with ideograms and have little interest in learning about the world outside their community."

Thousands of Chinese migrants were coming to Italy every year, but they managed to remain invisible for a long time. Most found work in garment work-shops that kept them out of sight and far removed from mainstream society. Newcomers like Pei, however, were changing all that. By working at a bar, she had stepped into the very heart of contemporary Italian civilization—a place where people came not only to sip their cappuccinos and down their espressos but to share life's news with old friends. In the bar, Pei poured drinks for men who gathered to celebrate a birthday and she poured more when they came to-gether to mourn a death. She congratulated a particularly happy man when he bought a round of drinks for his friends and tried to comfort the miserable ones who drank their sorrows away with wine. It was here in the bar where Chinese immigrants became actors on the Italian stage, no longer stagehands who hid behind the heavy curtains that cloaked the windows of a garment workshop. Every dark and bitter cup of coffee Pei brewed gave her a chance, however brief, to interact with Italians. This was how she judged them. Not by what she heard or by what she might someday read. She judged Italians by the way customers treated her, and she found herself drawn to the kindness of many strangers. Some of her customers had been to China before.

"Next time I go to China, I'll bring you with me," one man teased, leaning over the bar counter.

Pei played along and nodded her head enthusiastically at the offer. "*Sì signore*," she said. "*Mi piace.*" *I like.* A few customers even coaxed Pei into giving them her mobile phone number. When the old men called her, Pei flipped open her pink cell phone and put the receiver to her ear, rolling her eyes and speaking broken Italian: "*Uuuh? Sì, sì . . . Uuuh? Domani. Sì, sì, sì.*" Even though she seemed annoyed by the frequent phone calls, the minute-long exchanges left Pei feeling needed or even missed.

Everyone back home in China warned Pei about the foreigners. The *lao wai*. "Those *lao wai* bosses can't be trusted," they said. "You will be cheated out of your wages and you won't even know it!" But Pei's experiences in Italy told her otherwise. A few weeks after she first arrived from China, she found herself adrift in a crowded train station. Passengers brushed past her, lugging suitcases and enormous backpacks. Sweat beaded on her forehead as she approached a few stationary travelers, her train ticket crumpled in her clammy hand. All she could hear was the sound of her own hammering heart when she plucked up the courage to step forward and speak: "Padua? Padua?" It was the only Italian word she could muster in that moment—the name of the city she needed to head toward. Pei was surprised when the Italians pointed her in the direction of the right platform. "Even if you can't speak the language, the Italians are very smart. They can figure out what you want," she said. Then there was the time Pei went into a government office to pick up her newly minted ID card.

"*Buongiorno signora*, how can I help you?" the clerk asked. Dry mouthed, Pei blinked. Thoughts scrambled around in her brain and a choking sensation clogged her throat. The clerk saw the panic in her eyes, turned to his computer, and accessed an online translation website. His fingers moved swiftly across the keyboard, and within seconds his sentence was translated into a string of Chinese characters. Pei heaved a sigh of relief. She leaned closer, nodded her head, then typed a few Chinese characters in response. With the click of a mouse, the Italian translation appeared a few seconds later. It was almost instant communication. "I think the Italians are very nice and have excellent manners," she said. "They go out of their way to help you."

Pei discovered Italians weren't as bad as they were made out to be. Sometimes, it was her fellow Chinese emigrants she needed to be wary of. An extensive and powerful network helped a newcomer like Pei find a job in a bad economy. But her working arrangement—typical for new emigrants arriving from China—left her completely dependent on her employer. Pei called her boss *Ayi*. It means Auntie and it is an affectionate, respectful title given to female relatives or close friends of the family. Ayi hailed from the same mountainous county Pei and her family came from, Qingtian. To come from the same hometown meant that you were automatically friends, neighbors, comrades, even family. Pei lived with Ayi, ate meals with her, and worked side by side with her every day at the bar, but Ayi was not her friend and certainly not her family. It seemed nothing she did was right in Ayi's eyes. There were many rules and Pei tried in vain to follow them.

"Stop making that strange sound with your tongue!" Ayi chided when she overheard Pei rolling her Rs.

"Use both hands when carrying the tray!"

"Do not mop the bathroom floors until the last customer leaves!" Ayi scolded one night. But the next day, as Pei waited for the bar to empty out, Ayi was furious. "Why are you not cleaning the floors?"

"I am sorry, Ayi," she apologized, grabbing the mop. But she made a mental note: "When I am my own boss, I will remember what it was like to be a worker," she thought. "I will treat my workers as partners. People I can work with, not people who work under me." As a chilly fog descended upon the town in late November, Pei shivered when she went outside to put the patio furniture away. As she stacked the chairs one on top of the other, her raw hands made contact with the frigid steel. Her blisters tingled like the prick of a hundred needles. Soon after that, Pei began wearing gloves to work. Ayi spoke up in an exasperated tone: "Child, surely it isn't that cold outside!" Pei said nothing, but after stumbling home one night at the end of another long shift, she wrote it all down in her diary: "This kind of life lets me profoundly feel what Mama experienced those five years when she was all by herself in a foreign country. What an isolating life!"

Pei's isolation was compounded by feelings of deference and gratitude, especially when Ayi reminded her that she was doing her a favor. "We did not have to take you in," she said. "It was only because your mother called me so many times that I agreed to hire you." Pei's mother was the first to come to Italy. She found work in a garment factory near the city of Padua where she met Ayi. Now Pei's mother worked on a mushroom farm one hundred miles away. She wasn't able to get her daughter a job at the farm, and she didn't want Pei working for a stranger. She remembered her friend from the factory. Maybe she needed a pair of extra hands at the bar in Solesino? At the time, it seemed like a good place for her Pei. In many ways, the Chinese aren't so different from the Italians. Both communities rely on *raccomandazione*—personal connections. In Chinese, it's called *guan xi*, and such relationships pave a smoother path for emigrants like Pei. *Guan xi* helped her find a job and a place to stay. *Guan xi* can get you a loan in order to kick-start a new business venture. *Guan xi* can introduce you to your future husband or wife, if matchmaking is what you need. In other words, *guan xi* can hook you up in more ways than one. No doubt *guan xi* can get you far, but it can also make life more difficult for you. Workers who wish to maintain good *guan xi* with their bosses might be afraid to say no to an extra shift or to ask for a raise. Pei was entitled to a day off and, after a month's work, to a 50 euro raise. But she said nothing. She didn't want to sour her *guan xi* with Ayi. A new emigrant often knowingly entered into such working arrangements. Pei insisted it wasn't exploitation. It was an opportunity, she said. A chance to acquire new skills and gain better prospects. During those hard months in Solesino, Pei learned to hold her tongue and tried to be thankful for her job. That's what it is like to be raised Chinese, she said. You are taught to desire nothing, to accept everything, and most importantly, to eat your own bitterness. "I am learning to keep my grievances in my heart," she wrote in her diary. "No one will hear my pain. I must swallow my tears. When I one day leave this bar, I will be grateful to them for the experience!"

LEAVING CHINA

By a stream and a hill is a little town
With narrow streets and small houses
There are not many shops but I have bought cakes
And one can buy wine at the New Year
By a stream and a hill I have a brother
This little town is my home

—Chinese coolie song

She was only twelve years old, but she remembers watching the clock that cold February morning. The skies were gray, and the clouds gathered up in tight bales, ready to burst with rain. Ye Pei watched her breath waft out in front of her like incense blowing off candle sticks. Ten minutes past seven. That was when her mother left for the airport. She was not allowed to go with her, and Pei remembers being sent off to school instead. Gasping for breath in between sobs, she grabbed her book bag as tears flowed down her red face. Leaving China was her father's idea, not her mother's. But it was her mother's visa that came through in the end, and she was forced to pack her bags and head to Italy alone. Pei's mother, Fen, had absolutely no interest in going abroad. Fen was a stay-at-home mom—the one who took care of the kids while her husband worked on the assembly line, stitching leather shoes in a factory about forty miles away. The couple often spent months at a time apart. Even so, their feelings for each other remained strong. Her husband, Shen, was a strong man with a tanned, pudgy face and kind, oval eyes. Physically, he was the exact opposite of Fen, who was just five feet tall, with pale skin that wrapped tightly around small bones. The two had known each other since childhood and for the longest time, Shen called Fen his *tutu*, his "little rabbit." When he came home to visit after his many months in the factory, he cupped his thick hands to his round face and called to his wife in a high-pitched coo: "*Tooooo-tooooooo!*" Fen was just twenty years old when she married Shen. A year later Pei was born. While many families in China are bound by the one-child policy, rural families are allowed to have a second child if the first is a girl. And so two years later Ye Mao, a boy, was born. It was Shen who always wanted to go abroad. He earned the equivalent of just a few dollars an hour working at the leather shoe factory, and like everyone else from Qingtian, he had heard about the riches he could make in Europe.

They say the people of Qingtian have been leaving the barren mountains behind for three hundred years for a chance to make it rich elsewhere. The rocky terrain left too little fertile land for farming and made it difficult to support any sort of major industry, except one. Rocks were mined from the cliffs, and some young men apprenticed as soapstone carvers, spending months inside dusty workshops transforming uncarved blocks of semiprecious rock into stunning sceneries and landscapes. Shen hadn't dabbled in rock sculpting in his youth, as many of the other local men had done. His stubby hands were not designed for such careful and fine sculpting. But he had grown up hearing the stories of famed Qingtian stone carvers said to be the county's first migrants. They walked across Siberia to get to Europe, where they peddled those beautiful hand-carved soapstones on the street. There was the tale of one particular rock carver who had traveled from Qingtian all the way to the land of windmills and wooden clogs. The lucky man had a chance encounter with the Dutch queen, and when he presented her with his most exquisite sculpture depicting two lions playing with an oversized pearl, the queen praised its beauty. Her public admiration sent Dutch aristocrats rushing to the streets to offer Chinese peddlers large sums of money in exchange for stones. Then there was the other famed sculptor who had the chance to display his work at an island in the East China Sea where a band of foreign tourists purchased some of his carvings. The sale inspired him and a small group of carvers and traders to embark for Europe on a French boat leaving from Vietnam. By the early 1900s, it is said enough Qingtian natives were making the trip for one of them to operate a hotel in Marseilles to accommodate new arrivals and run a parallel business recruiting sailors for European shipping companies. Whether these stories are true or not, they inspired generations of people to emigrate, fueling the belief that Europe was a gold mine for opportunity and fortune.

The Chinese have been leaving China for centuries, crossing land and sea in search of wealth and opportunity. One of the most famous travelers was a navy admiral in the imperial Ming Dynasty who embarked on seven epic voyages that sailed as far as Africa nearly a century before Christopher Columbus's arrival in the Americas. Zheng He was an imperial court eunuch— kidnapped as a boy from his home in western China and ritually castrated—before he rose to the top of the imperial hierarchy, becoming a chief aide and key wartime strategist. Zheng He was eventually chosen to lead one of the most powerful naval forces ever assembled: from 1405 to 1433, he journeyed throughout Southeast Asia, to India and to the Middle East before reaching East Africa. Along the way he gifted gold, porcelain, and silk to his hosts, and in return his fleet returned to China with exotic goods like camels, zebras, giraffes, ostriches, and ivory. The voyages allowed the admiral to establish trade relations, draft practical maps, and record sailing directions. But this age of discovery did not last long. Late Ming emperors, fearing that seafarers might trade, amass wealth, and one day plot against them, began discouraging travel and overseas trading. They even decreed anyone who left and came back should be beheaded. China turned inward, and a formal ban on emigration remained in effect until 1893. Despite this, legions of Chinese people, largely merchants, traders, and laborers, continued to leave in the nineteenth century. It was never the migrant's intention to leave the homeland permanently. No, the idea was to sojourn—temporarily migrate elsewhere, struggle and save, and then return home to China a rich man.

Not everyone could afford passage abroad. Scores of Chinese workers were kidnapped and then bought and sold on the ruins of the African slave trade. Coolies—a Hindi word used by the Portuguese to describe hired workers in India—came to mean transient laborer; in Chinese the word *kuli* means bitter strength. Chinese coolies rushed to California, to Canada, and to Australia to pan for gold. They worked as sailors for European shipping companies and eventually came to cluster in the port cities of London, Hamburg, Lyon, and Rotterdam. Coolies went to India, to South America, to Africa and pretty much anywhere there was a living to be made—anywhere outside of China. Migrants poured forth from the coastal Chinese provinces, faint with hunger but full of hope, eagerly searching for stability that was missing in the homeland. China was a divisive and hierarchical place prone to famine and ravaged by natural disasters, economic crises, war, and rebellion. People were desperate to get away from it all.

In the eighteenth century, when China attempted to suppress the opium trade, British warships sailed into the Pearl River Delta and violently overthrew the country's coastal defenses, forcing the Chinese to agree to a series of humiliating treaties and concessions. The Taiping rebellion killed more than twenty million people between 1850 and 1864 when a man claiming to be

Jesus's younger brother enlisted a massive army and tried to bring about major political and religious change. The Japanese occupied the country from 1937 to 1945, pillaging cities, brutally murdering citizens, and raping and mutilating women. When the Japanese left, the Chinese turned on each other. It was the Communists who eventually triumphed over the Nationalists, and the country's new leader, Chairman Mao Zedong, began subjecting his people to various social experiments, starting with the Great Leap Forward in 1958. Mao forced peasants into collective farms, causing mass starvation; then he kick-started the Cultural Revolution in 1966, forming a Red Army of impressionable youth who forced their college professors to work as peasants and laborers in the fields and factories. The Red Army murdered those suspected of bourgeois sympathies, and it is estimated as many as seventy million people died in the course of a decade. In recent years, China has witnessed more bloodshed, prompting more waves of migration. With such a tumultuous history, it's not surprising why so many Chinese have sought better fortunes abroad.

The first time I heard about the Chinese Labor Corps was when a local historian in Qingtian mentioned that 140,000 Chinese men were recruited by the Allies during the First World War to fill a critical labor shortage at the Western Front. He said 2,000 men were recruited from Qingtian and that the Corps represented one of the first major waves of migration from China to Europe. I searched online and pored through history books to learn more. I discovered the Chinese Labor Corps fulfilled many duties including unloading cargo ships and trains, chopping down trees for timber, and maintaining docks, railways, roads, and airfields. Skilled mechanics repaired vehicles and worked on tanks. Some historians say they even helped dig trenches. Later, after the Armistice, the Chinese stayed behind to clean up the mess. As late as 1919, Chinese laborers remained in France and Belgium to help clear the rubble, bury the dead, and clean up the battlefields. Those who enlisted in the Chinese Labor Corps were promised daily wages, food, clothing, and medical support. Contracts drafted by British and French recruiting officers also pledged regular payments for the laborers' families. Such rewards were tempting enough to encourage thousands of men to sign up for three years of work on the front lines of a war they knew very little about. For a country searching for a new national identity, participating in the war was a chance for China to gain a foothold in the emerging international order.

Most of the laborers recruited by the British came from the northeast provinces of Shandong and present-day Hebei. The French also recruited laborers from China's southern provinces. Some of the men were soldiers or former soldiers, though a large number were skilled workers like carpenters, blacksmiths, and mechanics. Recruiting officers seemed to prefer enlisting men from the north of China, who were deemed bigger and stronger than men from the south. A YMCA communiqué described the men as having "superior physique and greater endurance." Meanwhile, a *New York Times* article in 1917 reported "the best selected stock" was going to France, with a "large percentage" of them six feet tall. After the war, many of the surviving Chinese laborers returned home to China but a few thousand stayed behind. They found factory jobs in France and some married French women, despite French and Chinese governments discouraging the unions. They formed the first rooted Chinese community in Paris, setting up the city's first Chinatown around the Gare de Lyon train station. The Corps was the largest ethnic minority group to participate in the Great War, but I was surprised to discover how their contributions have been largely forgotten, their stories left out of official histories. "How many lives have vanished into obscurity?" I thought. "And how many other Chinese immigrant tales are left untold?"

No one knows exactly how many ethnic Chinese live outside of China today, but it is estimated there are about sixty million out there. Collectively they make up the largest diaspora in the world. Wherever the Chinese have gone, they have gained a reputation for their *kuli*. Even today, at least seven in ten Americans describe the Chinese as hardworking, competitive, and inventive, according to the Pew Research Center. In the early days, migrants set off with the promise to work so hard they would spit blood from their beating hearts. They pledged to send money home to care for their families and to one day return dressed in silk robes. While they sweat and toiled overseas, their hearts remained in China. This passionate attachment to the homeland was rooted in the idea of filial piety—revering parents while they were alive—and ancestor worship—honoring their spirits when they were dead. The Chinese kept detailed genealogical records, and wherever they went, they maintained an intense preoccupation with origins and identity. Far away from home, this preoccupation only intensified and manifested itself in "Chinatowns" that sprang up all around the world. No matter how far they ventured, China remained the center of the universe. China, *zhong guo*, literally means "the central nation" or "the middle kingdom." And when children like Ye Pei studied maps in school, China was always at the center of the atlas, with the Americas to the east and Europe to the west.

Ye Pei's father earned no more than a few dollars an hour working at the leather shoe factory some forty miles from Qingtian. This was a typical wage for a factory worker in China, but it was a fraction of what Shen's neighbors and friends were earning in Europe. When he returned home to see Fen and the kids, he was besieged with reminders of wealth that could be earned if he dared to venture abroad. The migrants no longer sent money home to build houses made of stone and wood. Now they built modern apartment buildings for their extended families and commissioned massive hillside tombs to honor their ancestors. They dressed their loved ones in name-brand clothes and cruised around Qingtian in luxury cars. In China, great importance is placed on one's "face" or *mianzi*. When talking about *mianzi*, the Chinese are not referring to a face that can be washed or shaved, but to a face that can be "lost" and "fought for" and even "granted." To lose face is to be disgraced; to fight for face is to find a way to preserve your dignity; and to grant face is to give someone a chance to regain his lost honor.

Shen did what any respectable Chinese man would do. He fought for his *mianzi* and decided he too would go abroad. He set his hopes on Italy, where he planned to work in a factory doing what he did best—stitching leather shoes. There were ample employment opportunities for unskilled workers in the country's textile industry, and everyone in Qingtian was talking about it. *Yidali* was a place where you could "get rich quickly." Shen submitted an application for a worker's visa to the Italian consulate in Shanghai and expected to hear back soon. Weeks turned into months, months into a half-year. Still, he received no reply. Shen grew impatient. On a whim, he asked his wife to put in an application. "Just to see what happens," he said at the time. It took just two months for Fen's application to be approved. She spent the next few days crying at home. The pounding in her chest refused to go away as she thought about leaving her husband and her children behind. She would be moving to a strange country where she did not speak the language and where she knew no one. "My heart is not prepared for this," she told Shen, who held onto his wife's cold hands, feeling perhaps just as awful as she. Shen had never planned on his wife going to *Yidali* alone. After all he was the man of the house, the breadwinner, the one who always took care of the family. Why would the consulate approve one visa and reject another? Emigrants are never given an answer to this question. The people in Qingtian hold fate accountable. It makes leaving more bearable, as if it was never your decision to make in the first place. *If you are born in Qingtian, you are destined to leave.* But everyone leaves in their own time, whether they are ready or not.

Fen looked her children in the eye and told them she would be home in a few years. Pei and Mao nodded solemnly, not realizing how much they would grow and change by the time they saw her again in Italy. Fen's visa was arranged by a Qingtian man who ran a Chinese restaurant near Venice. On paper, he hired her to be a cook in his kitchen. Off the record, she paid him $19,000 for his "help."

Fen asked for many favors and borrowed as much as she could from family and friends. But when she arrived in Italy, the restaurateur took the money and told her there was no work. She scoured the classifieds in the local Chinese-language newspaper and found a job in a Chinese-run factory in Padua, a city thirty miles west of Venice. She worked thirteen hours a day, but she didn't have to sew. She took a notepad and pen and went around the factory keeping track of the merchandise and stock. The factory's main task was to remove "Made in China" labels on clothes and replace them with "Made in Italy" tags. Fen did not tell her children about the Chinese restaurant owner who took her money without offering her the employment he promised. Nor did she tell them about how frightened she was when she first arrived, unable to speak a word of Italian. She didn't tell them how she had bounced from factory to factory before she was able to find steady work. And because Ye Pei wouldn't have known where the city of Padua was, when Fen first telephoned home, she told her daughter she was calling from Venice.

"That's the water city, isn't it?" Pei asked. "There are lots of bridges and when you open the door, there is water everywhere. The water comes right up to your doorstep, doesn't it?"

"Yes," her mother said. "It is very beautiful. There are gondolas everywhere." Pei remembered reading about Venice in a schoolbook. Now, hearing her mother's voice through a garbled phone connection, she longed to be there with her. Together, they could wander across those crescent-moon bridges, roam through narrow alleyways, and watch Venetians ride their sleek, black boats to run even the simplest of errands, like going to the grocery store. She wasn't sure if she would be brave enough to get on a gondola herself. She didn't know how to swim and was deathly afraid of water. "You have to listen to your father from now on," her mother said. "I'll be home in two years."

"At first, I believed her," Pei told me when we first met one spring day in 2011. "But it has been five years now and she has not been back to China since."

In Qingtian, meeting people who dreamed of a life abroad was easy. Getting them to open up about their dreams was not. I was looking to meet migrants who were talkative and candid, honest and open-minded. While the Chinese people can be extremely straightforward about some things—"What's your age?" "How much money do you make?" "Why aren't you married yet? You're so old!"—it was difficult to find people who were completely truthful about their feelings. During my first month in Qingtian, I encountered at least one or two potential migrants every day. A young man, who told me he wanted to go to Spain, washed my hair at a salon. A sales rep, who dreamed of going to Holland, tried to sell me a gym membership. One young woman, considering going to Italy, helped me with my China Mobile phone plan when I first arrived in Qingtian. Zhan Junjun was dressed like a stewardess in a navy blue pantsuit with a matching handkerchief tied around her neck. She was nineteen years old, professional and courteous, and during our brief conversation, she told me she was planning to go to *Yidali*—Italy.

"Why Italy?" I asked.

"My sister is already there," she said.

"Where does your sister live?"

"Rome . . . I think."

"And why are you motivated to go abroad?"

"Well, everyone's doing it," Junjun replied with a shrug. And then, because I was asking her so many questions, Junjun got suspicious. She leaned forward, her voice dropping to a whisper. "Are you one of those people who . . . you know . . . " She trailed off and I leaned forward, waiting to hear the end of her question. "You know . . . " I met her gaze and raised my eyebrow. She tried again: "One of those who . . . " Finally, she gathered enough courage to spit it out: "Someone who brings people out?" Brings people out. It took me a few seconds to understand what she meant. Then I felt my cheeks burn. Junjun was asking if I was *she tou*, a snakehead, the Chinese word for human smuggler! I shook my head and bashfully told her no. Like the coyotes who smuggle people across the U.S.-Mexico border, snakeheads are Chinese gang members who smuggle people out of China to other countries. They often use stolen or altered passports and improperly obtain visas. Sometimes they form bogus business delegations and tour groups as a way of evading immigration controls. Smuggling is different from human trafficking, where people are bought and sold into forced labor and sexual slavery. Those who are smuggled willfully agree to being illegally transported into another country.

A few weeks after I first arrived in Qingtian, I visited the old family home in the village of Shabu. There, in the drawer of an old dresser, my husband's great-uncle kept a book that charted six generations of family genealogy that I hoped to see. I boarded a grubby bus headed west toward the village of Shabu where more than half of the 439 households shared the same surname as my husband Marc—Guo. Great-uncle was a retired farmer who lived in a rustic two-story structure of faded timber. Holding up weathered terra-cotta roof tiles was a network of interlocking wooden supports, one of the most important elements in traditional Chinese architecture and China's major contribution to worldwide architectural technology. Craftsmen had cut the wooden pieces to fit perfectly so that no glue, screws, or bolts were necessary to hold the roof up. Two pairs of portraits hung side by side on the old walls: photographs of Marc's great-grandfather and great-grandmother, and drawings of Marc's great-great-grandfather and great-great-grandmother. Like all old portraits, these ancestors watch over the house with solemn black-and-white expressions.

Great-uncle retreated to his bedroom to retrieve the tattered book from his dresser. A bare lightbulb swung from the ceiling of the room cluttered with shoe boxes and shopping bags. In the center of it all stood an antique canopy bed carved out of rosewood. The wood was now faded and worn, but I could still make out carvings of plum blossoms—which represent renewal, perseverance, and purity—and cranes—representing happiness and immortality. We stood in his open-air courtyard, sipping leafy green tea and soaking in the sunshine on that cold winter day, poring over all the dates and names that had to be read in the traditional Chinese way—vertically and from right to left. I saw a long tradition of going abroad: great-grandfathers, grandfathers, grandmothers, aunts and uncles and cousins that had settled all over Europe. They went to Holland, Belgium, France, Germany, Italy, Spain, Portugal, and Austria. Great-uncle had four children himself—his three eldest daughters all lived in Spain and the youngest child had yet to leave. His name was Guo Zhongyi, but everyone in the family called him by his nickname: Ah Dai. As I turned the thin, yellowing pages of the family book, I learned that it was my husband's great-grandfather who first went to Holland, where he sold peanut cookies on the street. The Chinese peanut trade began in 1931 when an unemployed Chinese seaman began making and selling what the Dutch called *pindakoekjes*, small cookies made of peanuts and caramelized sugar. The idea spread and soon the Chinese *pinda-man* became a familiar sight throughout the Netherlands. With the money he earned, my husband's great-grandfather returned to China to build the house in Shabu where Marc's great-uncle now lived. It was proof that going abroad was the only way to feed one's family.

For as long as people have been leaving Qingtian, they have been sending money home. Remittances were first used to construct homes like the one in Shabu. Later, many families built apartment buildings that could house several generations of one family all in one building. Once they took care of the living, they turned to the dead. Massive stone graves were carved out of steep hillsides to honor the family's ancestors. Emigrants then sent money home to help pave new roads and mountain paths, to renovate temples, and eventually to build new bridges over the rivers linking one town to the next. They erected statues in local parks: a sculpture of Napoleon Bonaparte on his horse was a gift from French migrants, a figure of Johann Strauss wielding his gold violin was bank-rolled by migrants in Austria, and migrants in Italy paid for a not-so-accurate replica of Michelangelo's David. In Florence, the renaissance masterpiece is fully nude and carved out of marble. In Qingtian, David was forged out of copper and the censors had stepped in—covering David's groin with a large copper leaf. Remittances also went toward new schools and later toward funding local businesses like hotels, coffee shops, and karaoke clubs. Qingtian, once a quiet backwater county, was consumed with development, rapt in the clamor of jackhammers and drills.

For a long time, Ah Dai wanted to go abroad. The timing, however, was never right. When he was younger, everyone urged him to stay home and study. Life overseas was too *xinku*, too bitter on the heart, the family said. So Ah Dai stayed in school, but like many children in Qingtian, he struggled to find incentives to study hard. If he was destined to leave, why did grades even matter? Ah Dai managed to finish high school and then he prepared to go abroad. But that year, the European economy took a turn for the worse. As many as one million emigrants—a third of all foreigners in the country—lost their jobs when Spain's construction bubble burst in 2008. Ah Dai would have to wait for the economy to recover. Not far from his home, he found a job in a factory where he drilled screws into electricity meters. He earned less than $250 a month. In 2010, even though the situation in Spain continued to look grim, Ah Dai's family began the paperwork to get him a visa anyway. He knew nothing about Spain and had no intention of learning Spanish before he made his way abroad. He had never heard of *tapas* or *sangria* and couldn't name a single Spanish delicacy. When I asked him where he was going to stay, he thought for a second, then turned and shouted to his mother, who was in the kitchen across the old courtyard: "Mama, where does my older sister live?"

"*Ma-deh-lee!*" she shouted back. Madrid, the country's capital. It was a month later when the eldest of Ah Dai's sisters, who had been in Spain since she was thirteen years old, returned to Qingtian for a short visit. Guo Wei was now thirty years old, a mother of three, and the owner of a store outside Madrid that sold small household products. When she returned home to Qingtian that year, she brought a gift for her brother. Ah Dai cradled the device, admiring its luminous screen. It would be months before the iPhone 4 would be available for sale in China. Ah Dai showed off his new toy over lunch at his house in Shabu one day. It had cost his sister about $800 to purchase it—about four months of Ah Dai's pay at the factory—and he understood very well that it was foreign money that allowed his sister to give him such a present. I met many emigrants in those early months who, like Ah Dai, told me "getting rich" was the number one reason why they wanted to go abroad. In many ways, he was a very typical young emigrant. But I was hoping to meet someone who was a little more curious about the outside world, someone actively preparing for his or her journey overseas.

I decided to look for places where emigrants might gather. Across the county, posters were stapled onto crowded bulletin boards—all of them advertising help with going abroad.

Exit the Country visas.
Learn Italian in just 2 months.
Going Abroad? Learn to Cook.

The black-and-white poster for a cooking school caught my eye. I followed the signs to the Exit the Country Chef Training Center one morning where I found students gathered in a dimly lit commercial kitchen. They were watching a young man in a white chef's jacket slice a cucumber and a carrot with the utmost precision. Shling! Chop! Chop! A steel blade diced and carved the vegetables, making contact with the chestnut cutting board beneath. Most of the students were young men, but there were some women too. Nearly everyone was in their twenties. One student hovered behind the chef, taking notes. Another stood right in front, capturing the action on his digital camera. The chef put down his knife and lifted a plate up for everyone to see. Slivers of cucumber and carrot had come together to form palm trees, a sunset, and a sandy beach. In China, people don't ooooh and aaaah. The students expressed astonishment with a synchronous: "Waaaaaaaah!"

"The examiners will not be tasting your food. They will judge each dish by appearance only," the chef told the class. "Just make sure everything is cooked thoroughly. You cannot present food that is raw." The students were preparing for a national cooking exam that usually required at least a month's worth of training. Most of the students, however, had just started attending classes at the Exit the Country Chef Training Center. The exam was scheduled for the end of the week. A pass meant you received an "Occupational Qualification Certificate" issued by China's Ministry of Labor and Social Security. It was supposed to be hard proof that you knew your way around a kitchen. But I didn't have much confidence in the candidates. The chef had said himself: examiners judged each dish only by how the food looked, not by how it tasted. "If you can't remember how to make a certain dish during the exam, just watch the person next to you," the chef went on, glancing around the room with a reassuring look. "We are all in this together."

The cooking certificate could be used to find work in restaurants across China, but all the students at the school were planning to work overseas. Most were hoping to emigrate to the Czech Republic or Hungary. The rest had their hearts set on Finland, Romania, Spain, and Holland. I sat beside a young woman named Jiajia, who had long, dark hair and teal-colored contact lenses that made her eyes look alarmingly cat-like. She told me her plans to work in a Chinese restaurant in Budapest. The cooking certificate would bolster her visa application, Jiajia explained. "The Hungarian government favors emigrants who come with some sort of employable skill," she said. Jiajia spoke with an airy confidence and calm that set her apart from the young girls who giggled and whispered to each other during class. I learned that she had recently graduated from university.

"But what good is that?" Jiajia asked. "I'm unemployed." Across China, there were too many graduates and not enough jobs. There were six times the number of graduates than there were a decade ago, and China's job market hadn't evolved fast enough to absorb all six million of them. The Chinese economy was providing greater opportunities than ever before, but "tough competition makes it a real challenge to find a good job," Jiajia said. Even with her degree, Jiajia's salary in China would be meager compared to what she could earn washing dishes in Hungary. "It's one euro to every nine yuan," she reminded me. "That's the reality." I met several other girls in class that day who were in similar situations. They had graduated from university and were either unemployed or unhappily employed. All of them were hoping to forge a better future somewhere else. I had expected to run into country bumpkins and high school dropouts at the cooking school. Instead, I found educated young women willing to drop their diplomas and their pride to make fried rice in a foreign country. It made me think of all the dish washers and servers and cooks I'd seen working in Chinese restaurants in the West. I thought of the girls who served me stir-fried vermicelli in Barcelona and the man who wrapped dumplings in Bordeaux. I thought sheepishly about the Chinese delivery guy in New York who brought me my General Tso's chicken through rain, snow, and sleet. Most of these emigrants probably didn't go to college—but then again, what did I know? I never asked and they never told. How much do we *really* know about the people who cook for us, serve us, and clean up after us? Every one of them has a unique story about leaving home. It made me stop and think—what are these people giving up to pursue the emigrant dream?

The next morning, students at the cooking school sat behind old wooden desks lined up in front of a faded blackboard. Du Lirong, director of the Exit the Country Chef Training Center, stood waiting. Like most of the men in

Qingtian, he was not tall, but he held his ground with strong features: a set of bushy eyebrows, greasy black hair, and a gruff voice. Director Du cleared his throat and began: "This is serious," he said. "This is a national test. You cannot be late. The older students will have no problem getting up. It is the younger ones I am worried about." Director Du began to pace. "You, young people, are always on the Internet until three or four in the morning. There are always one or two of you who do not show up on time." He stopped pacing and stared hard at the young man seated near him before moving on. He emphasized cleanliness and reminded everyone to bring a towel to the exam. He told the women to tie up their hair, take off all jewelry, and remove fake nails and nail polish. No sandals and no high heels. Jiajia took note. And the men? No dyed hair. "You walk in with yellow and green hair, looking like a panda," he growled. "People don't like that. You'll make the examiners uncomfortable and you will look like a hooligan." Director Du took a breath and then continued. "All right, now let's talk about Shanghai." If students passed the cooking exam and the rest of their papers were in order, they could submit a visa application to the appropriate consulate in Shanghai. The final hurdle was a face-to-face meeting with a consulate official. For many hopeful emigrants, this is where things can go wrong. Director Du told story after story of failure:

> "When the embassy asks how long you trained, make sure you tell them one to three months. If you say anything less than that, they'll tell you to go back and study some more."
> "Once, the embassy official asked a student, 'What can you cook?' The student replied: 'Nothing.' The official asked: 'Not even egg fried rice?' 'Nope,' said the student. So the embassy sent him home. You don't want this to happen to you."
> "Another student was once asked by the embassy: 'How much are you paying people to bring you out?' '$20,000 to go to Sweden,' the student replied. He was finished. The correct answer is: 'I'm going to work for relatives. Their restaurant is busy and they need workers. I didn't pay anyone to bring me out.'"

A steely silence washed over the room as Director Du spoke of hopeful emigrants who had foolishly spoiled their chances of going abroad. I could hear the frantic scratching of lead on paper as students vigorously scribbled in their notebooks. Director Du picked up a stack of papers and began handing out sheets. Typed in black font were questions students could expect to encounter during the embassy interview. Sometimes an emigrant's fate hinged on questions like:

Q. When making rice, what is the water to rice ratio?

A. 1:1.2

Q. What do you need to make soya sauce?

A. To make soya sauce, you need soya beans or soya bean cakes, wheat bran, and salt.

Q. How long does it take to make tea-infused eggs?

A. About an hour.

Q. When you put an egg in boiling water, how long does it take to cook the egg?

A. (trick question!) Put the egg in cold water first before bringing the water to a boil.

Across China, the national cooking exam is typically held just once a year. But there is so much demand in Qingtian, the exam is held once a month. People from all over the country come to take advantage. There were forty-six students preparing for the exam that week; twelve had come from outside the county and one candidate had traveled clear across China from as far away as Yunnan, a western province sharing a border with Tibet. Later that week, Jiajia and her classmates rose early one morning and filed into an empty classroom where they answered a host of multiple-choice questions before demonstrating their cooking prowess in a test kitchen. All but one of the candidates passed. "I don't know what happened," sighed Director Du. "It's as if he didn't study at all. I don't think he read any of the materials." Jiajia said the exam was a cinch. She had removed all the color from her nails and tied up her long, dark hair. At one point in the test kitchen, she couldn't remember what to do next, but she remained calm. She tilted her head to the right and eyed the person next to her for help. With the cooking certificate in hand, she was now taking her passport photos and gathering documents for notarization. But the week after the exam, Jiajia also started a new job. She was offered a position in the sales department at a local bank. In a tight white blouse and dark pants, she sat behind a smooth, dark desk in an office she shared with four other young bank employees, mulling over her new situation.

"Now that I have this job, who knows if I will go abroad?" she said. "I'll see how much I like working here at the bank and I'll see how far my application to Hungary goes. I'm not sure what to do now."

There was so much uncertainty in a migrant's life. Will I stay or will I go? *When* will I leave and *where* do I go? When I get there, what will it be like and will I like it? Will I ever return home to China? There were too many questions and so few answers. Some migrants, eager to somehow prepare for the journey ahead, believed the best way to ready themselves was to start with the tongue. Language was the key to success. You could be the most industrious worker there ever was, but if you couldn't put more than two words together, you were nothing. Hard workers survived. Big talkers prospered. But how to flutter your tongue fast enough to get that R to roll? And was it possible to gather so much saliva deep in the throat for that guttural *ccccht!* sound necessary in so many Germanic languages? The foreign-language schools in Qingtian boasted a wide curriculum, offering classes in Italian, Spanish, Portuguese, German, French, English, Polish, and Czech. I knew there was a good chance of meeting passionate and loquacious emigrants there.

In big Chinese cities like Beijing and Shanghai, foreigners and foreign-language schools are commonplace. But in a small county like Qingtian, where foreigners are still rare, it was a shock to find so many posters advertising language schools and tutors. I followed a series of pink signs down a main road. At the corner where an old man sold small tanks of water brimming with goldfish, I turned right and entered an alleyway before making a quick left behind a seedy apartment building. The lane was lined with trash. I found a dark stairway and climbed up to the second floor where, through an open door, I saw a man and woman sitting behind battered wooden desks in an apartment that had been converted into a classroom. I had reached the Longjin Road Foreign Language Training Center. I was looking for Xu Mengqiu, the school's principal teacher.

"Hi, do you know where Teacher Xu is?" I asked the two students.

"She's napping," said the man. He was typical of Qingtian men—short and thin—but with a sturdy build and a hazel glow that remained with him all year round, even in the winter. He had a set of piercing eyes, the kind that paid attention to everyone and everything.

"You're here to learn Italian, too?" he asked, putting his hand on a beige book that I saw had both Chinese characters and Italian words printed on its pages.

"No, I'm researching a book about the overseas Chinese from Qingtian," I told him. "Maybe I can interview you sometime?"

He was quick to answer. "But I'm not an overseas migrant."

"Ah, but you will be," I replied just as quickly. "Maybe if you have some free time one day, we could meet and uh, get a cup of coffee." He looked at me and laughed. It wasn't a good sign. "No need to be shy," I continued, trying to save the conversation. "I just want to hear your story. Maybe you can tell me why you want to go abroad, what your dreams are, that sort of thing."

"Oh, us?" he said, turning to look at his classmate. He laughed again. "We don't have any dreams." I didn't know it at the time, but when it came to dreams, this man had many. Our conversation ended as awkwardly as it began when I asked him for his contact information. He reluctantly gave me his phone number, and he wrote his name in Chinese characters and then spelled it out phonetically in *pinyin*: Chen Junwei. And then he said: "You can try to find me, but I don't drink coffee."

I was relieved when Teacher Xu got up from her nap and wandered into her cluttered classroom. She was sixty-one years old, with permed black hair and reading glasses that sat on the tip of her nose. She spoke with an almost guttural voice that projected to the far ends of the classroom. I later learned she was quite the Chinese opera singer. Teacher Xu once taught English at a Qingtian elementary school, and though she retired nearly ten years before, she continued to teach privately and with a whole new repertoire. She taught Spanish in the mornings, Italian in the afternoons, and Portuguese in the evenings. On the weekends, she held tutorial classes for those who needed extra help. Each student paid a flat fee of less than $100, and Teacher Xu encouraged them to learn as long as they needed to. On average, students took lessons for about a month before going abroad, and she estimated that six hundred students went through her school each year. She spent a lot of time in her Italian and Spanish classes teaching students how to roll their Rs.

"If you can't roll your R, you can just say 'L'—but really try to roll it if you can," she urged in Chinese. "Stick your tongue up . . . RRRRRR . . . come on, together now. . . RRRRRR." Teacher Xu was a grammar nut who had a good grasp of all the conjugations and tenses that European languages required. But she was unable to carry out even a simple conversation in any one of the languages she taught. This was symptomatic of many foreign-language teachers in China. They could read and write to a certain degree, but colloquial everyday dialogue was clumsy and stilted. Teacher Xu always spoke to me in Chinese. In all her sixty-one years, Teacher Xu had never been abroad. She spent her days and nights speaking the patois of so many foreign lands—lands she had once hoped to visit. She had a son in Barcelona, but he was struggling. After ten years, he hardly made ends meet running a small convenience store in the city. It didn't look like Teacher Xu would have a chance to go over to Spain anytime soon.

"*Ge-lazie! Per il tuo regalo bellissimo!*" the Italian class thundered one afternoon. *Thank you for your beautiful gift.*

"*Regah-lo,*" Teacher Xu emphasized.

"*Regah-lo!*" the students shouted back.

"In Chinese culture, when you receive a gift, you might put it away and open it up later when you are alone," Teacher Xu explained. "In the West, it's rude not to open a gift in front of your guest. So you have to take the gift, graciously thank them, and open it up right then and there. *Per il tuo regah-lo bellissimo!*" she repeated. Chen Junwei furrowed his tan brow and gripped his pencil as he scrawled notes in the margins of his book while muttering the phrase over and over again under his breath. *Per il tuo regah-lo bellissimo. Per il tuo regah-lo bellissimo.* He was by far the most diligent student in the class. After the lesson was over, he often stayed behind to help other students with their homework and to look up new vocabulary in Teacher Xu's thick Chinese-Italian dictionary. I could see that Chen was everyone's friend. He organized social events after class and on weekends. When Teacher Xu needed to cancel or make sudden changes to the class schedule, she would often ask Chen to contact students on her behalf. So when I asked Teacher Xu to introduce me to her favorite, most outspoken students, I should not have been surprised when I arrived at the school to find Chen waiting for me.

"We've met before," I told him.

"I know," he said with a laugh. "You never called!"

We sat down in an empty classroom, and without the need for a cup of coffee, Chen began to tell me his story. He and his wife had been separated for nearly ten years. She was now working in a leather shoe factory near the city of Ancona, and Chen had stayed in China to care for their young son. He told me he was optimistic the entire family could reunite in Italy before the end of the year.

"My wife said to me: 'Language is so important. You absolutely, positively must learn the language before coming here.' She gave me this one task to complete before I meet her in Italy. I cannot let her down," he explained. He was probably the oldest student in the class, and sometimes he was embarrassed about his age. But he was determined to keep his promise. "I am doing this because I love my wife," Chen said. "It is because we love each other so much that we have made this sacrifice. To be apart, for so long." Chen was candid and sincere, and I was happy to meet a Chinese person who spoke about such intimate topics with ease, especially with a stranger. For him going abroad was not simply a habit, a *xi guan*, it was crucial. "I want to take my wife on vacation to Yunnan or to Anhui to see the famous Yellow Mountains because we never had a real honeymoon together," he said. "I want to take my wife to Venice, the water city. I heard it is very beautiful." Although Chen had never been to Europe before, he liked to imagine what Italy and what Italians were like. "I imagine Italians to be very good people, people with good moral characters," he said, sitting up straight. "They would have manners and they are probably very courteous and very kind." As well as caring for his son and attending Teacher Xu's classes, Chen occasionally helped out at his brother's shoe factory in a neighboring town. He hoped his skills would come in handy. "Italians are famous for their leather shoes so I think it is the right place for us to go," he said. "Italy is also famous for wine. I am excited to taste their good wine. Oh, and of course noodles. What is it now?" He scratched his head. "Ssss-pa-getty!" he beamed. "I have seen that word many times in my book and I remember it. Sss-pa-getty!" Chen could not wait to see his love, to take her to Venice, and to sample pasta and Italian wine, but his ten-year-old son did not share his enthusiasm. China was the only home he had ever known. "One thing I really regret is not giving my son a home with a mother's love," Chen said. "I told him, 'We are going to Italy to be with Mama.' It is best that we are all one family again." But to Chen's son, Mama was just a stranger who called every so often on the telephone. Curious, excited, and motivated, Chen was the perfect emigrant to follow on his journey from China to Italy. Except for one thing: his visa application was taking unusually long to process. As the months passed, Chen watched many of his friends come to class, grinning widely with news of yet another approved visa. Chen would attend the celebratory dinners and give cheerful toasts. They clinked green beer bottles together, and Chen smiled, genuinely happy for his friends and their imminent journeys, but inside he felt an awful twist in his stomach. In truth, the pain was felt several inches higher. "My heart is breaking," he told me. "I can't stand waiting any longer."

When the brown, naked trees suddenly burst to life with cherry blossoms, I knew spring had come. Winter's gray haze gave way to a cloudless blue, and I was happy that I lived in the Chinese countryside where pollution did not choke the skies. I had been in Qingtian for more than three months and had met many who dreamed of emigration. Some were more prepared and passionate about the dream than others. Ah Dai seemed so clueless and nonchalant. Jiajia was hopeful but conflicted. And Chen, so romantic and passionate, was enduring a long, painful wait. Would I have the opportunity to follow up with any of them in Europe? Would they get their visas? Decide to go? Or end up staying in China? Meanwhile, I wanted to meet the children emigrants had left behind. I liked visiting local schools because the students were always excited to have a visitor.

I stood in front of the classroom, moon-shaped faces staring back at me. The school's internship co-coordinator, Qiu Guanghua, told the high school students that a visitor from abroad had come to speak to them. Now, three dozen almond-shaped eyes were trained on me. "A foreigner?" they whispered. I felt their eyes fall on my jet-black hair, on my round face and slanted eyes. I looked just like them. Chinese. Not the kind of foreigner they expected.

"Our guest comes from America!" Teacher Qiu said excitedly.

"What kind of language do they speak in *Mei Guo*?" one boy said from the back of the room. *Mei Guo*. America. The Beautiful Country.

"They speak *Mei Guo hua*!" Another boy replied confidently. *They speak American!*

"*Ben dan!*" said one girl, spinning around in her chair. *No, stupid.* "They speak English in America."

Suddenly, someone spoke out in English. "Hah-low!" the girl said. She straightened up in her chair and grinned at me. "How arrrr you? I am fine-ah! Sank you!" she giggled, completing the rudimentary English conversation all by herself.

"Hi, everyone," I finally said in English, when there was a moment to speak. "I am a Canadian who went to school in America. And in America, you're right, we speak English."

Stunned, the three dozen students were now eyeing my lips. My lips that betrayed me every time I spoke in China. The lips that told the Chinese that while I looked like them, I was a foreigner. My lips that spoke perfect American English. I switched into Chinese then, a language I had worked hard on improving the past few years.

"I have come to Qingtian to learn about the overseas Chinese," I said. "I am very happy to know you."

"Hands up," Teacher Qiu called out. "How many of you here have parents who are abroad?" Hands crept up slowly, fingers first, reaching toward the ceiling. In all, we counted more than two dozen hands. Teacher Qiu chose a few at random and ushered them out of the classroom. I interviewed many teenagers at the Qingtian County Vocational High School that spring. Most told me they had not seen their parents in years and that they had been raised by grandparents for as long as they could remember. Their parents were busy working in the kitchens of Chinese restaurants in the Netherlands, while others were dabbling in the wholesale trade in Spain. Many students told me their parents were in Italy, sewing clothes and handbags and stitching leather shoes in Chinese-run factories.

"Mama spent nearly five years in a factory in Italy," said the sixteen-year-old girl with the face of a doll. She had gleeful eyes and she spoke a little too quickly, but I liked how straightforward she was and how she wasn't afraid to speak her mind. Pei talked about the day her mother left for the airport, how her mother had cried when her visa was approved, how her father ended up staying behind to raise both her and her younger brother. And how, at the end of the summer, the three of them would finally be reuniting with her mother in Italy. Then the girl rested her chubby cheek in the palm of her hand and spoke dreamily about Venice, the wondrous city on the water.

It was Pei's last summer in China, and she spent much of her time practicing her eight-teeth smile. For days she gripped a chopstick sideways between her teeth until her cheeks quivered and her jaw grew sore. "I feel like someone is holding a gun to my head and telling me to smile," she grumbled. "I look like a mindless automaton." But this meticulous smile—which revealed exactly eight teeth—was expected of the *fuwuyuan*, the Chinese server. Pei practiced as much as she could. Her teachers at the vocational high school emphasized that no matter her mood, no matter how foul a day she was having, the most insufferable customer was always right—and always entitled to the perfect smile. It was advice Pei would remember months later when she started working at the bar in Italy.

Her summer internship at the four-star hotel in Qingtian's urban center sent her scurrying across the glossy tiles of the hotel's exclusive restaurant, tending to hungry patrons who hollered, "*FU-WU-YUAN!*" whenever they needed more tea or wanted their dirty dishes taken away or if they wished to complain about the food, which they often did. During her internship, Pei put her high school lessons to use, remembering precisely not only how she should smile, but also how she was to stand, walk, sit, and squat like a lady in the event she dropped something on the floor and had to find an elegant way to bend down to retrieve it. Though the school curriculum had included some basic English lessons and chapters in her Chinese-language textbook covered such topics like "What is American Express?" and "Touring Hangzhou's Famous West Lake," her teachers "basically prepared me to be a world class *fuwuyuan*," Pei told me that summer, rolling her eyes. Still, she took her job very seriously. She dressed neatly in a bright red top and black trousers and was tasked with laying out the china and placing bottles of beer and wine on large round tables. When the busboys brought food out from the kitchen to the server's station, Pei learned to balance the heavy platters on one hand. She looked taller at work, probably because she was careful to maintain her posture. She straightened her back, elongated her neck, sucked in her tummy, and carefully folded her hands one on top of the other in front of her stomach. When she flashed her perfect eight-teeth smile, she looked stiff yet refined. Pei earned 800 yuan a month, the equivalent of about $120, and she felt privileged to be spending her final days in China in such luxurious surroundings. What made her job even more fun was that Li Jie had also landed an internship at the very same restaurant in the very same four-star hotel.

Li Jie had never kissed a girl before Pei. He had never even held a girl's hand before she had grabbed his for the first time that spring. Li Jie welcomed Pei's advances, was smitten by her bubbly, outgoing personality, and liked to listen to her ramble on about her day, telling story after story without ever taking a breath in between. Pei was more seasoned than he. She had recently broken up with another boy and admitted that she only latched onto Li Jie "because of his height." He was six feet—an entire head taller than her—and she liked the fact that she could wear high heels and still raise her chin to look into his eyes. When they kissed, she pressed her toes into the ground to reach him. It wasn't long before she began to notice Li Jie's other good traits. For one, he had a nice smile and later she decided that he was a good person. He didn't particularly know how to be a good boyfriend. When Pei's friends weren't feeling well, their boyfriends brought them hot soups and medicine. Li Jie never did that. And it annoyed her when other girls flirted with him in front of her face. Li Jie didn't flirt back, but he never did anything to stop them from hooking arms with him or resting their heads on his shoulder. The entire class knew about their relationship—Pei made sure of that—but around her father and grandparents, she kept him a secret. She relinquished Li Jie's hand if they saw an Auntie rounding the street corner, and she darted out of the room and dropped her voice to a whisper if he happened to call her when she was with family. More than once, her father eyed her suspiciously and asked, "You don't have a boyfriend, do you?"

"No, Ah Ba, of course not," she always said, quickly changing the topic.

Every night, when Qingtian's urban center flickered to life, the two drifted in and out of shops and stopped to snack at the food carts. Pei felt carefree and in love. From the rooftops of the newest buildings, laser beams cut through the evening fog and colorful LED lights lit up each floor, smearing bright colors in the dark waters of the Ou River. The archways on the county's biggest bridge lit up too, and alongside the river, glowing red characters spelled out the county's official slogan: *Build a harmonious, prosperous new overseas Chinese town.* Pei and Li Jie took it all in, their faces brightened by the neon glow. For decades now, emigrants were pouring money into their home county. They opened shops with foreign names. France Bordeaux sold imported red wine. There was lasagna and Spanish *jamon* at La Fite restaurant. And Verona café served authentic Italian espresso. The coolest hangout was J.J. Bar, but Pei had never gone inside. She said the prices were too high, and a bar like that was no place for a respectable sixteen-year-old. "Generally, when people think of a bar, negative associations like drunkenness and loose women come to mind," Pei explained to me. "After a few years in Italy, maybe I can save up enough money and return to China to open a bar here in Qingtian," she said. "But if it is my own bar, it will be a place to eat and drink. Nothing more."

There was nothing scandalous about J.J. Bar—except perhaps the notoriously flirtatious but harmless owner, James Xu. James was a thirty-five-year-old bachelor with a passion for rock and roll and a knack for sweet talking. His J.J. Bar was an oddity in Qingtian: housed in a beautiful loft of exposed red brick, it looked like it belonged in New York, with its mismatched furniture, worn wooden floors, and tarnished taps in the unisex bathroom. On Fridays, the bar hosted open-mic nights and the kitchen made amazing calamari. Above the bar, the names of beers, wines, and cocktails were spelled out with pastel chalk in perfect English, a rarity in a country famous for its Chinglish—nonsensical English in Chinese contexts. At Qingtian's illustrious Prague Impression Restaurant, I encountered some of the finest examples of Chinglish on the menu: *Sizzling secret makes tofu. The pickle pseudoscianena polyactis. Unique flavor wax gourd.* And, my favorite, *Mei dish of burning flesh.*

J.J Bar's cool atmosphere and English menus had me convinced James was an emigrant who had spent time abroad, maybe in the United States. When I met him in his office, which looked something like an Apple Store, he was standing next to a stainless steel coffee machine swiping a newly purchased iPad 2. He had a small belly, the kind that told you he enjoyed his food, and he wore a white chef's jacket that he casually left unbuttoned. He had a soft, smooth voice, and he liked to use a little English as he spoke to me, adding "very good," "OK," and "yes" at the end of his sentences. I soon learned that the look and feel of J.J. Bar was entirely inspired by James's obsession with American pop culture. He had never been to Europe or to North America, but drew inspiration from the hundreds of American movies he had seen over the years.

While a new Qingtian was being forged, with its bars and fancy restaurants, old Qingtian continued to flourish. In narrow alleyways, women sold freshly steamed tofu and bare-chested men hawked vegetables from old wicker baskets balanced on spindly shoulders. Bicycle rickshaws stirred dust when they rolled past idling luxury sedans. And every morning, I could hear the frantic squeals of a pig being slaughtered. Just two blocks from the four-star hotel, a man in a dirty apron laid out bloody stumps—chops, tenderloin, trotters, ears, and snout—on a stained wooden board attached to the back of his motor bike. He tied a plastic bag to the end of a wooden stick and waved it lazily over the meat to keep the flies away.

The four-star hotel was the tallest building in all of Qingtian, with its revolving front door, high-ceiling lobby, sprawling ballroom and conference facilities, massage center, and restaurant. An entire floor was dedicated to karaoke, called KTV in China. The people who came to dine at the hotel restaurant were emigrants who had returned to China from abroad. Pei noticed their diamond rings and Louis Vuitton handbags. The men wore Italian loafers and Paul Shark polo shirts. And they were always doling out gifts to friends and family—boxes of Marlboro cigarettes, Ferrero Rocher chocolates, and wads of cash tucked inside red envelopes. With these gifts, they were proving to everyone that they had "made it" in the West. As sixteen-year-old Pei stood there in the four-star hotel restaurant, hands carefully placed one on top of the other and flashing her eight-teeth smile, she could only imagine what opulence awaited her in Europe. *The possibility to make a true fortune!* She imagined returning home, her luggage crammed full of gifts from Italy—wine, chocolates, and leather shoes—and treating her friends and family out to a sumptuous dinner and a night of karaoke. They might someday even be guests at this very hotel, she thought. Not every migrant found success overseas. Pei understood that. Only the successful ones could afford to come back to China every year. The emigrants who hadn't quite made it yet—emigrants like her mother—didn't come home. It wasn't that she couldn't afford the plane ticket. What she couldn't afford were the gifts and the red pockets and the dinners that friends and family expected of her. She couldn't afford to show off. Pei hoped to one day be the kind of emigrant that could come home to China as often as possible. She wanted to clutch a designer handbag and eat at the most expensive places in town, too. As a student, she rarely had the chance to splurge on a meal. But when she did, Pei found the spaghetti at one particular restaurant especially delightful. Most teens her age were preoccupied with maintaining an abnormally small waistline, but Pei was a girl who liked to eat. Lalacomte Beef and Coffee was one of the newer places in town, despite the menu claiming "153 years of family ownership" and the ancient-looking decor. There were velvety pillows and gilded armchairs, ornamental mirrors, faux-marble busts, and fake oil paintings. Steak was served Chinese-style—a well-done piece of beef sizzling on an iron platter, smothered in black bean sauce and topped with an egg cooked sunny-side-up. A straw came with your knife and fork so you could poke the runny egg and suck the yolk out. It cost just a few extra yuan to add a side of *yidali mian*—Italian noodles—cooked way past *al dente* and tossed in a sauce that looked and tasted like ketchup. Pei always slurped the noodles, staining her lips red, thinking how much she might like Italy if pasta tasted like this. Pei spent most of her summer working at the hotel restaurant. Sometimes she found herself working twelve or fourteen hours a day because her manager wanted her to stay behind to help with banquets or other evening functions. Even so, she never felt tired. She always made sure her purse was stuffed full of candy. And she liked to treat herself to an extra large cup of sweet, frothy bubble tea. The sugar rush allowed her to spend many nights at the Internet café with Li Jie. The next morning, the two walked back to the four-star hotel to start another day's work having not slept at all.

The family crammed their suitcases full of dried everything. Dried bamboo, dried river shrimps, dried squid, and dried *yangmei*—Qingtian's famous crimson fruit. They packed pumpkin seeds, beef jerky, pork jerky, parched weeds, withered herbs, and wild mountain grass Pei's grandmother plucked with her own hands and dried in the hot sun. The family even managed to fit a rice cooker in one of the suitcases. The August humidity felt as heavy as a shroud as the car rose up toward the expressway, passing under a bridge with red letters that welcomed people to Qingtian first in Chinese, then in English, Spanish, Italian, and French. *Welcome! Bienvenido! Benvenuti! Bienvenue!* There were no signs that bid farewell. Pei gazed out the window, watching scenery fly by like paint thrown on a canvas. The road leading out of her home was once an old two-lane highway that snaked slowly alongside the Ou River. But since the new expressway was completed in 2005, leaving Qingtian got a whole lot easier. It took just two hours to get to the city of Wenzhou, where the nearest airport was.

If the people of Qingtian are known for their tales of migration and soapstone sculptures, then the people of Wenzhou are known for their ambitious entrepreneurs. Isolated by the mountainous terrain and far from Beijing where Chinese leaders bickered about private business and free markets, the Wenzhounese began forming informal credit networks in the 1980s and early 1990s that allowed businesses to grow without the help of state-owned banks. As private enterprise flourished, the people of Wenzhou became famous across China for their cunning sensibilities and flair for business. Along the way they picked up a rather peculiar nickname: the Chinese Jews. Wenzhou bookstores are stocked with publications like *Fierce Wenzhou People: The Jews of the East and Their Money-Earning Knowledge*; *Study the Secrets of Enterprise and Wealth with the Wenzhou People*; and *Jews of China: The Zhejiang Business Legend*. Other titles like *The Feared Wenzhou People* and *Wenzhou's Property Stir-fryers* paint a more loathsome picture, describing how speculators have pursued quick returns with aggressive forays into a number of different industries including coal, cotton, oil, and real estate, pushing up property prices in cities like Hong Kong, New York, and Vancouver. The people of Qingtian, with their distinct history and culture, tend to distinguish themselves from their Wenzhounese brothers and like to consider themselves to be nicer and less aggressive counterparts. But no one can deny the connections between the two peoples: a combination of Wenzhou business sense and Qingtian's migration networks have leveraged the people of southern Zhejiang both abroad, as traveling migrants, and at home, where dusty hamlets along the Ou River have been transformed into booming factory towns.

The best way to see those factory towns is driving along the Jinliwen expressway. Eight family members accompanied Pei and her family as they sped past lush valleys and deep gorges. Every few minutes, the wind howled as they plunged into the dark insides of a mountain. There were twenty-nine tunnels in all, the longest one stretching for over two miles. Soon, factories emerged below the expressway. Giant billboards appeared by the side of the road, first for buttons, then zippers, then jungle gyms, trampolines, slides, and swing sets. The factories started off as small family-run workshops that focused on manufacturing things that didn't require much technology or investment. The factories quickly increased in size and production but continued to churn out small and simple objects. They made playing cards in Wuyi, neckties in Shengzhou, and billions of socks were produced every year in Datang. One-quarter of all shoes bought in China were made in Wenzhou, where Shen had worked all those years. Southern Zhejiang province had become an ocean of small commodities, with every spot along the Ou River developing an export niche—even Qingtian. But the county didn't export things. For hundreds of years, Qingtian's biggest export has been people.

Inside the terminal, behind a wall of glass, Pei peered at the white bulbous nose, triangular wings, and long, narrow tube marked with tiny, round windows, like the portholes of an ocean liner. The plane looked smaller than she had imagined, but when she stepped on board, she was surprised to see so many little seats packed inside. More family members had come to the airport to say good-bye. She counted at least fifteen people. There were aunts, uncles, cousins, Pei's grandfather from her father's side, and her grandmother from her mother's side. "When will we see each other again?" her grandmother had asked, grabbing Pei's hands in hers, a steady flow of tears running down her cheeks. "Or will you be like your mother? And not return home for years?" Pei bit back the urge to cry and instead forced a smile to spread across her face. Hiding her emotions to protect her grandmother, she replied: "Of course not." But she knew it was a lie. In truth, it would be a long time before she could return to China. The plane shuddered as its engines thundered to life, roaring as it charged down the runway and lifted off. Pei's heart alternated between excitement and trepidation. They were served breakfast, a watery rice porridge made with green beans. Pei scooped two spoonfuls into her mouth before unbuckling her seatbelt so she could run to the little room at the front of the plane where she vomited in the small, steel toilet bowl. They stopped at the Shanghai international airport for a layover, where father and son snacked on grapes, oranges, and spicy duck necks. Pei stole away to sneak a phone call to Li Jie. "I'm in Shanghai," she whispered. Li Jie was silent on the other end, and she knew that he was crying. They wept quietly together, sniffling into the receivers of their cell phones. "Wait for me; I will come back," she told him. Fen had uttered similar words to her husband, when they said good-bye five years before. An ocean away, she rubbed her small, pale hands together and waited anxiously to see her husband and their two children again.

EAST MEETS WEST

Very soon I will leave this home. This word home doesn't mean much to me anymore. I can so easily leave one place and move to another. Hard to believe, isn't it?

In a crowd of white faces stood a Chinese woman in the arrivals hall of Milan's international airport. She had pale skin and small feet, two physical traits the Chinese consider a sign of beauty. In another life her dainty figure and complexion might have indicated stature and wealth—but not in this life. In her hair, which was thicker and more textured than the average Chinese woman, she clipped a jeweled brooch. She did this whenever she had somewhere to go—to distinguish the occasion from days spent in the factory or the farm. At home in China people had always pointed at her thick, wavy hair and accused her of being a foreigner. Chinese women typically had straight and silky hair. Only foreigners had curls. "Such a trait must have come from outside of the country!" the gossiping Aunties chuckled among themselves. But as far as Fen knew, her ancestors had lived in Qingtian for generations. Now, outside of the homeland, her waves and her curls—once the subject of much speculation and debate—went unnoticed. In fact, her hair was exceedingly plain compared to the embellished hairdos all around her. Fen knew the *lao wai* spent hundreds of euros at the salon. She didn't have that kind of money, and even if she did, she would never spend it on her hair. Most days her hair was matted down with sweat, tucked under a blue hairnet. Fen considered hair salons to be a *lao wai* extravagance. After five years in Italy, that's still what she called the Italians. *Lao wai*. Foreigners. Except *they* weren't the foreigners on this soil—she was.

Fen thought back to the time when she first stepped foot in this airport. Coming off a long flight from China, her eyes bleary and her thick hair tangled, she searched the crowd for a flicker of a familiar face but did not find anyone waiting for her. Travelers coursed by, some striding confidently toward the terminal's sliding doors, others pausing briefly before dashing toward a pair of open, outstretched arms. Fen stood alone in the bustle of it all, and it quickly became apparent how completely and utterly useless she was in this new land. She couldn't read the script on the menu at a nearby café. She couldn't even ask where the nearest toilet was. It was this feeling of utter helplessness that she vowed to overcome. She would work day and night so that she could one day be independent and free of all obligations—free of waiting for bosses that didn't show, free to find whatever job suited her, free to gain some kind of control over her own fate. At the same time, Fen acknowledged there were many who endured much worse than she had. She knew many migrants who paid snake-heads to smuggle them out of China. She heard all the horror stories: dozens of people packed into safe houses like animals, stuffed into the trunks of cars, herded into the back of vans, loaded onto small boats to cross borders over hushed waves in the dead of night. Some migrants were essentially sold into slavery—their families threatened by bullies and goons back home if they did not continue to work like a slave to pay off their debts.

Fen was left alone with her thoughts for hours before the restaurateur finally arrived at the airport to pick her up. He did not apologize for making her wait, and then he told her she would have to start looking for work because he did not have a job for her at his restaurant. Fen's fingers smudged the black ink of Chinese newsprint as she scoured through the classifieds and found mostly garment factory jobs. They all said the same thing: *Sewing in garment factory. Paid per piece. Room and board provided.* She bounced around from factory to factory before finally finding one that suited her. The factory boss was from Zhejiang and so were many of her co-workers. Together, they cooked familiar foods and spoke the language of their own soil. With few connections in this new life (none that would help her anyway) and without the ability to speak Italian, working for a garment workshop was the only job Fen could find. A Chinese boss didn't mean the job was a good one or that the boss was reliable. Fen knew that already, having been burned by the Chinese restaurateur who took her money and didn't give her the job she was promised. But it was still better to work for someone she could at least communicate with. At the factory, Fen was pleased when she was given a more clerical kind of job, keeping track of numbers, boxes, shipments, and deliveries. It was much better than spending her days hunched over a sewing machine. And she was relieved she wouldn't be forced to find work in Prato, a place she was urged to avoid.

Many migrants spoke about Prato with dread. Prato was a place where the rhythm of your life was chained to the frantic pulse of a sewing machine. A place where, behind a veil of curtained darkness, you often lost track of the sun and didn't know whether it was day or night. Where your worth was measured by the number of garments you could sew in a day. They told one another to avoid Prato, yet so many Chinese migrants inevitably found themselves there. Tuscany's second-largest city is just west of Florence and about an hour's drive from the Leaning Tower of Pisa. In the shadow of such prominent attractions, Prato is lesser known to most tourists, though it has long been famous around the world for its textile production. The city has been producing silk and fine wools, which traditional artisans have crafted into high-end clothing, since the Middle Ages. When the first Chinese immigrants arrived in the late 1980s, they began sewing for local Italian companies. They had no particular skills or connections but could offer two guarantees—that the orders would be completed quickly and delivered at the lowest possible price. Those two guarantees would soon become essential as the Italian economy began to slow and show signs of strain.

Pronto moda means fast fashion, and it is the Chinese claim to fame in Prato. As word spread that there were jobs to be had in Italy, thousands of poor Chinese, mostly from Wenzhou, Qingtian County, and its surrounding regions, began flooding into the region in the early 1990s. Many were smuggled in by snakeheads. All of them were seeking a better life and the chance to make a fortune. Chinese migrants soon started opening their own workshops. They rented abandoned workspaces from locals who, in a time of intensifying global competition, were happy to sell off their family businesses. The Chinese workshops were typically family-run and usually consisted of a husband and a wife and no more than ten workers. If their children were old enough, they most likely helped out in the afternoons after school. The workshops produced goods faster and cheaper, offering the flexibility and high productivity their Italian counterparts lacked. Orders were accepted even if they involved night and holiday work. Workers moved from factory to factory and stayed for days or even weeks to complete orders on time. Factory bosses covered up the windows with heavy black curtains. This prevented the workshop's florescent lights from disturbing the neighbors at night, but the curtains also allowed the garment workers to stay hidden from the outside world. Factories with a little more experience gained contracts with some of the country's larger and more prestigious fashion houses through Italian intermediaries. Factory bosses in Prato told me they had stitched garments for Dolce & Gabbana, Prada, and Giorgio Armani in the past. For a while, many of the workshops had their hands full with this sort of work. But high-end clothing, while lucrative, had its limitations. The workshop's schedule and profits were ultimately determined by those fashion houses, and competition among Chinese-run workshops was fierce, with factory bosses trying to undercut each other by promising lower prices and faster turnarounds. Some workshops began to shift their focus to the medium to low-end market. They introduced a newer, cheaper, and faster production method that cut out Italian intermediaries and freed themselves from any control the fashion houses previously imposed. Garments were designed, stitched, and sold all in the same place. *Pronto moda*—fast fashion—was born.

Fen's factory kept a frenetic pace and a demanding schedule, but the working conditions were not nearly as harsh as those found in Prato. Fen even grew to like her job. She enjoyed the freedom to move about the factory floor, and there was steady work despite the business operating in stealth. Occasionally the workshop was shut down at a moment's notice. Harried workers were told to gather up their things, and the sewing machines and long rolls of colorful textiles were hauled to a new location to dodge an incoming raid or police sweep. It was as steady as work got for Chinese migrants, who were used to constant change and made seemingly big decisions like switching jobs or moving to another city as swiftly as they stitched fabric together in the factory. Fen thought back to her last moments in China and remembered promising her young daughter she would return home in a few years' time. She said it to comfort both herself and Pei, but the truth was Fen didn't know what opportunities awaited her in Italy. It was only when she began working at the garment factory, earning ten times more than what she would earn working in China, that she knew she had to stay. Fen grew accustomed to spending her days and nights in the factory. Every month, she waited for pay day. She sent most of her earnings back to China where Pei was dreaming of gelato, gondolas, and crescent-shaped bridges.

It was two years before Ye Pei's eighteenth birthday when Fen realized she needed to make some major changes in her life. Family reunification was a long and complicated process, and after five years in Italy, she was still nowhere close to eligibility. The first condition required Fen to have her own accommodations that could not only house her family but also pass a government health and hygiene inspection. She also needed proof of a steady income. To be eligible for family reunification, both her children had to be less than eighteen years of age. Still working at the garment factory, Fen was living in a dorm-style apartment she shared with a number of her co-workers. And though she had been working day and night for five years straight, she didn't have a paper trail to prove it. Chinese bosses always paid in cash, and no one logged all those hours spent in the workshop. Then there was the problem of describing her job to others. She imagined filling out the visa application form for her family and going to the embassy for an interview.

"How long have you been in Italy for?" the embassy official would ask.

"*Cinque anni.*" Five years.

"*Va bene*, and what do you do for a living?"

"I cut 'Made in China' tags off clothing and sew on 'Made in Italy' labels in their place," Fen would say with a grim smile. Her dream of bringing her husband, her son, and her daughter, Pei, to Italy was unraveling fast. First things first—she needed a new job that would prove she was legally employed, a job she wouldn't be afraid to tell others about. Would she consider working for an Italian? It was around this time Fen received a call from a distant uncle who had emigrated to Italy years before. Relatives in China had passed Fen's number to him, and when her cell phone rang that day, she was overjoyed to hear a familiar voice.

"I knew you had come to Italy, but I had no way of reaching you!" she exclaimed.

"It is good to hear your voice," he said. Then he asked if she would consider working on a mushroom farm near the coast.

"Run by foreigners?" Fen asked.

"Yes, Italians," the uncle said.

"How much is the pay?"

"800 to 1,000 [Euros]. Sometimes more. Depends how much you work."

"How long are the hours?" Fen asked.

"Not as long as in the factory."

"And room and board?"

"No, you have to find your own home and cook your own food." Fen did the math in her head. At the factory, despite the long hours, she still managed to save much of what she earned because her food and lodgings were provided for. How would she go about securing a place to live on her own? "The farm bosses are very helpful with that sort of thing," her uncle said.

The chambers dripped with humidity and stank of dung. Fen edged down the aisle, reaching for creamy heads that emerged from the refuge of the warm, dark soil. Dozens of manure beds were stacked on giant metal shelves that stretched from the floor to the ceiling of each chamber, but that didn't deter Fen, whose fast hands could gather hundreds of mushrooms in a day. She was grateful for her job at the farm, just as the farm owners were grateful for their Chinese workers. After all it was the Chinese who saved them. When the farm first opened in 1978, the goal was to provide jobs for local Italians. There was plenty of work in the summer thanks to the tourists who flocked to the nearby beach resorts. Sunbathers roasted on the sand, swimmers frolicked in the warm waters of the Adriatic Sea, and boardwalks sizzled with kebab and seafood. At night, the lights of beachfront discos danced on the loud dark waves. But come winter the sandy dunes cleared out, restaurants shuttered for the season, and the resorts went silent and dark. In 1978, seven local families decided to start an enterprise that could keep restless locals occupied through the cold winter months. They opened a twenty-five-hectare farm specializing in the cultivation of oyster mushrooms. By 1996, only two families remained in the business—the Magnanis and the Simonis. They expanded the farm to forty hectares and built a large indoor complex so they could start cultivating white and brown mushrooms. The farm's production continued to increase, but it also became harder to find Italians willing to get their hands dirty.

It was in the 1990s when immigrants came flooding into the country and the farm owners realized these newcomers were hungry for work. The first hires were Albanians, Macedonians, and Romanians. When the first Chinese immigrants showed up a few years later, the farm owners knew they were saved. "We found the Chinese to be very good workers, willing to work weekends and willing to work hard," said Frederico Magnani, the son of one of the farm matriarchs and a handsome twenty-two-year-old botany student who was poised to take over as soon as he was finished with his studies at the University of Bologna. Frederico grew up in the family home just meters from the farm and was just seven years old when he began growing potatoes, tomatoes, watermelons, and all sorts of lettuce greens. Frederico said he preferred the peace and quiet of the countryside, where he could breathe in the scent of the earth and hear the magpies sing. The Chinese workers said they liked Frederico's easygoing nature, which contrasted with the benevolent yet intimidating personas of the farm matriarchs.

The first Chinese worker at the farm was a woman who spent many years working in a garment factory. She was painfully quiet and kept to herself, but she was an excellent worker. "We asked her if she knew others who needed a job and now we have more than fifty Chinese workers," Frederico said, adding that they have since mushroomed into one of the largest fungi farms in all of Italy. "We need the Chinese and the Chinese need us." The farm did more than provide jobs to Chinese immigrants; they also offered a solution to one of the biggest challenges migrants said they faced—finding a place to live. "We're not like those Italian women with their immaculate homes, beautiful gardens, and spotless kitchens," one migrant admitted. "By comparison, our homes can really be an eyesore." The migrants planted seeds harvested from their home villages in China and grew leafy vegetables Italians had no names for. They hung wet laundry outside their homes on makeshift ropes that sent socks, panties, and hosiery flapping in the wind.

But the biggest concern was the Chinese kitchen. Standing outside a migrant's home, the crackle of a stir-fry could be heard and smoke could be seen billowing out the windows. And so, only the oldest, most dilapidated homes were rented to the Chinese. The farm owners used their connections to find places for the workers to stay. Fen, who did not have a driver's license or a car, needed a residence within walking distance of the farm. With their help, Fen found a house to rent and submitted an application for family reunification. Then she waited anxiously for her husband and two children to arrive. She wondered what it would be like to live with them in the same home, and she hoped they would not be disappointed with their new lives. Whenever I asked Chinese migrant mothers about reuniting with their children, they often insisted the transition would be a smooth one. "The bond between a mother and a child is very special," they would say. "Of course I will be able to recognize my own children!"

※

We sat on the plane for thirteen hours. I almost couldn't bear to sit any longer. When we arrived in Italy I wanted to call you, but I don't have an Italian SIM card.

Pei started every journal entry with three Chinese words: 亲爱的. *Qin ai de*. My Love. She wanted to share her daily experiences with Li Jie, but it was difficult with the time and distance between them. He had never left China before, and Pei felt it was impossible for him to fully understand her new life. So she began to write it all down, in the very diary Li Jie gave to her as a gift before she left China. He said the diary was to help her recall her own experiences, but Pei wrote in those pages every day in the hopes that Li Jie would read it himself when he one day joined her in Italy.

On the plane she tried to imagine her mother, Ah Ma, in a new country. She remembered Ah Ma as a gentle and demure woman who preferred to stay at home, shuffling around the house in her pajamas. She remembered Ah Ma scrubbing the kitchen tiles and Ah Ma curled up under a blanket watching television. What did Ah Ma look like now that she had been living among strangers for so many years? When they finally stepped off the plane and into the airport, Pei tried not to stare at foreigners, who had light-colored hair, pale eyes, and big noses. The men had shiny hair they slicked back with gel. They wore pointy leather shoes and Pei liked the smell of their cologne. Some women painted their lips a bright rouge. Pei admired their skinny legs and round breasts. Others had complexions that were as dark as chocolate. A few women wrapped their heads in colorful scarves; some covered their faces entirely with a dark veil. Pei had never seen anyone like that before. At home, such characters would have attracted a curious mob—and that was when there was just one or two of them. Never in her life had she seen so many strange-looking foreigners all in one place. She noted the time: 8:15 a.m. In China, it was already 2:15 p.m. Although she came from a country that spanned five different geographic time zones, she never thought about time differences. China has maintained just one standard time since 1949: Beijing Time. The sight of so many *lao wai* and the six-hour time difference was enough to convince Pei she had indeed stepped onto unknown shores.

Suitcases of all shapes and sizes streamed past as the family waited for their bags. Pei wondered what was taking so long. All three suitcases were overweight and had been stuffed to the seams like a dumpling during the Chinese New Year. But the ticket agent at the Wenzhou airport let them through without any penalty. Perhaps their bags had burst open while being transported and Italy's customs officials were rifling through their belongings. Would they find the dried river shrimps and *yangmei* bayberries she had so carefully packed away? "We're going to be fined," Pei told her brother. "I just know it." A loud thump interrupted her frets. The bags, still bulging but unopened, had finally arrived. The family gathered their things and set off one by one into the arrivals hall. They had prepared a little test for Ah Ma.

Fen's eyes darted from one dark head to another until they landed on a familiar, pudgy face. "I'm here!" she called to Shen, frantically waving her arm.

"*Laopo!*" My wife! His voice rang out loudly. That was her cue. Pei ventured out, pulling her luggage along with her. Blood rushed to her cheeks as soon as she saw her father standing next to a woman who looked even smaller and paler than she remembered.

"Ah Bai!" Fen waved, using her daughter's nickname in dialect.

"Ah Ma," Pei said softly, no louder than a whisper. At last, Mao made his entrance. He was fifteen years old, skinner and taller than Pei, with thick, messy hair and glasses. Mao strolled forward confidently, but his mother's eyes passed over him as she continued to scan the crowd. It wasn't until he waved that Fen peered into the face of the lanky teenager and saw the son she once knew. "Ah Mai," she said warmly. "If you didn't wave, I wouldn't have known it was you." The two children stared at their mother, who looked like a smaller version of her former self. She had been on her own for too long, Pei thought. They stood in the arrivals hall, a little bewildered.

"*Laopo, xin ku la,*" Shen said, his hand resting on her back. *My wife, life has been tough on you.* Though Fen's heart fluttered inside her chest, she was now paralyzed with emotion. The children did not stand as close to their mother as they should have, and they did not embrace. It wasn't the Chinese way. Instead Fen asked what many Chinese ask their loved ones whenever they meet: "*Ni men chi le ma?*" Have you eaten yet?

> *I had expected to see tall skyscrapers, but here there are none. People live in homes that are two stories tall.*

Fen's uncle, the one who had introduced her to the mushroom farm, waited in a van outside the terminal for them. They piled in and set off on a four-hour drive. Pei could not sit still as she craned her neck looking for skyscrapers. She saw none. Instead, a landscape of medieval castles and crumbling farmhouses stretched out into the distance. The *autostrada* was similar to the highways in China, except the big green signs had the names of places Pei had never heard of.

REGGIO EMILIA
PARMA
MODENA
BOLOGNA

They headed east out of Milan and toward Emilia-Romagna, a province blessed with a charming countryside, historic architecture, and unparalleled cuisine. The area owes its beginning to the Romans who built a road in 187 BCE bisecting the flat, foggy region. Along Via Emilia are historic towns featuring restored medieval and Renaissance *palazzi*. Bologna, the cultural and intellectual center famed for its arcaded sidewalks and grandiose medieval towers, is in the middle of everything. Parma and Modena lie to the west; the Adriatic Sea, with its resort towns, beaches, and bars, to the east. Italians rarely agree about anything but most will concede the best food in the country can be found in Emilia-Romagna—also known as Italy's culinary heartland and sometimes referred to as Italy's "stomach." This is the birthplace of tortellini, fettuccini, ravioli, and lasagna. *Prosciutto crudo*, a rosy ham sliced razor thin, is cured in Parma. Reggio Emilia is where you find Parmesan cheese. For centuries, balsamic vinegar has been made in the ancient city of Modena. The signature dish in Bologna is tagliatelle al ragu, ribbons of egg noodle topped with a rich, meaty sauce. And who could forget the region's famous sandwich, the *piadina*—a pita-thin bread filled with prosciutto and mortadella, put under a grill, and served hot with cheese oozing at its sides. Pei's stomach growled, but not because she knew anything of the region's legendary cuisine. In China, it was already 5 p.m.—time for dinner. As they neared the coast, the car turned off the *autostrada* and Pei saw olive groves and vineyards planted in neat rows on the sloping contours of the earth. Green leaves flapped in the wind and clusters of full-bodied grapes hung down like pearls. They drove inland along a road that traced the tops of those gentle slopes, passing a number of industrial-looking buildings at the bottom of a valley. "That's the mushroom farm," Fen pointed. Again, the sight of villas and farmhouses surprised Pei. She wondered where the canals and gondolas were and how far the water city was. The car headed uphill past a few homes, each with a well-kept yard and tidy rows of vines and olive trees, before turning up onto a gravel driveway and rolling to a stop in front of an old two-story house with peeling yellow paint and a crumbling terra-cotta roof. It was 12:40 p.m., 6:40 p.m. China time.

"We're here," Fen announced.

Both Pei and her brother responded at the same time: "Where?"

"Home."

"This is our house?" Pei asked, peering at the cracks in the concrete walls.

"Can we live in this house?" her brother said, eyeing a rusty tractor that sat in an overgrown yard surrounded by coils of corroded barbed wire.

"Just come in and you'll see."

> *I struggled with jet lag. In broad daylight I was yawning repeatedly and I could think of nothing but sleep. Indeed, I looked at the clock it was already past 11 p.m. in China. But here, it was the middle of the afternoon and the fierce sun shone down on me as if to remind me that this was reality.*

They climbed out of the car and stretched their legs. They had been traveling for nearly twenty-four hours. Large green jugs, the kind that looked like they were used to store wine, lay scattered about near the gravel driveway. Weeds sprouted from the interlocking brick path that brought them to the front of the house where a couple of fig trees stood next to a muddy field. The house was in utter disrepair. Long cracks stretched across the facade and chunks of yellow had fallen off the walls, exposing grey concrete underneath. A single front door opened up into a dusty room with an old fireplace and a sagging floor. A staircase brought them upstairs where they found three bedrooms, a bathroom, a kitchen, and a dining room, all connected by a long, narrow hallway. Rent was nearly $700 a month and was paid to the old woman, a friend of the mushroom farm owners, who lived across the street in a pristine three-story home tucked behind a wrought-iron gate. There were at least two cars parked on their paved driveway at all times and perched on the cantaloupe rooftop was a satellite dish. Pei and her family didn't own a television. They bought secondhand bicycles so they could get around a little easier.

"You each get your own bedrooms," Fen said excitedly. Pei entered the kitchen and saw an old cast-iron, wood-burning stove in one corner—a relic left behind by the landlord. Then she saw that her mother had purchased new appliances for the kitchen: a refrigerator, microwave, and a stove. On the table were dishes her mother had prepared earlier that morning. Chinese stir-fries, boiled dumplings, fruit, and even a bottle of champagne. Pei's father popped open the cork.

"It's a special occasion," he said. "We must drink!" No one in the family liked champagne very much, but they all took obligatory sips, the golden bubbles rising to the tops of their glasses in a dizzying froth. Pei turned to look at her mother. It was true she looked a lot older than she remembered, but there was something else about her. She exuded a quiet sense of competence. "Ah Ma has taken on so much responsibility," Pei thought. "She's the one taking care of our family. All of us, even Ah Ba, depend on her now." Months later, Pei would come to understand that it would be up to her to take care of the family, too. That night, Pei pulled the creaky shutters down over her bedroom window. Her mother said burglars often targeted Chinese residences. "They know the Chinese keep a lot of cash at home," she told Pei. "Make sure you close all the windows and shutters every night and before you leave the house." It was already 2 a.m. in China and Pei had no way of contacting Li Jie. She wondered if he had stayed up, waiting for her call.

> *So, there are also flies, mosquitoes, and ants outside of China, too. I wonder what would happen if the small insects in Italy encountered the insects in China. Would they say "hello" to each other in Italian? I would hope so! Maybe I think too much . . .*

Pei got a better look at her surroundings over the next few days. Their old house was perched at the top of a hill overlooking a valley. On a clear day, you could see the Adriatic—a blue-grey mass pooling just above the horizon—in the distance. Recreational cyclists zipped past the house in their sleek helmets and colorful spandex, riding hills that dipped and swelled like waves in a sea. Their house might have been old and crumbling, but the rest of the street was lined with pristine, gated villas that overlooked private vineyards and olive groves. Birds sang loudly in the trees. And every house on the street had at least a few pet dogs. No matter their size, these dogs dutifully guarded the gates of each home, barking ferociously at anyone who walked past. Pei was careful not to get too close, especially after one man made a point to yank his dog in the opposite direction the minute she neared. Though her Italian wasn't very good at the time, she could still make out a few key words: *Cinesi. Mangiano. Cani.* Chinese. Eat. Dogs. "Obviously this man wasn't speaking to his dog," Pei said angrily. "Those words were meant to hurt me." For centuries, people around the world have been eating dog meat. Ancient Romans feasted on their canines, butcher shops in France and Belgium sold dog meat during the nineteenth and early twentieth centuries, and dog meat was also consumed in Germany and the Netherlands, though usually only in times of war and famine. Today, the tradition of curing dog meat into jerky and sausages continues in Switzerland. In China, people have been eating what's often called *xiang rou* or "fragrant meat" since at least 500 BCE. In some Eastern cultures, dog meat is believed to have medicinal properties like generating heat and promoting warmth in the body. Pei admitted she had eaten dog meat before in China. "It was delicious," she told me rather sheepishly. "But I would never admit that to an Italian."

Italy is no place for an introvert. For many, striking up a conversation isn't merely a matter of being polite. Conversation is far too important to be cut short. But if you don't speak the language, conversing can be rather awkward and difficult. In the mornings, as powdery sunlight sifted in through the shutters, Pei often awoke to a strange gurgling sound coming from a workshop next to their home. The space belonged to the landlord, and some of the neighborhood men would gather there to make red wine or to tinker with machinery. "Make sure you always say 'hello' to the foreigners," Fen told her children. "Otherwise, Italians will think you are rude. They say *buongiorno* to you; you say *buongiorno* back. It's that simple." Pei had already learned this phrase when she was still in China, but her phrasebook used Chinese characters to sound out Italian words. *Buongiorno* came out sounding like *puo-en-ju-er-nuo* and *grazie* sounded like *ge-la-zie*. It was not a fashionable or exotic accent and Pei felt her words were coming out rough and ugly to Italian ears. There was one thing she could say with confidence: *ciao*. She used *ciao* every day to say hello and good-bye. She said *ciao* to her neighbors in the morning, in the afternoon, and at night.

She spent the next month at home, exploring the hilly neighborhood on her secondhand bike. "Having no car in Italy is like having no feet," Fen said. "So you must learn to ride." Pei never needed a bicycle in Qingtian. How ironic, she thought, that a Chinese girl would be forced to learn how to ride a bike in Italy. In the mornings, when her mother went off to work, Pei cruised alongside her father, Shen, who had taken up running in an effort to lose some weight. She gripped the handlebars until her hands turned pink, teetering to the left and to the right. Going downhill terrified her and she fell repeatedly, scraping her elbows and knees on the pavement. In the afternoons, Shen worked in the muddy field next to their house. He tilled the soil with a shovel and spade, got down on his hands and knees, and buried the seeds below a layer of fertilizer. Everyone else in the neighborhood planted flowers and tended to olive groves and grapevines. In a few months, bamboo shoots, balls of lettuce, and blades of bok choy would sprout from Shen's muddy garden.

Pei wrote in her diary and recorded new Italian words every day. She noticed the locals liked to speak with their hands. There was the waggy finger-pointing pose. The shrugging of shoulders with the palms facing upward toward the sky. Some Italians connected index fingers to thumbs and shouted, *"Perfetto!"* And if someone was angry, he slid his hands under his chin as if to say, "I don't care." The family purchased SIM cards that allowed for cheap long-distance calls to China. In the early mornings, Shen called home and shouted greetings into his phone to ensure his family and friends could hear him all the way from Italy. If you stood outside his bedroom window, even before the orange sun had spilled out over the horizon, you could hear him holler at the top of his lungs: "Have you eaten yet??!"

The family preferred to cook at home, but getting to the grocery store was not easy. It was a thirty-minute bike ride to the nearest supermarket, and to get there, you had to travel down what Pei considered a death-defying hill. Getting home was no easy task either. Pei couldn't decide which was more onerous—speeding down that hill or having to push a heavily loaded bicycle back home. The more groceries they bought, the more difficult it was for them to transport those items home. Things like bottled water and toilet paper were large and cumbersome and could only be purchased if they managed to hitch a ride to the store with one of Fen's colleagues. That's when the family bought in bulk. They stacked half a dozen cases of bottled water and toilet paper rolls in one corner of the dining room—enough to last them several months. The supermarket was one of the largest Pei had ever seen, but there was very little she had an appetite for. They called Emilia-Romagna Italy's "stomach," but when it came to eating, Pei came to say one phrase over and over again: *Wo chi bu lai*, which roughly translates to "I can't stomach it." She said it when she tasted salami for the first time. The chewy texture made her feel as if she were eating raw meat. "*Wo chi bu lai*," she said. When her mother made spaghetti bolognese at home, Pei said it tasted different from the noodles at Lalacomte Beef and Coffee. She pushed her plate away and said: *Wo chi bu lai*. She was told eating salads were good for her (it would help her lose weight!), but all she wanted to do was stir-fry that crisp lettuce in some oil and garlic. "Eating something raw just seems wrong," Pei said. "I don't think I can stomach this, either." The family agreed Italy was indeed a fine country: the air was clean, the sky was always blue, and the people were well-mannered. The only problem was the food. "There just isn't a lot of good food around here," Mao often said gloomily. "There is nothing to eat." In September, they celebrated Pei's seventeenth birthday. Shen cooked all of his daughter's favorite dishes, and Fen invited another Chinese family to share in the meal. Ying Ying, a skinny girl with long hair and droopy eyes who was just a few years younger than Pei, lived at the bottom of the hill. Both her parents worked on the mushroom farm with Fen. The two families packed into the tiny kitchen for dinner, smacking their lips, clinking glasses of wine, and digging their chopsticks into the hearty dishes laid out before them. But Pei and Ying Ying did not exchange one word until Fen said: "Why aren't you two talking to each other?" Pei and Ying Ying turned to look at each other for the first time and broke into giggles. For the rest of the night, the girls could not stop chit-chatting and eventually broke away from the family, Pei spilling all her secrets to Ying Ying. She talked about Li Jie and about life in China. Ying Ying listened enthusiastically to her stories. That night, Pei declared Ying Ying her best friend in Italy.

It was soon after her birthday dinner when Pei learned her mother had found her a job. A friend had recently purchased a bar near Venice and agreed to take Pei in. She would live and work with this woman and her family and she would learn how to mix drinks, how to brew the perfect cappuccino, and most importantly, how to socialize with Italians. Every Chinese migrant seemed to be investing in a bar. It was a good idea for Pei to learn as much as she could about it. This friend, whom Pei called Ayi, promised to enroll her in a local school where she could take part-time Italian lessons and work part-time at the bar. It sounded like a good arrangement.

"This is the best way for you to learn Italian quickly," Fen told Pei.

"Ah Ma," Pei said. "Why can't I find a job in a factory like you did?"

"Absolutely not," her mother said firmly. "It's very hard to improve your Italian in the factory surrounded by Chinese people all day."

Pei was determined to take on this new challenge. If she was able to learn Italian well, she could help her parents open their own business. They wouldn't have to work for others anymore. Everyone back home in China always talked about the importance of being your own *lao ban*, your own boss. It was as important a rite of passage as marriage and having children. Being a business owner put you in charge of your own fate. Every migrant went abroad with this dream, and Pei felt it was her duty to help her parents achieve it. Filial piety was an old Confucian philosophy, but it remains a key virtue in modern Chinese culture today. For Pei, this meant showing respect for her elders and deference to their opinions and kowtowing in front of ancestral tombs. Now that she was older, it meant supporting her parents and helping to take care of the family. Pei believed she could do it. Even though she was now the *lao wai* in a foreign country, she had Ayi and her family to guide her and show her the way. She was confident she could learn quickly and grew excited by the prospect that she would be living and working close to Venice. The water city and its great canals still shimmered in her dreams at night.

> *Very soon I will leave this home. This word* home *doesn't mean much to me anymore. I can so easily leave one place and move to another. Hard to believe, isn't it?*

For the longest time, Italians owned and operated Bar Girasole. Men lingered on its sizable patio sheltered by a green and white awning. From there, they could see the looming blue spire just a few blocks away. Next door, a small flower shop burst with the colors of spring: shocks of yellow daisies, sprays of citrus tulips, and bold red roses. The sweet fragrance of freshly cut stems lingered in the air for only a moment before it was overpowered by the aroma of roasted coffee beans. Bar Girasole's outside walls were a sunny yellow, and customers felt warmth and welcome as soon as they stepped inside its blue-painted walls. When a Chinese family purchased the bar a few years back, locals worried the establishment would fall to the wayside. Chinese business owners tended to skimp on a few Italian conventions—freebie appetizers, décor, and lighting—but this family was different. They kept the pretzel bowls full and all of Bar Girasole's lights on. The Chinese began investing in bars when work at the garment factories started drying up and restaurants saw fewer and fewer customers. The economic crisis may have caused some consumers to hold back on dining out or purchasing new clothing, but the Chinese had a hunch: Italians might still be willing to pay for their daily cappuccino. It cost just 1 euro a cup at most bars—a small price to pay for a time-honored Italian tradition. It's not clear who was the first person to make this hypothesis and test it out, but the idea spread throughout the migrant network quickly. Soon, buying a bar was the new business opportunity every Chinese migrant had on his or her mind. The owner of Bar Girasole also came from Qingtian County. Ayi had the coarse hands of a worker, and the lines in her face and the ruddiness of her cheeks were that of someone whose skin had been thickened by the country sun. Often, her eyebrows knitted together like she was bothered by something. That was to be expected, for the woman had a lot on her mind. Together with her husband and her two grown children, Ayi managed the bar seven days a week starting at six in the morning and closing well past midnight. The bar was constantly busy, the aroma of roasted coffee beans thick in the air. Old men liked to play card games or try their luck at the digital slot machines. Ayi stood behind the bar next to her daughter, a young woman in her late twenties who wore black-framed glasses and pulled her thick, dark hair back into a ponytail. The two watched over the cash register, the spring of the till jumping open as often as steam shot out of the stainless steel coffee machine.

"We have a spare bedroom in the apartment. Ye Pei can stay there," Ayi told Fen and Shen, who had accompanied Pei to Solesino on her first day. Ayi would provide housing and food, and Pei would earn 500 euros, less than $700, a month.

"Thank you," Fen said quietly.

Ayi turned to Pei. "You can start by washing the dishes."

Fen and Shen took a seat next to the bar and watched their daughter roll up her sleeves. Pei kept her head down and tried not to look at them. She wanted to be as professional as possible, to show Ayi she was focused on the task at hand. She scrubbed hard to get the stains out of the tiny white cups that never stopped piling up next to the sink. In between cups, she grabbed a towel and wiped the counters. Eventually, she began clearing dirty dishes off tables. After she completed each chore, Ayi always found something else for her to do. Pei moved about the bar with a broom, ignoring the tingling in the soles of her feet. When the hands of the clock joined together at midnight, her legs began to tremble. She had never stood for so long in her life. It was 2:30 a.m. by the time she was let off work. Fen and Shen didn't like to see their daughter work so hard, but they took solace in the fact that she would be living under the care of someone known to them. They would never allow Pei to live and work with a stranger. Ayi was a friend and she had come from Qingtian, too. Those who came from the same hometown always took care of their own.

*I thought I could do very well on my own, but at the sound of
the door slamming shut, I couldn't control the tears. At that
moment, I wanted Mama and Baba to come back, but I knew
that was not possible.*

Fen and Shen stayed the night with Pei in her new room and left early the
next morning, back to the house by the mushroom farm one hundred miles
away. As they left, the door of Ayi's apartment shut with a hollow thud, and
Pei let out a small cry that was pregnant with pain and surprise. When she left
China just one month earlier she did not cry, not even when her grandmother
gripped her hands and asked when she would return home. It was easier not to
cry then, for she was the one doing the leaving. Now she was being left behind.
She wanted to dash to the door, cast it open, and call to her parents to take her
home with them. But "home" had taken on so many different meanings in the
last month. Was China her home or was "home" that house on the hill with the
peeling yellow paint? She wanted to know how long she might have to stay with
Ayi and her family. How long would she have to work at the bar? Pei swallowed
all these questions. The last thing she wanted was for her parents to worry about
her. She didn't want to be a burden. She rubbed her eyes and drew a shaky
breath. "Today, I have a choice," she thought. "I can sulk or I can smile." Pei
decided she would choose the latter.

*In front of them, I must pretend I am very happy. If I feel like
I'm about to cry, I have to smile. If I show weakness, they will
look down on me. No one is going to care about my sorrow. I
will not show anyone my anger.*

Appearances were everything. Pei already knew that, and like a soldier pro-
grammed for war, her body responded with unfailing precision: she sucked in
her tummy, straightened her back, held her hands one on top of the other, and
flashed her eight-tooth smile. She would be at Ayi's beck and call. She would
do everything that was asked of her—even scrub the toilets if that was what Ayi
wanted. She would learn how to make the perfect cappuccino. And she vowed
to learn Italian by speaking with customers as often as she could and memoriz-
ing her Italian-Chinese dictionary at night. In the shower, she held water in her
mouth, tilted her head back, and gargled in order to practice rolling her Rs.
That first week, Ayi and her daughter gave Pei a new name.

"How about Alessia?" they suggested.

"Alessia," she repeated. "*Mi chiamo Alessia.*" My name is Alessia.

CHINATOWN

*All migrants, not just Chinese migrants, look for a place where
they can start new lives, a place to plug into the diaspora. But
when migrants cluster together to form these immigrant neighborhoods, it can put native populations on edge.*

I watched Marc disappear behind a gray, nondescript door. The customs
official motioned to us just as were getting off the plane in Pisa. Then he
pointed to Marc and led him away. "Don't worry. Stay calm," said Carina
Chen, the businesswoman we were traveling with. She grabbed me by the arm
and pulled me forward. "Just keep walking and don't look back. They do this
all the time." Carina flew from Barcelona to Pisa every weekend and said it was
normal for customs officials to target the Chinese for random checks, but I was
distraught. Just what was the officer checking for? "They're just going to ask
him a few questions," Carina told me. "He'll be out soon." We sat at a table in
front of a McDonald's a few meters away from the door, but I couldn't help but
turn around every few minutes to see if it would open. I wondered what kinds
of questions they were asking Marc, and I worried how effectively they were
communicating since Marc didn't speak Italian and it didn't seem the customs
officer spoke much English. Behind the gray door, only a few words were said
in rudimentary English:

"What are you doing in Italy?" the officer asked.

"I'm here as a tourist," Marc said.

"Let me see your passport." Marc took out his Dutch passport and watched
the officer flip through it. "Your bag." Marc handed over his backpack. The

officer unzipped it and began unloading its contents, laying them out on the table one by one. Marc's DSLR camera. A toothbrush. A pair of boxers. A set of earphones. Pretzels from the airplane. The officer looked disappointed. "OK," he said, gesturing toward the door. I waited five minutes before the door finally swung open and Marc came striding out. He made eye contact and gave a slight nod of the head. He was fine.

We followed Carina outside the terminal to a car rental depot where we climbed into a two-door Fiat. Carina sat in the driver's seat, set the radio station to play Italian pop music, and kept her eyes trained on the winding road ahead as we sped west on the *autostrada* toward Prato. Her husband, Pang, usually did the driving when they visited every weekend, but it was a busy time for their wholesale operation in Barcelona where they sold the latest and trendiest "Made in Italy" clothes at bargain prices. This weekend Carina had come to Prato alone, and she was kind enough to allow us to tag along. As soon as we pulled off the *autostrada*, Carina drove on wide lanes flanked by massive warehouses. We had arrived in an industrial district called Macrolotto. Everywhere, I saw signs in both Italian and Chinese: Perfect Pronto Moda. Lucky Pronto Moda. Pronto Moda Forever. I checked my wristwatch. It was close to 11 p.m.

"Are any of the warehouses still open at this hour?" I asked.

"Most of them only open this late in the evening," Carina answered. "If you try to come during the day, you'll find many of them are closed."

Carina spoke better Italian than she did Chinese—that's because she was born and raised in Italy. When she was a child, her Chinese family ran a workshop stitching leather handbags near Rimini, a resort town on Italy's east coast. Her husband, Pang, had spent years helping his mother run a Chinese restaurant in the area. The two met outside a local Chinese school where Carina was a student. Having emigrated from Qingtian to Italy as a teen, Pang's Chinese was pretty good. He was at the school only to scout out pretty girls. He spotted Carina, who had long black hair, a fair complexion, and a vivacious laugh. By the time they married years later, both their parents' businesses had folded. The young couple had to figure out a way to take care of their families, but there were few options as Italy's economy stuttered to a halt. Carina and Pang visited a relative in Barcelona who ran a successful wholesale business selling clothes imported from China. They decided to move to Barcelona in 2006—just in time to catch the tail-end of the economic boom in Spain.

Carina drove past more warehouses before pulling into a parking lot. "Dinner first," she grinned. "Prato has the best Chinese food in all of Italy." We walked into a cloud of gray. Through the haze of cigarette smoke, I saw dozens of Chinese people seated around large round tables. "*Mamma Mia*, I'm no longer in Italy," I thought. "This is China." Everyone was dressed in black winter jackets and I shivered, noting the heat wasn't turned on. We took a seat and saw southern Zhejiang delicacies—hearty soups, fried razor clams, and steamed duck tongues—rotating on turntables in a steady orbit. "We haven't just returned to China," I exclaimed. "This could be Qingtian!" A high-pitch screech followed by a low boom confirmed another suspicion: a late night karaoke party was under way at the back of the restaurant. We ate quickly before climbing back into the Fiat. That night, we visited at least a dozen wholesale outlets with Carina, who haggled hard for her purchases. She ordered 150 beige coats, each one costing her twelve euros. A slinky gold sweater that looked great with a pair of black tights caught her eye. She ordered 80 pieces and paid in cash. Carina strolled up and down one of the cavernous warehouses, leafing through metal racks crammed full of clothes. She eyed a gray tank top that came with a matching faux cashmere sweater. A nice ensemble for the working woman. A salesperson in knee-high boots and a fanny pack around her waist approached and asked for nine euros a set. Eight Euros, Carina countered. The saleswoman said 8.50 was her lowest price. "No deal," Carina said. She noticed many of the warehouses were selling knitwear ponchos and shawls. But the weather wasn't very chilly in Barcelona and she wasn't sure they would sell in Spain. It was now close to 1 a.m. and Carina was calling Pang to update him on her purchases. When they first moved to Barcelona, the young couple worked tirelessly to establish their wholesale business in the garment district not far from the city's Arc de Triomf. Two years later, more than a million immigrants lost their jobs when the housing bubble burst in 2008, and as both Spanish- and Chinese-owned businesses shuttered all around them, Carina and Pang defied the odds by expanding their business. They opened several more shops across the city and began traveling to Prato every week to keep up with demand. Their work and travel schedule was grueling, but Carina and Pang seemed indefatigable. When she finished giving her update and got off the phone, Carina announced we were finally heading to the hotel for some rest. "We start up again early tomorrow morning," she said.

The parking lots outside many Chinese-run *pronto moda* warehouses are lined with the cars and trucks of wholesalers who have come to load up on inexpensive "Made in Italy" clothing. They buy in relatively small quantities, and most manage to avoid import tariffs thanks to the fluid borders of the European Union. The *pronto moda* garments are then resold in shops around the world to unwitting consumers who may be shocked to discover the clothes are made by Chinese hands. When I shared this revelation with friends and family, they never looked at "Made in Italy" labels the same way again. Neither did I. "The workmanship in Prato's Chinese factories is mostly poor but always in vogue," Carina explained. "Actually, a lot of the stuff made in China is of better quality. The only problem is they are always a little bit behind." I was dizzy as Carina sped around Macrolotto the next morning, making multiple stops and placing numerous orders. The Chinese own nearly 45 percent of the city's manufacturing businesses, and all the buildings in Macrolotto looked the same. Carina had a hard time orienting herself, spinning her tires on the same roundabouts before finally pulling up to the right warehouse. She was looking for a particular stylist who did an exceptionally good job of creating high-fashion look-alike garments. Carina and Pang were often browsing fashion websites and walking around Barcelona's high-end shops for inspiration. Sometimes they bought a particular garment they liked and e-mailed photos to the designer in Prato. By the time they arrived in Prato on the weekend, the prototype was ready for inspection. Not every garment they ordered sold well, but Carina said experience was teaching them to make better choices. Recently, they were having more hits than misses. What makes *pronto moda* so successful? Some like to credit industrious Chinese immigrants, but there's another more quantifiable reason: *Pronto moda*'s location in an industrial district allows entrepreneurs to purchase fabric, dye all the garments according to the current fashion trends, and purchase accessories, all in a very short period of time. Carina and Pang could replicate the latest fashions and have those garments designed, produced, and delivered to their stores in Barcelona within a week. The fastest boat from China couldn't deliver that. Now, whenever I am shopping, I run my hands over clothes made in Italy and inspect labels for hints of where they might have come from. "Did these shoes come from Prato?" I wonder. "Did a Chinese migrant makes this sweater?" I stand in my closet and wonder how many migrant stories are woven into the fabrics that hang there.

The fire started at Teresa Moda in the middle of the night on a Sunday. It most likely began in the corner of the garment factory where there was a camp stove being used to cook meals. Then it swept through the cramped space, quickly creeping up on the workers who were sleeping nearby. There were no emergency exits and the windows were blocked by bars. Rolls of fabric leaning against the wall lit up like giant candlesticks. The flames melted a mountain of plastic coat hangers, devoured bags of newly cut garments, and charred the blackout curtains over the windows. Seven workers—two women and five men—died. One of the dead suffocated as he tried to escape through iron bars on the windows. Police said it took days to identify them all because relatives were too scared to come forward. When they finally did, the community enlarged photos of the victims and affixed them to the door next to a handwritten sign that read: "Sorrow Has No Color." Dozens of bouquets were left at the entrance to the workshop, and a few days later, hundreds of people, both Chinese and Italian, attended a candlelight vigil in a rare showing of solidarity and sympathy. In the weeks that followed, four Chinese citizens were placed under investigation on charges of multiple manslaughter, failure to uphold workplace safety measures, and exploitation of illegal workers. Then, prosecutors issued arrest warrants for eleven people, Chinese and Italian, including a City Hall employee, on charges of issuing false residence permits to more than three hundred Chinese immigrants who paid $820 to $2,050 each for the papers. Law enforcement officials gave numerous interviews to the press, saying they have struggled for years to rein in illegal and unsafe practices. In the two years leading up to the fire at Teresa Moda, officials performed more than 1,500 checks on garment and textile operations in Prato—more than half of those businesses belonged to Chinese citizens. As a result, more than 1,700 fines were issued, about 400 undocumented immigrants were identified, and more than 350 companies were shut down for various violations. Still, officials said they were severely understaffed when it came to keeping tabs on the more than 8,000 factories in Prato's textile and garment manufacturing sectors. Officials complained that Chinese workers were reluctant to cooperate with Italian officials, and labor leaders said they had failed to convince the workers to fight for better conditions. "If you want to build consensus, you have to offer them opportunities, residence permits, and new jobs; show them it's better to be legal," a labor union representative told the *New York Times*. "Instead, when factories are raided, the workers are brought to the police station, fingerprinted and given a paper that tells them they have to leave Italy." During my research, I encountered sporadic cases of Chinese migrant workers going on strike or leaving a garment workshop in protest of poor working conditions. But for the most part, workers were too afraid to defy their bosses for fear of deportation and even retribution against their families in China. Most prefer to pay off their debts, save money, and move on with their lives.

Carina knew many who survived Prato's notorious garment workshops. Her friend Jimmy Xu was forced to spend years in one when he was indebted to an uncle who helped arrange his passage from China to Italy. With the help of snakeheads and a set of false papers, Jimmy left his home in Qingtian and traveled first to Switzerland then through Belgium to Italy before finally arriving in Prato where he worked at his uncle's workshop. Inside, living and working spaces were one and the same. The fragrance of stir-fry lingered in the air that tasted of hot glue and metal. Wet laundry hung from the ceiling, and a portable gas-powered stove was pushed into one corner of the room while some workers slept in cardboard cubicles not far away. Jimmy spent at least twelve hours a day bent over a sewing machine, his small hands racing to feed reams of cloth past a shuddering needle. Mountains of half-finished garments piled on the floor next to him. Such atrocious working conditions were no secret among the Chinese, and Jimmy had heard all the horror stories. Still, tens of thousands of migrants like him continued to make the journey from China to Italy. Why did they come? Because for many, while Prato was harsh and remuneration was poor, salaries still equaled ten times the average worker's wage in China. And amid the tales of isolation, hard work, long hours, and unbearable living conditions emerged stories of success: migrants who managed to save and borrow and make the right connections so they could escape Prato and open a business of their own.

To pay off his debt of nearly $15,000, Jimmy sometimes worked fifteen hours a day. It didn't take him long to regret leaving China, but going back home wasn't an option. "I was very poor and very tired, but I didn't say anything," he said. "I didn't want my family to worry about me." Jimmy learned to sew quickly and in silence. His uncle had a vile temper and often chastised workers if he caught them talking to one another. "We would work all day and not exchange one word," Jimmy recalled years later. "I was a robot without a mind." In the beginning, he earned just 500 euros each month. Later, when he learned to sew quickly, he could earn double that. "The only time I was happy was pay day," he said, "but then I had to give it all back." He shared a bedroom with seven other workers and rarely ventured outside the workshop except to wander up and down Via Pistoiese, the heart of Prato's Chinatown. It's a short walk beyond the city's medieval walls, past the cathedral with the stunning Renaissance frescoes; an area the local Italians have nicknamed the area *San Pechino*—Saint Beijing. Here, the Italian bakeries and cappuccino bars have disappeared and given way to storefronts with Chinese signs. There are travel agencies, money-wiring shops, immigration consultants, and Internet cafés— shops and services devoted to maintaining the link between migrant hometowns in China and the diaspora. Outside a supermarket selling Chinese groceries is an electronic job board flashing the latest garment industry jobs. Every day dozens gather on the sidewalk, puff on their cigarettes, and stare at the listings that crawl across the board.

Decades before the Chinese came, Via Pistoiese was a street occupied entirely by Italian artisans. Agnese Morganti's family is one of the few Italian families that still live and work here today. Since 1973 the Morgantis have been a retailer of spare parts for industrial machinery. Like a traditional Italian business, and not unlike a Chinese one, all family members are actively involved in the business. "The building itself is not only a shop and a warehouse but also a home," she explained. Agnese remembers she was just a child when the first Chinese family moved into the house next door. The year was 1992. "My grandparents made friends with them. They would help my granny if she locked herself out and even gave us Christmas hampers filled with Chinese foods. The presence of the Chinese in the area was still barely noticeable. Still, you would see a couple of lanterns here and there hung by the entrance of the very first Chinese restaurants." Agnese said she often overheard people in the neighborhood complaining about the Chinese. There were jokes about the newcomers stealing pets and cooking them in smoky kitchens and quite a few laughs about those migrants who, try as they might, could not roll their Rs. "Such comments never won me over. For a kid, it was all so fascinating," Agnese said. "I just found it fancy, exotic, and extravagant."

Not everyone sees the birth of Italy's Chinatowns the same way. The Italian-language press regularly publishes stories perpetuating a "yellow peril"—a term used widely in America one hundred years ago—and local governments try to stem what they characterize as an "Asian invasion." In Treviso, just outside of Venice, politicians outlawed the hanging of red lanterns in front of stores. "It's spoiling the appearance of the city," the head of the council's town planning department told a daily newspaper. "The Chinese put up all sorts of stuff: lanterns, lions, dragons, there's even one [establishment] that did its whole front in Oriental style." The city's deputy mayor agreed: "Treviso is a city of Veneto and Padania; it's certainly not an Oriental city," he said. In Forte dei Marmi, a resort town on the Tuscan coast, the local government slapped a ban on the opening of kebab shops, Chinese takeaways, Indian restaurants, and other purveyors of "ethnic food." "This measure has nothing to do with xenophobia. It is about protecting and valuing our culture," said Forte dei Marmi's mayor, Umberto Buratti. And in an elementary school in Milan, a school was closed because there were "too many foreigners" enrolled according to a law set by then-prime minister Silvio Berlusconi that proclaimed foreign children could not make up more than 30 percent of a class. Thankfully, the law was abolished by a new education minister the following year, and the school, now considered a model of integration in Italy, was reopened. The bans and decrees are just the latest expression of nationalism that has been sweeping across the country as Italians struggle to hold onto their traditions in the face of globalization. Fears about immigration and the economy have heightened as the recession drags on and the wealth of Italian families has plunged. To some Italians, the Chinese seem to have only gotten richer—not just in Italy but in China and all around the world—and their tendency to flaunt their newfound wealth with luxury cars, flashy clothes, and designer handbags has only made things worse. In Prato, part of the resentment has indeed been cultural, but what seems to vex most is how the Chinese are beating the Italians at their own game. The immigrants have managed to navigate Italy's notoriously complex bureaucracy and build a flourishing, if underground, sector while many Italians have gone out of business. "The Chinese are very clever and very well organized," a police officer, who regularly deals with Chinese immigrants near the city of Bologna, told me. "To avoid the authorities, they have created their own rules, they solve their own problems, and they operate in their own little world. And they deliberately choose to stay silent, so the newspapers don't write about them and the police ignore them."

All migrants, not just Chinese migrants, look for a place where they can plug into the diaspora. For many people, that starting point is their own ethnic group—people they know or people with whom they share a common language. When migrants cluster together to form these immigrant communities, it can put native populations on edge. To them, these enclaves are alien and threatening, denounced as dirty and disease ridden, and condemned as permanent and irredeemable slums. But the contrasting truth is this: these neighborhoods are a nucleus of entrepreneurship, ambition, and social organization, providing migrants with cheap housing, jobs, and informal loans to help kick-start businesses. The people here are not all passive victims; many of them are opportunists who work hard to forge a better future for their families and hope their children will enter mainstream society and one day leave Chinatown behind. In this way, these neighborhoods are the most effective pathway to social and economic integration.

The Chinese are the fourth-largest immigrant group in Italy behind the Romanians, Albanians, and Moroccans, but they seem especially numerous because they tend to cluster in their Chinatowns. Rumors and misgivings have spread quickly. During my time in Italy, aside from the allegations that Chinese kitchens were making dog soup and perceptions that all Chinese people look alike, I heard whispers suggesting immigrants were agents and spies for the Chinese Communist Party, bent on world domination, and this: *I cinesi non muoiono mai.* "The Chinese never die." In the opening chapter of *Gomorrah*, a nonfiction account of the decline of Naples under the rule of one of Italy's most notorious organized crime networks, journalist Roberto Saviano describes a horrific scene: dead bodies spilling out of a shipping container bound for China.

> The hatches, which had been improperly closed, suddenly sprang open, and dozens of bodies started raining down. They looked like mannequins. But

when they hit the ground, their heads split open, as if their skulls were real. And they were. Men, women, even a few children, came tumbling out of the container. All dead. Frozen, stacked one on top of another, packed like sardines. These were the Chinese who never die. The eternal ones, who trade identity papers among themselves.

A port crane operator in Naples described the scene for Saviano. He saw the bodies fall—bodies that were being sent back to China so they could be buried in their hometowns. But why is it said that the Chinese never die? Some believe the visas and identification papers belonging to the deceased are passed onto undocumented immigrants who assume a new identity in order to stay in Italy. A third party is believed to profit from such transactions—perhaps the Neapolitan mafia known as the *Camorra* or the Chinese triads, which follow the diaspora wherever they go. The idea that "the Chinese never die" is so pervasive in Italian society that even those who are more open-minded about issues of immigration are unsure what to think. "Of course we don't believe these rumors are true," one Italian university professor told me, "but I can't help but wonder why is it that I have never witnessed a Chinese funeral before."

If these Italians visited the mountains in Qingtian County, they would have found their answer. They would have seen the enormous stone graves, and they would have witnessed families burn paper euros and perform the ritual kowtows. Many Chinese migrants still consider themselves sojourners whose wish is to be buried in their own native soil. Today in Qingtian the graves have grown so numerous and so large, the local government has outlawed traditional hillside tombs and encourages people to bury their dead on small plots of land in Western-style cemeteries. But the people in Qingtian have continued to build the tombs anyway, and the government has responded by sending crews out in the middle of the night to inflict the greatest dishonor on the dead—extinguishing incense sticks, knocking over altars, overturning rocks, and spray-painting tombstones. To protect the graves, families try to make new tombs look old by covering them in brush. I saw many of these old-looking new graves in the mountains not far from where Marc's grandfather is buried. His family always said how lucky they were to have purchased a plot years before the ban came into effect.

When my friend Sun Wen-Long hears "the Chinese never die," his normally cheerful face turns a solemn white. Wen was born and raised in Italy and speaks with a thick Bolognese accent. Italians say his accent is so good that if they close their eyes they are sure he must be a native of Bologna (which he is), but when they open their eyes they are surprised to see a young Chinese man with long black hair in a typical Italian style. His Italian name is Valentino, which I think is a fabulous name, but Wen thinks it sounds too feminine and prefers to go by his Chinese name. Wen is a college student in Bologna and a volunteer for ASSOCINA, a group of second-generation Italian-born Chinese dedicated to creating dialogue and bridging the gap between Italian and Chinese cultures. When Wen hears "the Chinese never die," he will tell you how he recently lost his mother to cancer and how she is buried in a family plot just outside of Bologna. He will tell you how his grandfather, who came to Italy more than sixty years ago, purchased graves for the entire family. "They could easily have decided to stay in China and have a tomb there in the mountains of Qingtian, but they chose to stay in Bologna where their children, grandchildren, and friends spend their evenings playing mahjong, where they had built a life," he said. "My grandfather Joseph knew that his tomb in China would have fresh flowers just once a year. Here in Italy, I can honor him when I want to, because this is where my family has put down roots." Wen says he's not alone. "In Italy there are so many kids and so many families of Chinese origin who despite all the problems, despite the economic crisis, despite the difficulties of integrating into Italian society, have chosen to live and work in Italy, and chosen to die here." Yet Wen grows ever more frustrated with the country he calls home. For more than five years he has been part of a battle to reform Italy's citizenship law, joining an alliance of twenty-two civil society organizations that are campaigning for citizenship to be based more on "soil" than on "blood." Their slogan: *L'Italia sono anch'io.* I am also Italian.

In Italy, the children of immigrants are not granted Italian citizenship at birth. Instead they are forced to adopt the citizenship of their parents. For eighteen years, Wen was considered a citizen of China, and he remembers, as a young teen, trying to sign up for something as simple as a local soccer league. In order for him to join, he was told it was necessary to request a document from the government of China certifying that he wasn't playing in a Chinese sports league—that of course would be a conflict of interest. It didn't matter that Wen had never even been to China or that he couldn't even speak Chinese very well. It took six months to get the right documents before he was finally allowed to play. The experience showed him that he was an outsider in his own home. Wen became eligible to apply for Italian citizenship on his eighteenth birthday. "I waited eighteen years to officially be Italian, but I have felt Italian all my life," he said. Though Wen feels this way, many Italians don't see him in the same light. That young man with the perfect Bolognese accent and the long Italian hair that whips around his face as he plays soccer with his friends on a weekday night? He can't be a *real* Italian. No, he will always be Chinese. In recent years Wen has started to see himself that way, too.

The woman spearheading reform to Italy's citizenship law was Cecile Kyenge, a Congolese-Italian politician who was appointed Italy's first black cabinet minister in 2013. During her short ten-month tenure, she faced a torrent of abuse from Italy's right-wing Northern League party and its anti-immigrant supporters. She had bananas thrown at her while she was standing at a podium during a political rally. She endured racist taunts like "Congolese monkey," "Zulu," and "the black anti-Italian." One of the League's most senior figures likened her to an orangutan, another accused of her wanting to impose "tribal traditions" on Italy, and a councilor with the League, a woman, even called for her to be raped. Meanwhile, Kyenge has kept up her mantra that Italy is a tolerant country. "I have never said Italy is racist. Every country needs to start building awareness of immigration and Italy has simply arrived very late," she said.

For a century, Italians left their homeland in droves. An estimated twenty-six million Italians migrated elsewhere from 1876 to 1976. Chronic unemployment, low wages, worsening agricultural conditions, and a turbulent history were just some of the reasons why. In the beginning, men left their families behind and moved from one province to another in search of seasonal work as agricultural laborers. Even within their own country, these workers faced intense discrimination. When employment opportunities within Italy dried up, they traveled afar, scattering across Western Europe. Others journeyed to Canada, the United States, Brazil, and Australia. In their new homes, they endured what almost all migrants must face—miserable living conditions and the hardships of adapting culturally and linguistically in a new land. They sent money home, and those remittances helped keep Italy's economy afloat. Then the tides began to turn.

Migrants began showing up on Italy's shores in the 1970s. Truckloads of Albanians arrived half-starved and hopeful for another chance at life. Then came migrants from Romania, the Ukraine, Bangladesh, and China. In recent years, Italy has also borne the brunt of an influx of asylum seekers attempting to cross the Mediterranean to reach Europe. Many of the migrants are men, women, and children fleeing conflicts in the Horn of Africa and the Middle East. Packed into rickety and rusted fishing boats that are hardly seaworthy, they wash up near the closest Italian territory to North Africa: a rocky island called Lampedusa that has become synonymous with death and despair. Italy has repeatedly requested aid from the European Union in managing refugees, but has been turned down. In 2011, at the height of the influx when more than sixty-two thousand migrants arrived in Italy, boats carrying hundreds and even thousands of people were arriving in Lampedusa every day. Today the flow has slowed, although not by much. In 2013, more than forty thousand migrants came to Italy via Lampedusa, and thousands more have drowned in shipwrecks near the island's coast. Next to orange buoys and fishing nets, blue body bags perpetually line Lampedusa's sandy harbor.

Right-wing, anti-immigrant politicians in Italy have experienced a surge of support as fears rise over the flow of asylum seekers and migrants have been made scapegoats for the country's economic woes. The Northern League political party even unleashed a series of xenophobic posters, one of them depicting a Native American wearing a traditional feather headdress with the headline: "They underwent immigration. Now they live on reservations. Think about it." Just over a million foreigners were living in Italy in 1990—2 percent of the country's entire population. Today, there are more than four million foreigners here—that's 7.5 percent, and this number doesn't even take into account the children of immigrants born in Italy. A national Catholic charity recently projected the country's foreign-born population will make up 23 percent of Italy's population by 2063. Italy was once a country people left behind. Now, it is overwhelmed with newcomers. With a shrinking economy and relentless recession, immigration is a difficult reality to swallow for most of Italy—especially in a place like Prato.

※

Less than forty-eight hours after she landed in Tuscany, Carina Chen was finished with her *pronto moda* orders. I wanted more time to explore Prato, so as Carina caught a flight back to Barcelona on Sunday evening, Marc and I booked a hotel room in the center of the old city. Before Carina left, I asked for some advice. Had she been to the old city before? Where should we go and what should we see? "I'm not really sure," she said. "I've just been to Via Pistoiese . . . " Though she took weekly trips to Prato, she had just enough time to visit the warehouses in Macrolotto and have quick meals in Chinatown. She also made sure to drop by a shopping mall near her hotel and buy a bag of *cantucci*, a type of biscotti studded with roasted almonds, for her two young children. But she had never explored the old city. Not even once.

Our Lonely Planet guide advised us to visit the city's famous textile museum. Housed in a converted mill right in the center of town, it is described as a symbol of the local textile manufacturing industry. Inside, precious textiles are on display, recovered from burial chambers dating back to the third century

CE. There are sacred velvets and damasks from the thirteenth century, Italian embroideries from the fifteenth to twentieth century, ancient texts documenting the development of the local industry over the last quarter of the nineteenth century, and a gallery of Italian hand looms, spinning wheels, spoolers, and warping machines. There's also a smattering of contemporary textiles and film costumes made from locally produced textiles. I learned that following World War II, Prato's textile industry was booming. And that by the early 1980s, the area was considered a "model industrial district." The museum acknowledged that Prato was forced to abandoned its traditional wool businesses to compete in a new and changing global market. Today's factories are smaller enterprises that have shifted their operations to producing specially designed textiles such as cotton, viscose, linen, silk, yarns, and knitwear. We left the museum brimming with knowledge about the rich history of this textile town, yet I couldn't help but notice the absence of recent history in the exhibitions. Nowhere in the textile museum did I see the words *pronto moda*, nor did I see one exhibit mentioning the Chinese presence. As soon as we exited the museum, we looked west toward the crumbling city walls that were built during the Renaissance. Today, it is a barrier that divides the Chinese world from the Italian one, and I came to a realization: while Prato is home to the highest percentage of Chinese in Europe, reaching nearly 50,000 in a city of 190,000, and has attracted the largest concentration of Chinese-run industry in the continent, the Chinese in Prato are literally living outside the walls of mainstream society. The tension in this city is apparent, with many locals bitterly accusing the Chinese of destroying their home and ruining the "Made in Italy" brand. The Chinese in Prato argue they have helped rescue the city from total economic irrelevance. If it weren't for the Chinese, some say, there would be no *pronto moda*. The Chinese didn't take jobs away from Italians; the Chinese saved Prato.

That evening a hotel employee recommended we try La Vecchia Cucina di Soldano, an old trattoria not far from the center of the city that served many local specialties. Still not accustomed to the Italian tradition of a late dinner, we hungrily waited until 8 p.m. for the trattoria to open. The restaurant was warm, cozy, and dimly lit, with an eclectic mix of paintings and antiques hanging on the walls. A few customers were already seated at small red-and-white-checkered tables when we entered. But as soon as we stepped through the doors, the place seemed to freeze over. Forks stopped in mid-air and all eyes were on us. On our black hair. Our faces. My Chinese eyes. A waiter rushed forward to seat us. He helped us navigate the menu and made excellent recommendations. Marc and I spoke quietly in English, and I noticed the restaurant had grown even quieter as nearby patrons listened to us speak. Dinner started off with bruschetta and spicy salami, followed by ravioli with ragu sauce, and *bistecca alla fiorentina*, which is steak topped with arugula, lemon, and chunky Parmesan cheese. The food was delightful indeed, but throughout the entire meal I felt as though we were being watched. An uncomfortable aura seemed to surround us. "Do you think Chinese people ever eat in that trattoria?" I asked Marc when we were back in our hotel room that night. Prato may have been home to one of Europe's largest Chinese communities, but it occurred to me that Chinese immigrants rarely entered the old city and maybe never dined at the local Italian restaurants. For one, eating out wasn't cheap. And the Chinese, who I know to be deeply prideful, probably preferred their own cuisine. Maybe another reason why we didn't see immigrants within the old city walls was because, like Carina, they were all too busy working.

When news of Prato's deadly fire fanned across the Chinese migrant network and reached Jimmy Xu, the former garment slave was not surprised to hear it. He had long since left Prato. As soon as he repaid his smuggling debt to his callous uncle, he packed his bags and traveled east, as far away from Tuscany as he could. He ended up in the coastal city of Rimini—the same Rimini where Carina grew up and where Ye Pei would soon arrive—where a cluster of Chinese factories still thrived on subcontracting work for Italian fashion houses. A friend of his had managed to open his own workshop and Jimmy went to help. "I was a changed person," he said. "I could get a drink after work, have a beer with my friends. We talked during the day at the factory. Can you believe we were actually allowed to talk?" Four years later, he opened his own factory where he assembled clothes for high fashion companies, gaining contracts with Hugo Boss, Versace, Dolce & Gabbana, and Giorgio Armani, among others.

Life was quieter in Rimini. There is no Chinatown and Chinese garment factories are scattered across the countryside. Jimmy set up his own workshop in a concrete warehouse next to a farmer's field. On my first visit, I remember driving along a country road before taking a sudden right turn down a gravel path, past a warmly lit house where an Italian family was probably sitting down for dinner. I remember continuing down the bumpy road in complete darkness. By the time I could make out Jimmy's workshop in the twilight, we had already pulled to a stop in front of it. The doors were closed and the windows were blacked out by dark curtains. As soon as I stepped out of the car, I could hear the whir and clatter of sewing machines. I pulled the heavy metal door to the side and a beam of white light spilled out into the darkness. I stepped into the glow and found myself in a spacious room with high ceilings, bare cement floors, and about a dozen tables each with its own sewing machines. Jimmy and a Chinese woman were bent over two of the machines, running colorful reams of fabric through them. "Welcome!" he shouted over the deafening clang. They were stitching flags that had blue, white, and red horizontal stripes and a red dragon crest.

"What country does this flag belong to?" I shouted over the noise.

"I'm not sure," Jimmy shouted back. He'd spent the last three days stitching six thousand such flags. Recently, he was taking a lot of flag orders. He was sewing flags for a Dutch soccer team and stitched Swedish and American flags too. The woman working by his side was his wife, a girl from Qingtian he married shortly after leaving Prato. They had two young daughters who rode around the factory on their pink tricycles as Jimmy and his wife continued to sew into the night. I visited several Chinese workshops in and around Rimini. Some made swimwear and hemmed handbags; others crafted suede stilettos and jeweled flats. All of them were hidden away in innocuous structures behind heavy metal doors and dark curtains. Every factory boss complained about the economic crisis. They said work had slowed significantly in the past few years and they didn't receive many orders from the large fashion houses anymore. Good workers were also difficult to find because anyone with any skill opted to open their own workshop. No one wanted to work for somebody else. Many of the workers, who were often dressed in thick, puffy pajamas and slippers brought over from China, expressed a desire to find another job, but felt they didn't have any transferable skills—they only knew how to sew and they couldn't speak very good Italian having spent so much time in a factory among Chinese workers. As the economic crisis dragged on and subcontracting work dried up, Jimmy began taking on smaller and smaller jobs.

"Once I received an order for two hundred flags," Jimmy said. "The company told me it was a Chinese flag, but I had never seen it before." The flag was brightly colored, with six red rays of light radiating from a golden sun in the sky and a pair white and green lions spinning a circular yin-yang symbol. Weeks later, Jimmy was watching television one night when he saw the flags featured on a local news report. A group of Tibetans brandished them during a protest. "*Tah-mah-de!*" Jimmy cried out, cursing in Chinese when he saw the flags fluttering across the screen. He hadn't recognized the Tibetan Independence flags because the flags are banned in mainland China. Jimmy often reminisced about better days when he was stitching pants for Dolce & Gabbana and earning at least $8 a pair. Now he made just 14 cents a flag. Even so, he vowed never to return to Prato no matter how hard things got.

✠

Europe's first Chinatowns were established in the early nineteenth century when Chinese sailors jumped ship in Liverpool, Hamburg, Marseilles, and Amsterdam. Like the Chinatowns in America, these early sojourners were Cantonese men who sailed from China's southeastern Guangdong Province. And like the early American Chinatowns, these men took to cooking and laundering—jobs they were familiar with from a life at sea. Setting up in these European port cities was a strategic move; migrants could easily stay in touch this way and have convenient access to trade and shipping routes. Though early Chinatowns in Europe were dominated by Cantonese migrants, peppered throughout Europe were hundreds of migrants from Qingtian County who had made their way to the continent by sea and, as legend had it, by land via Siberia. The Qingtian migrants spread out all over the continent peddling soapstones and hawking trinkets in small towns and villages, preferring to avoid the cities where the Cantonese held sway.

As I traveled across the continent, I visited Chinese communities in six different European countries. During each visit I dined in Chinese restaurants, went shopping in Chinese-run stores, and met with local characters who showed me how every Chinatown had its own distinct history and flavor. The Chinatowns in northern Europe—in the UK, Belgium, and Holland—were much older and continued to be dominated by Cantonese immigrants. The Chinatowns in southern Europe—Spain, Portugal, Italy—were relatively new and had been built up by immigrants from southern Zhejiang. The largest Chinatown in Europe can be found in Paris. The first Chinese neighborhood, which was established near the Gare de Lyon train station, has long since vanished. But a thriving Chinatown, sometimes called *Petite Asie* or Little Asia, exists today in the south of Paris and is home to some fifty thousand people who have come not only from China, but also from Vietnam, Cambodia, Laos, and other parts of Southeast Asia. In the 1980s a second Chinatown in Paris emerged in the eastern district of Belleville. Here, the *Quartier Chinois* or Chinese Quarter was established mostly by emigrants from Qingtian and Wenzhou.

I had heard a lot about Paris's Chinese Quarter before I actually got there. I remember the news reports describing more than eight thousand Chinese immigrants marching through Belleville in the largest protest ever organized by the Chinese community in France after a number of Chinese immigrants were violently attacked and robbed in the area. The Chinese felt they were being victimized. They said criminals were targeting shopkeepers and business owners who were known to carry cash home at the end of the day. They said Chinese women, who criminals deemed too weak to fight back, were being mugged. The violence seemed to be escalating because many of the immigrants were reluctant to report crimes to the police either because of a language barrier or because they didn't have legal working papers and feared deportation. Violence in Chinatown wasn't a problem only in France. I heard similar concerns in nearly every Chinese community I visited in Europe including Rome, where emotions were running high after a Chinese shopkeeper and his baby daughter were killed by two thieves in a botched robbery. The bullet passed through the baby's head and then struck her father in the heart, killing them both.

Belleville means "beautiful city," but the neighborhood does not live up to its name. It is just a few metro stops west of the Louvre, but it is a world away from Paris's broad boulevards and blue rooftops. The area has historically been a working-class district. Over the years, many immigrants have settled here: German Jews fleeing the Third Reich in 1933, Spaniards in 1939, Algerians and Tunisian Jews in the early 1960s, and an influx of Asian immigrants in the past decade. Bellevue's avenues are crowded with Chinese restaurants and dingy supermarkets. When thousands of people flooded the streets one day in June of 2010, it was a rare and striking sight for many. The chanting protestors held signs and banners that read, "Stop the violence! Security For All!" and wore T-shirts that said "J'♥ Belleville." Some waved Chinese flags, which gave some the impression that the protest was not about security in the neighborhood but about patriotism, but most came out to denounce what they saw as targeted violence against the Chinese. "It sometimes feels that, in the collective unconscious, everything 'Made in China' is worth nothing, including the human beings," one protestor said just before the first fists flew and smoke washed over the streets of Belleville. Eyewitnesses say the fight began when a bag belonging to one of the demonstrators was stolen. A scuffle broke out between a group of demonstrators and several youths who were watching the protest, and when police moved in with their batons and handcuffs, the crowd began tossing objects at the officers. That's when they fired the tear gas. Blind and enraged, demonstrators seized the bumpers of parked cars and overturned them, blocking traffic in the area for hours.

More than a year after the riot broke out, I arrived in Paris and jumped on the metro toward Belleville. A local contact had invited me to a gathering in the *Quartier Chinois*. "Most of the Chinese community will be there," he told me over the phone. "It is a good idea to attend." I was looking for a restaurant called Meili Cheng, which, like Belleville, means "beautiful city." As soon as I climbed out of the subway station and saw Chinese greens piled in cardboard boxes on the sidewalks, the steamed-up windows of a noodle shop, and several DVD stores, I knew I was in the right place. I made my way up the main strip and saw a posse of four men walking in front of me. As they passed the shops and restaurants, one of the men would poke his head in and shout: "Are you coming?" A few seconds later, a man would rush out and join the group. They continued this way for several blocks until the group swelled to nearly a dozen men. I wasn't sure where the Meili Cheng restaurant was, but I had a feeling if I followed this group they would bring me there. Each man was dressed in a dark jacket and had a cigarette in his mouth. I stayed behind them, the smoke blowing back into my face, until we made a right turn onto a small side street where I saw a large foyer illuminated by a sparkling chandelier. A cacophony of pounding drums and clashing cymbals broke out as two red-and-yellow-sequined lions danced about on the shiny floors. "Just what kind of gathering is this?" I thought. Lion dances were usually performed during the Chinese New Year. Inside, the entire restaurant was decorated in red and more than twenty tables had been booked out for the evening's event. A wedding? Then I saw the banner draped across the front of the room: "Welcome Home Mr. Zhong Shaowu."

If there is one Chinese law of the universe, it is loyalty to your own people. In the homeland, the loyalties are to your family and village. Outside of China, those loyalties are extended to those from the same county, region, or even province. During the early days of Chinese migration, sojourners formed clan associations to provide welfare services to their own countrymen who had no social security to depend on. Among the most important functions that clan associations served was offering funeral services—arranging for the remains of deceased migrants to be brought back to China. Today, some clan associations have become relics of the past as Chinatowns empty out and multigenerational Chinese families become more integrated into mainstream society. But in some European countries, where unskilled and uneducated Chinese migrants continue to stream in, clan associations continue to be very relevant, serving as a contact medium between migrants and their hometown or region. Whenever I attended Qingtian County clan association meetings, I always felt as if I were attending a sort of high school reunion. The clan members always started off every meal with a toast: "To coming home," they said, clinking small glasses filled with the potent rice wine, *baijiu*.

The Qingtian County clan association in Paris had reserved a seat for me at the Meili Cheng restaurant. I sat at a table with a dozen Chinese businessmen feasting on a twelve-course meal that included Peking duck, shark fin soup (which I politely declined), and lobster sautéed with ginger and scallions. The men lit cigarettes in between each course and stood up to greet others who came from other tables to make toasts. Then the speeches began. One after another, Chinese men took to the stage and spoke with bravado into the microphone about a man named Zhong Shaowu. They praised Zhong's bravery and said he had become a model for the overseas Chinese in France. The speakers pumped their fists in the air, their voices rising in crescendo, ushering the audience to erupt into applause. Finally, the man of the hour took the stage. Zhong Shaowu was a short man dressed in a pink shirt and gray tie. He held a glass of red wine in one hand, and his face was flushed from an evening of toasts and cheers. In a shaky voice, he thanked the crowd for coming to dinner, said he was grateful to come home, then quickly took his seat. I turned to the man sitting next to me, a Qingtian businessman who ran a sushi restaurant in the city, and asked: "Just what did this Zhong Shaowu do exactly?"

"Mr. Zhong just got out of jail," he replied.

Okay, not what I expected to hear. "In jail? What for?"

"For shooting a man!"

My eyes widened. "What? He shot a man? Did the man die?"

"No, no, he didn't die. Mr. Zhong shot him in the leg."

There was a lot of back and forth before I was able to piece everything together. One night in June of 2010, Zhong was leaving a wedding celebration in Belleville with a number of other guests when they were confronted by a band of robbers. The robbers were said to be North African immigrants who wanted their money. When the Chinese said they had no money on them, the robbers knew better than to believe them—the Chinese often carry a lot of cash with them, especially at weddings. Everyone was getting ready to hand things over when Zhong pulled out a gun. He fired one bullet in the air as a warning shot, but the robbers didn't budge. So he fired again, this time hitting one man in the leg. Although police concluded Zhong acted in self-defense, he ended up going to jail because his gun was not registered. But to the Chinese, Zhong was a hero—someone who chose to protect himself in the face of escalating violence in Belleville. A few weeks later, thousands of Chinese immigrants poured out onto the streets, calling for Paris police to enforce a safer neighborhood and demanding Zhong's release. It was all coming together now: Zhong's arrest in early June of 2010, the massive protest a few weeks later, and now, more than a year later, his homecoming.

In France, I continued to pursue my research to discover more about the Chinese Labor Corps. I wanted to know about the 140,000 Chinese men who were recruited by the Allies during the First World War, and I was eager to find hard evidence of the 2,000 men who were supposedly recruited from Qingtian. I asked members of the Qingtian clan association that night in Belleville if they had any leads, but they said most of the members of the Labor Corps had married French women and the clan had lost all contact with their descendants. I knew if I wanted to learn more about the Corps, I had to travel to the northwest coast of France and to Belgium, where there are two thousand Chinese graves spread out across seventeen cemeteries.

The historic Belgian city of Ypres was the center of intense battles between German and Allied forces during World War I. Today, the city's main central square is surrounded by gabled guild houses that are now mostly occupied by restaurants and hotels. At the western end of the *Grote Markt* square is the magnificent gothic *Lakenhalle* (cloth hall), which was one of the largest commercial buildings in the Middle Ages and served as a main market and warehouse for the city's prosperous cloth industry. The original cloth hall was constructed between 1250 and 1304 but was blown to bits during World War I. It took decades of painstaking construction to restore the hall to its former glory. The first floor is occupied by wool and cloth exhibits while the second floor houses the In Flanders Fields Museum, where I met a Belgian sinologist who was an expert on the Chinese Labor Corps. Philip Vanhaelemeersch was in the midst of translating a memoir written by a Chinese schoolteacher who had come to Europe as a member of the Corps. "In the West, the laborers were no war heroes. They fought no battles; they had no share in any of the great victories during the war," Philip said. "Their presence in Europe during the war was, at best, a footnote in the history books on the war." In addition to being fluent in English and Flemish, Philip was an authority on Chinese language and history. And at six feet four inches tall, he had a body that was all limbs. I was surprised when Philip brought me to his car, a compact two-door Volkswagen Golf. He pushed his seat as far back as it could go, and when he climbed in behind the wheel, his knees came right up to the steering wheel. "There is much to see," Philip said as we left the city limits in his little car, the landscape transforming into an idyllic countryside where cows and sheep grazed in green pastures next to fields of potatoes and yellow blooms of hop flowers. Then we started seeing the signs for the cemeteries.

Row upon row, the white headstones were visible from the road. At nearly every turn there was a sign for a cemetery. More than three hundred thousand Allied troops died here. Today, Ypres's population is only thirty-five thousand. From a distance, the graves at the Lijssenthoek Military Cemetery on the outskirts of Ypres all look the same. But when I looked a little more closely, I started to notice the differences. The tombstones with rounded tops belong to

British soldiers, the squared stones are German, and crosses mark the French graves. The stones with Chinese script belong to the Chinese laborers. Most of these men died between 1918 and 1919 from the Spanish Flu; others died from wounds and injuries received during the course of their duties; and some lost their lives during German air raids. As I walked past each tombstone, I saw that many of the men had come from Shandong Province or the city of Tianjin, north of Beijing. I didn't see any stones listing Zhejiang Province as a hometown. I asked Philip if he had knew anything about the two thousand men who were said to have been recruited from Qingtian. I was unable to find any mention of them in the historical documents I was reviewing. Philip shook his head. He too had heard the anecdotes but had not come across any solid proof. Philip said it was possible the men enlisted with the French, who did go farther south in China than the British in their recruiting efforts. But record keeping was inconsistent and incomplete during the war, and tracking bodies was difficult. Unlike the British, who buried the dead on the spot, the French sent many of the bodies back to China.

As we continued to walk through the Lijssenthoek Military Cemetery, I saw most of the stones were marked in Chinese with the laborer's name, some stones were unmarked, and some names had been carved onto plaques affixed on nearby stone walls—these were members of the Labor Corps whose bodies were never found. Inscribed on many of gravestones was one of four proverbs: Faithful unto death; A noble duty bravely done; Though dead he still liveth; A good reputation endures forever.

Next, Philip brought me through a network of deep trenches—a maze of narrow pathways dug out of the muddy hills—and talked about artifacts that were recovered from the front. There were bullet casings laborers had etched with Chinese characters reciting nostalgic poems, old photographs in which battlefield tourists posed with members of the Corps, and the trenches themselves, which as one British officer testified, the Chinese were experts at digging: "In my company I have found the Chinese laborers accomplish a greater amount of work per day in digging trenches than white laborers," he wrote. "Chinese laborers were always in blue or terracotta blouses and flat hats, hauling logs or loading trucks, always with that inscrutable smile of the Far East upon their smooth yellow face." As we walked through the maze, I noticed how Philip towered over the trenches, his head and shoulders rising above the muddy refuge. I looked at the muddy walls and thought of the brave men who cowered in this water-logged, rat-infested ditch, packed with rotting carcasses and reeking of death.

The sun was beginning to set and Philip told me there were still a few spots he wanted me to see. He drove farther into the countryside and onto a broken road when he suddenly stopped the car and told me to get out. Next to a farm-er's field, Philip whipped out a device in his wide palm. I peered at the quivering red hand and realized it was a compass. Philip pointed to the top of a sloping field that overlooked a small, running creek. A number of Chinese laborers were once buried here, but their bodies have since been moved. "Very good *feng shui* in these parts," Philip said. "They were buried with their feet facing the water." We got back into his car and drove up to a house where an older woman invited us into her kitchen for a drink. Philip and I had been conversing in English the entire day, but upon entering this woman's house, he took on a completely dif-ferent persona. The tall, bespectacled professor brimming with dates and names and histories became a tall, swaggering Belgian who began speaking in a dialect of Flemish that was completely unintelligible even to Marc, who spoke fluent Dutch. The woman filled our glasses with a foamy, golden beer, and Philip leaned his long arms over the table, casually asking the woman a few questions to start. As the woman answered, Philip noticed that I had stopped scribbling in my notepad. He turned to me and whispered: "*Ting bu dong*?" I looked at him and burst out laughing. Philip had asked me a very simple question in Chinese: "Can't you understand?" It was an incredible moment when I realized I was sip-ping beer in Ypres with a woman who spoke an unintelligible dialect of Flemish and a seven-foot-tall Belgian sinologist who spoke better Chinese than I did.

I listened to the woman talk as Philip translated. Like many of the locals in the area, she grew up hearing many wartime stories from her parents and grandparents. One night in November of 1917, five hundred Chinese laborers passed through the area and set up camp in the field just outside their home, which is now chock-full of Brussels sprouts. When one of the laborers came out of his tent to light a cigarette, the flame attracted the attention of a German pilot in an airplane overhead. A bomb was dropped, killing thirteen Chinese men. "Although forgotten soon after the war, the laborers remain present in the collective memory of the local population," Philip said. "If you pay at-tention to the small details of the changing landscape, you can still detect the Chinese presence here."

It was dark when Philip dropped me back in front of the *Lakenhalle* where we had met earlier in the day. My mind was brimming with facts, figures, and dates and blanketed with vistas of green fields and white tombstones. Not only had I finally visited Ypres, a place I had spent so many years reading about in history textbooks, but I had also learned a whole other story about the war—one left out of those very same books. Still, one thing continued to bother me. I had come to Ypres to learn about the Chinese Labor Corps, a group that repre-sented a major wave of migration from China to Europe, but I had also hoped to find a solid link to Qingtian, my husband's ancestral hometown and Pei's home in China. I had an hour or so before the nightly remembrance ceremony at nearby Menin Gate—a barrel-vaulted limestone archway dedicated to British and Commonwealth soldiers whose bodies have never been found—and so I looked around the *Grote Markt* square for dinner options. Across the way, I saw a red sign that read "New Shanghai City."

Inside, the walls were painted a deep shade of red and furnished with modern tables and chairs. Scrolls of Chinese calligraphy hung on the walls, and the menu was printed in English, Flemish, and French. The restaurant's owner, Leilei Ji, flitted from table to table making sure all her customers' needs were met. Dressed in a red T-shirt and black apron, I listened as Leilei switched easily from Flemish to rudimentary Spanish to English. Leilei and her husband, Xiaogang, had owned the restaurant for more than a decade. Before leaving China, they were schoolteachers in Qingtian. From Qingtian! At this point in my travels, I shouldn't have been surprised. I was encountering Qingtian restaurateurs in every corner of Europe. But meeting Leilei and Xiaogang was especially meaningful that day in Ypres. I learned that the couple had three young boys who were all born in Belgium. Leilei and Xiaogang were caring and conscientious parents who enrolled their children in after-school activities and didn't pressure them to help out in the restaurant. They closed the business for a day and a half every week in order to spend time with the kids. Leilei and Xiaogang said they had no intention to return to China. Belgium was their home. I ordered off the menu, asking the kitchen to stir up some rice vermicelli and fresh vegetables for a simple home-style meal. That night I left New Shanghai City, my belly full and my search for a Qingtian connection somewhat fulfilled. I had failed to nail down any concrete evidence that two thousand men had come from Qingtian to Europe as contract laborers during World War I, but there was living proof of Qingtian people in Ypres today. I thought about the Chinese Labor Corps: the men who were lucky enough to return home to China after the war, the thousands of men who settled down in France, the men who were buried in the earth beneath my feet. Did a good reputation really endure forever? So much history is lost because migrants didn't like talking about the past. Those who lived through the horrors of a sweatshop, the poverty of Chinatown, or the terrors of war swallowed their words and pushed those shameful memories deep into their gut, where over time, the tender ache of the past dulled and faded away. Many brought their silent stories to the grave. For who would ever want to remember eating so much bitterness? And how could such stories ever be dignified?

So much of the Chinese immigrant experience in Europe has been lost or forgotten, partly because there really is no cohesive narrative that explains where these people came from and why. Migrants came from different corners of China at different times and for different reasons. Ye Pei once told me she was happy I chose to write her story. She was already forgetting many of her early experiences in Italy and said she hoped the book would help her look back and remember everything as it was. I wondered what legacy Ye Pei and the migrants of her generation will leave behind. Would we one day find their stories in textbooks and in museums? Or will their struggles and contributions, like those of the Chinese Labor Corps and the Chinese workers in Prato, be so easily forgotten?

Overseas remittances have helped the people of Qingtian build newer and bigger homes above the older ones on this mountain. The peaks are reserved for hillside tombs.

The tradition of rock sculpting continues today in Qingtian, though the young men who pursue this trade often do not have plans to go abroad. The finest pieces of Qingtian rock sculptures can go for hundreds of thousands of U.S. dollars.

A replica of Vienna's famous gilded statue of Johann Strauss has been erected in Qingtian's riverside park. The statue was gifted to the county by the Qingtian clan association in Vienna.

A stark side-by-side comparison of two homes in Qingtian: the home on the left was built with the help of remittances; the home on the right was not.

We burn spirit money and bring flowers, fruit, and incense to my husband's grandfather's hillside tomb during the 2011 Qingming festival, also known as Tomb Sweeping Day or Ancestors' Day.

Chen Junwei goes bayberry picking on a hot summer day in Qingtian. Separated from his migrant wife for close to a decade, he hopes to reunite with her in Italy.

Much of Qingtian County is still rural. On rocky hillsides, farmers carve out small terraced rice fields where they can.

A tombstone belonging to a member of the Chinese Labor Corps in the Lijssenthoek Military Cemetery near Ypres, Belgium.

Ye Pei makes it to Venice on her 101st day in Italy.

Pei working at her uncle's bar in Falconara, Italy.

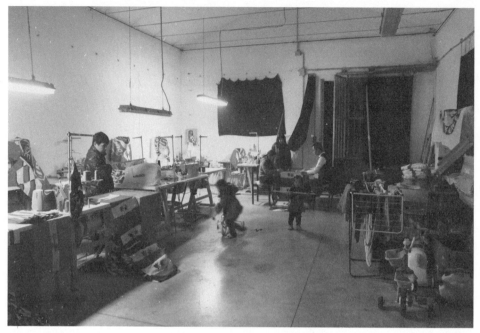

A typical Chinese-run garment workshop in Italy. Black curtains cover the windows and the door.

Workshop owner Jimmy Xu races to finish an order of flags due the next morning.

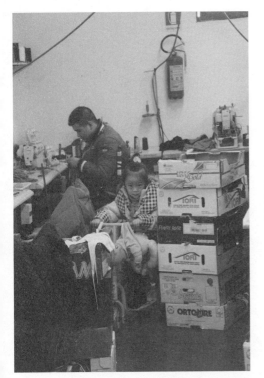

The child of a garment worker plays inside a workshop. The worker behind her is stitching bikinis for an Italian clothing company and piling them in the nearby fruit boxes.

Ye Pei picking white mushrooms at the farm near Riccione, Italy.

Pei's father, Shen, picking oyster mushrooms at the same farm.

Maria Chiara, the nun who speaks fluent Chinese, and Father Giuseppe Tong at the church-run Chinese-Italian Center in Savignano, Italy.

Ye Pei struggles to pass the Italian-language theory exam required to obtain her driver's license in Italy.

Ye Pei asks Italian-language teacher Lia Panelatti Santoro a question during weekly classes held at the mushroom farm.

Pei and her mother, Fen.

The Ye Family: (left to right) Shen, Pei, Fen, and brother Mao.

LA DOLCE VITA

*I smiled and told them I was adapting well. I really can't bear
to be separated from them. But in Europe, life is just like this.*

There are no canals in Solesino. No crescent-shaped bridges, no sleek black
gondolas, and no glittering lagoon. Venice, the water city, is more than
two hours away by train. Pei learned that in order to get there, she had to get
on a bus and head for the next town because there is not even a train station in
Solesino. She had taken extra long to get ready that morning: weaving her dyed
brown locks in and out of a loose French braid and pinning a glittery gray flower
to the side of her head. Over black leggings she pulled up a pair of pretty brown
boots trimmed with charcoal fur. And then she took out her long winter coat as
white as snow. She never wore this coat to the bar for fear it would get dirty. But
today, for the first time in ninety days, she wasn't going to be at the bar.

A silver fog draped down over Pei's head as she caught a bus and then a train
bound for *Venezia*. She gazed out the window as the train sped forward, chasing
the sun that eventually spilled through the sky, bathing the cabin in a morning
glow. Dark blue waves unfurled on either side of the track. Pei leaned forward
and pressed her face against the window, her breath fogging up the glass. Water
was everywhere. Across the lagoon, she could see them now: a cluster of tall
narrow houses built right on top of the water.

Pei had spent more than three months with Ayi and her family. Even so, she
still didn't know how to make a proper cappuccino. Ayi shooed her away whenever she hovered nearby, insisting Pei might upset a customer with a pathetic
cup of coffee. From afar, she watched jealously as Ayi's daughter handled the

machine, pressing beans and foaming milk. Instead of becoming a professional barista, Pei had become a professional cleaning lady. She spent most of her time bent over a dirty sink, a dirty floor, and a dirty toilet bowl. It wasn't just the issue of the cappuccino. Ayi and her family rarely spoke to her, unless it was to criticize her. One day, Pei noticed customers were glued to the television watching an Italian sitcom. The crowd laughed at the end of every punch line. Pei watched the screen and tried to follow the banter. When she chuckled along with the customers, that's when Ayi spoke up.

"Why are you laughing? You think you can understand what they are saying?"

"I can figure it out," said Pei, her cheeks turning red.

"Hmmph! She thinks she can figure it out . . . " Ayi muttered under her breath just loud enough for Pei to hear. That day and on many other days, Pei promised herself she would treat her workers nicely when she one day became a boss.

"The goal of being a *lao ban* is not so much about making money," she said. "I want to be a *lao ban* so no one can bully me." An aftertaste more bitter than espresso lingered on Pei's tongue as she contemplated her meager "five-hand" salary. After three months of work, she was still just making 500 euros a month. She had expected to get a raise after a month's work, but when it didn't happen Pei was too afraid to ask Ayi about it. She didn't want to sour their relationship. At the end of each month, she sent most of her earnings to her mother and kept about 50 euros for herself. Did Pei regret coming to Italy? No, never. She didn't believe in regret. Regret served no purpose. She only believed in planning for the future. Looking forward she realized if Ayi wasn't going to teach her, she needed to seek opportunities elsewhere. One such opportunity had already presented itself on a recent bus ride when Pei was pleasantly surprised to find a young Chinese woman on board. The two struck up a conversation.

"How long have you been out?" the woman asked.

"More than three months!" Pei said. It was the first time since moving to Solesino that she was able to chat so freely with another person. Her conversations with the bar's customers were brief and superficial, stilted by her limited Italian, and she was forced to watch her words in front of Ayi and her family. The last time Pei shared a carefree conversation was the night of her seventeenth birthday, when she had spilled all her secrets to her young friend Ying Ying. The memories of that night were already fading like a passing breath.

"I have a job at a bar, but I have not yet learned to how to make a cappuccino," Pei said.

"Well, you should come to my uncle's bar and learn," the young woman offered. Pei was drawn to her openness, her eagerness to help.

"Really?"

"Yes, the bar is in Padua. Just give me a call and you can come whenever you like!"

Pei decided she would call the girl after her day in Venice. Ayi was now granting her one day off during the week. She could take the bus to Padua and work at the bar for free. She didn't think it was important to ask for payment. An opportunity to use the cappuccino machine was compensation enough.

The water city drew closer as the train galloped forward with a rhythm and energy that matched Pei's own beating heart. She had slept only a couple hours the night before, legs tingling with excitement, unable to lie still long enough for sleep to overcome her. Restless, she rose from her bed in the middle of the night and opened her heavy Italian-Chinese dictionary, thumbing through its pages, mouthing the letters on the page, and rolling her Rs. Her tongue, which had once felt as languid and thick as polenta, now flickered nimbly, tickling the back of her teeth. Pei realized the Chinese phonetics printed in her phrasebook did more harm than good. Now she was training her eyes to follow only the Roman alphabet, paying close attention to the vowels and accents and the shape her mouth had to make in order to pronounce them. Her progress was slow, but it was the best she could do on her own. Though Ayi had promised to enroll her in a local Italian-language class for immigrants, that hadn't happened just yet. Her interactions with customers were mostly confined to bar vocabulary: *Spritz. Campari. Caffè Macchiato. Aqua Frizzante. Coca Cola.* Most of the time she couldn't understand what her customers were saying. But she learned to focus not on entire sentences but on the words she did understand. When it was truly a lost cause, she flashed her eight-teeth smile. It was the only way she could hide what she truly felt in her heart—stupid and illiterate.

She hid her feelings not only from the Italians but from her own family, too. During occasional phone calls with Li Jie, Pei told him she was doing well. Dwelling on her feelings only made her feel worse. Besides, Li Jie wouldn't know what to say to comfort her and there wasn't anything he could do to help her. When Pei called her grandmother in China, she was especially careful not to let on that she was unhappy. Telling the truth would only cause her to worry. She was even sparing with her complaints when talking to her parents, who telephoned her every afternoon in between her shifts to check in. Her mother called from the mushroom farm. Her father usually called a few minutes later. He had moved farther south to another city where he worked as a factory chef, cooking up meals for workers in a Chinese-run garment workshop.

The only time Pei could be honest was when she wrote in her diary every night: *Amore*, she wrote, using the Italian word for "my love." *I may look like I am brave and strong, but people do not know that behind this exterior, I am wishing I had an intimate friend by my side.* Deception was never her forte. From the time she was a little girl, she always let the people around her know what she felt. She cried when she was sad. She screamed when she was angry. "In that way, I was very immature," Pei said. "Now I know how to hide my feelings. This is a sign that I've grown up." Indeed she was the most cheerful barista there was—making sure to greet each and every customer as soon as they entered and exited the bar, all the while maintaining that ever-perfect smile. Even when she wasn't at the bar, she still went out of her way to be friendly. She said *buongiorno* to the old women walking past the laundromat, *ciao* to the man walking his dog, and *buonasera* (which means "good evening") to the clerk in the gelato store. As she waited at a bus stop for me one day, one of her regular customers from the bar saw her and asked what she was doing there. "My friends come here," she said in broken Italian. The grammar was off, her pronunciation shaky at best, but she was trying. Italians liked it when people tried to speak their language. But it wasn't only the language that posed a problem. There were many cultural differences Pei paid special attention to. In the Chinese countryside where she grew up, people rarely adopted such formalities as saying "hello," "good-bye," "good morning," and "good night." They asked each other if they had eaten yet. *Ni chi le ma?* But she wasn't in Qingtian anymore. She was making efforts to change her old habits, and she tried to change me, too. "The Italians don't like it if you don't say 'hello,'" she told me after I failed to greet a couple of old ladies as they passed us on the sidewalk one night. "That's why they think so many Chinese are rude."

> *Amore, tomorrow I will start writing to you in Italian. There will be many mistakes, to be sure. And you won't understand anyway. But if I want to learn, this is how it's going to be. I'm tired; I have to sleep.*

By the time Pei put her books away, only a few hours remained before the morning sun would rise. She made sure to tuck her Chinese-Italian phrasebook in her purse so she could rehearse a few phrases on the train the next morning. On the front cover was a photo of a bone-white church shaped like an octagon. The Basilica di Santa Maria della Salute was built out of the same Istrian stone that gave much of the city its luminous glow. For a long time now, she had envisioned standing before the lagoon and looking at this church with her own two eyes.

Venice had so many names: the water city, the city of canals, the floating city, the serene city, the "gateway to the Orient." Missionaries, merchants, and adventurers set off from Venice in search of new markets and travel routes as early as the twelfth and thirteenth centuries. Marco Polo was the most famous of them all. He is said to have spent nearly two decades in Asia, traveling across raging seas, harsh deserts, and treacherous mountains to reach the splendors of China. Pei remembered his name from stories in her school textbook. Polo was about the same age as Pei when he and his uncle embarked on their fabled journey, crossing the Gobi Desert to reach western China. He traveled to the city of Hangzhou, a place he called a "paradise on earth" in his book, *Il Milione*:

> Its streets and canals are extensive, and there are squares, or market-places, which, being necessarily proportioned in size to the prodigious concourse of people by whom they are frequented, are exceedingly spacious. It is situated between a lake of fresh and very clear water on the one side, and a river of great magnitude on the other, the waters of which, by a number of canals, large and small, are made to run through every quarter of the city.

To Pei, Polo's description of Hangzhou sounded very much like Venice.

The train raced across a brick and stone causeway called Ponte della Liberta, the Bridge of Liberty, before pulling into the railway station. Travelers spilled out onto the platforms, and trains heaved loud sighs, resting in their tracks. The train station was a modern, low-lying structure that remained as inconspicuous as it could in the ancient city. Pei followed the crowd through a drafty main hall and into the sunshine, stunned to see boats whizzing by on a waterway just a few steps from the station. There it was: the Canal Grande! She scampered down the wide steps and approached the glassy water, bending down to dip her fingers in. The myth of Venice was real. In straw hats and striped shirts, the gondolieri were poised like sculptures on glossy black boats. She pulled out her pink cell phone to snap a few photos. It was her 101st day in Italy. One hundred and one days since she left China and started her new life. Nothing had come easily in this country, but the helplessness and frustration that were weighing down on her for months finally lifted as she stood on that bridge, staring at the homes and gardens that rose from their own reflections in the placid waters. "It was my dream to come to Venice and now that I've done it, I feel like I can do anything," she said. "I can reach all my goals one by one, and really make something out of myself here in Italy." There were times at the bar, especially when her skin began to flake off, when Pei felt like even her own two hands were failing her in this new life. But the moment her fingers touched the icy water of the Canal Grande, something stirred within her. Coming to the water city was one small victory, one small step in the right direction. It was just ten in the morning when she marched across the bridge of the barefoot monks, the Ponte degli

Scalzi, and within minutes of entering the old city, she had found a gelateria where she ordered two scoops of ice cream. "*Due. Nocciola e pistacchio,*" she said, the words sliding off her tongue as though she had rehearsed this moment in advance. She gaped as a round ball of hazelnut was planted atop a creamy mound of pistachio. Then she gripped the cone with both hands and pressed the ice cream to her mouth, lips smeared in pastel green. "I have fulfilled two childhood dreams in just one day," Pei said. "One dream was to visit Venice. The other dream is enjoying an ice cream cone in the middle of winter."

It was afternoon when Pei realized she was lost in a Venice *hutong*. She wandered through a maze of alleyways behind the Canal Grande, passing under the long silhouette of narrow buildings, each one leaning harder into the next. Her Chinese guidebook explained that wooden stilts had been pounded into the soft bed of the lagoon and the chemical composition of the water had calcified the wood, transforming the stilts into sturdy posts. That wood was now resistant to rot and stood steadfast against the pull and push of the tides, immune to the weathering and disintegration of time. Still, Pei read on, the city was sinking. She turned the corner to find a mossy brick wall in front of her nose—a dead end. Many of the buildings in this *hutong* were homes, but Pei saw that most of the windows were pulled shut. Venetians were moving out of the water city in droves and settling in nearby cities that offered space, affordability, and an escape from the tourists. Pei retraced her steps, passing through a courtyard that looked vaguely familiar.

She had been lost once before. She had gotten off the bus one stop too soon and found herself alone and in the dark on the outskirts of Solesino. The main bus stop was usually easy to spot, even from afar. It was right next to the blue steeple that stood higher than any other building in town. But that evening, heavy fog swallowed the steeple from view. Pei wasn't sure which way to walk, and when she peered through the fog on that deserted road, her heart skittered uncontrollably as she realized there was no one else she could ask. It took her twenty minutes to find her way back into town, and when she finally staggered back into Ayi's apartment and into her room, she burst into tears. Now, wandering in a Venetian *hutong*, Pei was unafraid. She took a few more turns until at last she spied a thin sliver of sky. Then she heard a voice that lingered in her ear longer than usual. *Chee-eh-zi*! "Eggplant!" someone exclaimed in Chinese, just as someone in America might say "cheese." Then the pop of a flash and the snap of a shutter. A Chinese family floated by in a long and narrow gondola, posing for a portrait. "*Zhong guo ren*!" Pei exclaimed under her breath. *Chinese people!* The familiar sounds of her mother tongue filled her with a terrible longing, and her eyes followed the family in the boat until they disappeared around the bend.

Chinese tourists are the world's biggest-spending travelers, dropping $102 billion on foreign trips in 2013, and no place ranks higher than Europe as a vacation destination. They are the biggest-spending tourists in Italy, snapping up luxury goods and spending an average of 900 euros (more than $1200) a person. China's nouveaux riche have developed an insatiable appetite for designer labels. Prada, Louis Vuitton, Armani, and Gucci are idolized, and in most major European cities, hotels and luxury shops have hired Mandarin-speaking staff in order to woo more Chinese customers. The influx has been both a blessing and a curse for those who work in the industry. On one hand, the ailing economy has benefited from big spenders; on the other hand, some have come to bemoan the Chinese presence. The stereotypes are numerous: Chinese tourists don't tip. They don't line up. They move about in noisy groups. Many take to spitting on the ground. Chinese tour operators are notorious for bargaining down costs, booking hotels on the outskirts of the city and opting to bring their travelers to eat at ten-euro Chinese buffet restaurants. Chinese tourists were voted the second-worst behaved in the world, after Americans, in a recent survey of five countries. Pei wandered through Venice that day, turning her head at every phrase of Chinese overheard from a distance. She saw not only Chinese tourists but Chinese shopkeepers and bar owners as well. When she stepped into a local café, she was overjoyed to see a demure Chinese woman standing behind the bar.

"Where in China have you come from?" Pei asked her excitedly.

"Zhejiang," she replied.

"Me too!" Pei said. "Where in Zhejiang?"

"It's too small; you won't know it."

"I might know it; tell me."

"Qingtian."

"Qingtian!" Pei exclaimed. "I come from there, too!"

"Oh, really," the woman said dully. She gave her a "so what?" kind of look. Pei left the bar a little bit embarrassed and surprised that a hometown connection didn't provoke a warmer disposition.

She wandered along the Rialto, up the stone bridge to the central portico where she saw dozens of gondolas bobbing up and down in the waters, waiting to take tourists out on rides. The bridge itself and the streets that surround it were crammed with small shops selling precious murano glass, fine blown from spidery filaments. Delicate webs of lace were strung across the walls, and colorfully painted Carnevale masks hung side by side, displaying a range of human emotions. The faces of Harlequins, Punchinellos, and Pierrots eyed Pei as she picked out a pair of sterling silver earrings for her mother. "I don't know if Mama had the time to even come to Venice during her five years here," she said. "Her generation was so thrifty. All they did was save." Pei strolled into the Piazza San Marco, the basilica's gold and blue onion domes gleaming in the sun. She paused to see why a crowd had gathered around a display that showed a veiled woman holding a baby in her arms. Beside the woman were barn animals and piles of hay. She wondered who the baby was and why he seemed so important to Italians. Her phone rang. "*Pronto? Uuuuh? Sì, domani, sì, sì. . . . Uuuh? Sì, sì, sì. Uuuuh? Venezia oggi. Venezia. Sì, domani, sì.*" A customer was calling to ask where she was. "Yes, tomorrow, yes, yes," Pei stumbled about in broken Italian. "Yes, yes, yes. Venice today. Venice. Yes, tomorrow, yes." There were many lonely patrons at the bar eager to connect with Pei, the young and impressionable barista. But this particular customer, an elderly man, was a persistent one. He had repeatedly asked for Pei's cell phone number until she finally relented and wrote it down for him on a napkin. He called Pei every day, asking the same thing each time: Will you be at work today? Sometimes, the old man asked Ayi if Pei, and only Pei, could be the one to make his cappuccino. Those were the only times she had the chance to practice using the machine.

> *Sometimes I think I shouldn't complain. If I leave this job and take another job, it might be even worse. Then I'll really know the true meaning of "bad."*

The sky was turning indigo blue and Pei got in some last minute shopping before heading back to the train station. She bought a slice of pizza and sat on a bench on the platform to wait for her train. It never came. Ten minutes after her train's scheduled departure, Pei ran to a digital screen and saw to her dismay that her train had been rerouted to another platform at the last minute. It was gone now and that meant she was going to miss her last bus home. Pei bit her lip and took out her phone. Reluctantly, she punched in Ayi's phone number.

"Ayi, I am sorry; I have missed the train."

"Where are you?"

"Still in Venice."

Ayi sighed. "When is the next train?"

"In half an hour."

"OK. I will pick you up at the train station closest to Solesino."

Pei was furious at herself for missing the train and annoyed that she had to rely on Ayi to rescue her. "When I turn eighteen, I am going to get my driver's license," she told me. "Then I will be free to come and go whenever I please."

The next day, above the burble and clatter of the espresso machine, Ayi's daughter asked Pei about her day in Venice.

"It was wonderful," Pei breathed. "So much fun."

"I've been there before," Ayi's daughter said. "It's just an old city. Not very interesting at all. I wouldn't go back." Pei eyes fell, hoping her face didn't show how much she disagreed. I often heard Chinese immigrants in Italy speak this way. The Italy we know as tourists—the leisurely lunches, the bustling piazzas, Renaissance art—and the Italy we have come to read about in books like *Under the Tuscan Sun* and *Eat Pray Love*; that's not the Italy Chinese immigrants see. They are unimpressed with the country's villas and medieval towns. A Chinese woman in Milan told me she thought the city's *duomo* was "just a pile of rocks." Rome's coliseum was "crumbling and old." She was instead wowed by sparkling new structures that, to her, signified wealth: glitzy shopping malls, sports stadiums, and towering skyscrapers.

"In Venice, I had a really good Italian dessert in one of the cafés," Pei said to Ayi's daughter, describing a fluffy, layered cake that had a nip of espresso and liqueur and an after bite of chocolate.

"Oh, yes, it's called tiramisu," she replied. "But it's not Italian. It's a dessert from Spain." Pei, not knowing any better, simply nodded.

Still enlivened from her Venetian adventure, Pei gathered up her courage to call the young woman she had met on the bus. She was excited to travel to Padua and help out at the bar. Once she learned how to make a proper cappuccino, she could find a job elsewhere and escape from Bar Girasole. It took many rings before someone finally answered the phone.

"*Wei?*"

"*Wei?* It's me, Ye Pei. The girl you met on the bus a few weeks ago. The one working in Solesino."

"Oh, *ni hao* . . . " The young woman sounded distant. Pei pushed on, asking her when she could come to Padua next, but the woman cut her off.

"It's not convenient," she said. *Bu fang bian.*

"Then when?" Pei blurted, knowing she had asked one question too many.

"I'll . . . call you and let you know."

Pei hung up the phone and remembered her mother's words: "Don't believe everything people tell you." Skepticism didn't come naturally to her. Pei liked to believe there were people who did keep their promises, people who genuinely wanted to help others. There had to be another way. She remembered Ayi saying there was another Chinese family in town. It didn't take long for Pei to find their bar, which was just three blocks from Bar Girasole. Through the front door, she saw a skinny Chinese man behind the bar. He looked to be in his thirties, with hair that grew well below his ears in the Italian style.

"*Ni hao*," Pei said politely as soon as she entered.

"*Ni hao*," the man said, eyeing her curiously.

"I work at Bar Girasole, the one over that way," Pei said, gesturing with her hand.

"Yes, I know it."

"I heard there was another Chinese family here in town. Where are you from?"

"Wencheng," the man said, naming Qingtian's neighboring county. "And you?"

"Qingtian," Pei said proudly.

"When did you come out?"

"Just three months ago."

A woman with pretty eyes came out from the bar's back room and stood next to the bar owner.

"My wife," the man said.

Pei greeted the woman and then asked: "How long have you been here?"

"In Italy? More than ten years," the man said.

"So you must speak Italian well."

"Yes."

"I am so jealous! I find it so hard to learn."

"Oh, it will come in time," the man said. Pei thought he seemed kind. She decided to keep talking.

"The bar I work at belongs to my mother's friend," she explained. "But she doesn't let me operate the cappuccino machine. I was wondering . . . would it be all right if I came over here during my time off to practice?"

The man looked at his wife, who replied: "Sure, of course. Come anytime to play." Pei could not stop thanking them.

The average Italian drinks about six hundred cups of coffee in one year. Pei noticed the same people came to the bar every day, sometimes several times in one day, for their coffee fix. She herself had never tasted Italian coffee before. Every morning, she watched Ayi's daughter brew a cappuccino for breakfast, and she had formed the opinion that such an addictive drink *had* to be delicious. Her chance to have an authentic Italian breakfast finally came when she arrived at the bar one morning and learned that Ayi had accidentally brewed one extra cappuccino for a customer. The cup was hers, if she wanted it. Pei tried to hide her excitement as she wrapped her fingers around the tiny white handle, picking up the teeny cup up as elegantly as her blistered hands would allow. One quick sip led to a stunning revelation: coffee was not her cup of tea. What she had thirsted for was not so delicious after all. That night, she wrote in her diary: "I think I am happy with my water. Coffee is already bitter as it is, but pair it with a piece of sweet bread and the bitterness is even more extreme. The luxuries enjoyed by others are not necessarily the luxuries you want for yourself."

Images of the baby lying in a bed of hay next to barn animals appeared everywhere. She saw the baby on the lawns in front of people's homes, in store windows, and in the center of town. Pei learned *Natale*—Italian for Christmas—was fast approaching. She had never celebrated Christmas before, but in China more and more people were taking part in the Western holiday. She saw many pictures of the *sheng dan lao ren*, the *Christmas old man*, dressed in red and white and sporting a fluffy white beard. But she had never seen the baby in the barn before. As *Natale* drew near, the bar grew busier by the day. Customers crowded in, free from work and school because of the holiday. Many of the bars closed down for *Natale*, but Ayi made sure Bar Girasole stayed open for as many hours as possible. They worked on Christmas Eve, Christmas Day, and on New Year's Eve and New Year's Day, too. A day of rest meant a day's loss of business, after all. "We can't fish for three days and dry the nets for two," many immigrants often told me, using a Chinese proverb to illustrate their point. Some had come to see the wisdom in taking Sundays and holidays off—days many Italians reserved for the family, for visiting the market, for gathering at the same table for dinner, and sometimes, for going to church. "But the Chinese here have no God," one Chinese immigrant remarked. "We only worship money."

From behind the bar, Pei watched snowflakes drift down from the open sky, dusting the ground like powdered sugar. She saw children leaving tracks in that blanket of white, fathers joining them in snow fights, and mothers dragging the little ones in sleds. Pei had expected to visit her parents for *Natale*. Instead, the gifts she purchased in Venice sat in one corner of her bedroom. She thought about her mother and brother in the house with the peeling yellow paint, and she thought about her father who lived in another city cooking meals for Chinese factory workers. She wondered if he was joining her mother and brother for *Natale*. "In China, our family was split in two," Pei said. "Now that we are abroad, my family is split in three. We called it a family reunion. But it seems to me we have only grown further apart."

> *Right now all my thoughts are dedicated to learning Italian and working at the bar. If I don't contact you at times, please do not be upset, don't find it strange. I haven't changed. I just want to adapt to the European life.*

The days crawled by and Pei began dragging her feet on her way to the bar every morning. Ayi's home was just one block away, but her legs felt sluggish and heavy, and her chest pulled tight with dread. Her feelings oscillated between anxiety and eagerness—anxiety whenever she heard Ayi's cold criticisms and eagerness to appear useful under her watchful eyes. She didn't end up going to Padua to help out at that bar. The woman she met on the bus never did call her back. And though the other Chinese bar owner and his wife in Solesino encouraged Pei to drop in whenever she liked, Pei stopped going there after they kept asking her how Bar Girasole priced their drinks—one way business owners try to undermine the competition. Pei decided it was better not to hang out at the other bar, realizing if Ayi ever found out she would get in real trouble.

It was February when Pei called her mother with an important question. She had been working at the bar for six months and things were not getting easier. Pei asked her mother if she could come home. She didn't know if she would try to get another job and if that job would be in a bar. All she knew was that she needed to rest. Pei's mother agreed and the next day, Pei told Ayi that week would be her last. Ayi said nothing, only grunting in acknowledgment. Pei left the bar on a Friday, exhausted and bitter, fighting her own thoughts that urged her to remain grateful for the experience. She boarded a bus, then a train, then another bus that brought her close to the mushroom farm. From there, she plodded up toward her mother's house on the hill. Once there, Pei gave her mother the earrings she purchased in Venice so many months before. Then she mostly stayed in bed and slept.

�֎

Most of Falconara was still asleep when Ye Pei crossed the main square every morning on her way to her uncle's bar. She had already been entrusted with the keys, even though she had just started working for her Uncle Luigi that month. As soon as she turned the locks and cast the tanned wooden doors open at 8 a.m., customers started trickling in, most of them ordering their morning cappuccinos. Pei usually wore jeans and a tight-fitting long-sleeved shirt to work. She stood behind the bar, which was painted neon orange, next to pink plastic roses that leaned on one another in a tall, dusty vase. A beaded curtain swung about behind her, and about twenty nearly-empty bottles of liqueur lined the shelves. In Solesino, Pei had spent months watching Ayi and her daughter make cappuccinos. On the rare occasion she could touch the machine, she tried her best to replicate the sacred thirds. Here in Falconara, Uncle Luigi happily demonstrated the trickiest maneuver: creating the frothy milk. Now, the wooden handle of the brass portafilter felt like an extension of Pei's hand as she pressed the coffee grounds to ensure a dark brew. She turned her attention to the milk: a jolt of steam pushed through the stainless steel wand making a loud *pssssssst!* sound. Pei expertly lowered the wand into a stainless steel pitcher filled with pearly white milk and listened for a steady *ch-ch-ch* before swirling the pitcher to create a thick whirlpool. The milk stretched to fill half of the pitcher. Then she poured the frothy liquid into a small cup of dark espresso creating a golden *crema*. She smiled, wishing Ayi could see her now. Brewing cappuccinos all by herself, running a bar all by herself! Pei had spent about a month feeling sorry for herself as she stayed at her mother's in the house with the peeling yellow paint. "Half a year at the bar in Solesino and still unable to make a proper cappuccino!" Pei had scolded herself. "How much Italian did I really learn? Not much at all." And when would her family be able to purchase a bar for themselves? Not anytime soon. At that time, Pei had said she felt *wu nai*—the word meant helpless, but it literally translated to "unable to endure." Then she learned about a distant uncle who was looking for some help at his bar. Luigi was not Pei's direct uncle, but a distant relation—the son of a cousin of Pei's grandmother. Over the phone, he suggested Pei come visit for a few days. If she liked it, they could talk about her staying. She boarded a train and headed south. Romagna's vineyards gave way to a beautiful coastline. The waters of the Adriatic Sea were calm and blue.

It was usually late in the morning when Luigi rolled out of bed and walked straight into his bar, his mop of hair greasy and unkempt. He greeted customers with an obligatory *"buongiorno!"* before walking past the bar's bright yellow walls to the front door where he lit his morning cigarette. He wore the same clothes day after day—baggy navy slacks and a navy top—and everyone knew he was the barkeeper who slept in the back room. His single bed took up every inch of a narrow broom closet behind the bar. On a shelf nearby, in between dusty boxes of liquor, he managed to squeeze in a television and an old rice cooker. Luigi had two front teeth that stuck out in a goofy smile—a caricature of a Chinese man straight out of the racist political cartoons published so often in the Italian newspapers. But Luigi was anything but stereotypical. He was fiercely opinionated, engaging in lively debates with his customers about Italy and its corrupt politicians. His favorite subject, however, had nothing to do with domestic politics but with the politics of his homeland. "The Chinese Communist Party! What a bunch of liars! Corrupt!" he said in fluent Italian, throwing his hands up in the air as Italian men did when they berated their own government. "The *gong chan dang*," Luigi spat, using the Chinese word for the Chinese Communist Party, "like to encourage the Chinese people to love China. But what they really want us to do is love the Communist Party."

When her Uncle Luigi went off on his long rants about the Chinese Communist Party, Pei kept her head down and busied herself with washing the dishes and wiping the counters. "China has a huge problem and that's the one child policy," he continued. "What other country has forced abortions?" He talked about China's *hukou* system, an archaic household registration system that ties peasants to the land and deprives them of all social rights like health care, housing, and education if they were to move to the city in search of work. He spoke about Chairman Mao's Great Leap Forward and the Cultural Revolution. "Because of the Chinese Communist Party, all of the country was poor," he said, pacing behind the bar. "We all had to emigrate; we had no choice!" Luigi's stories were very different from the far more optimistic version of history Pei had learned in school. The Great Leap Forward and the subsequent famine were glossed over in her textbooks, the Cultural Revolution relegated to an addendum. Students are told it was a "difficult time" in China's history, but few are able to grasp the extent of the horrors that unfolded. Pei knew there were many things she had yet to understand. After all, she was just a "child" as the Ayi in Solesino always called her. What did she know? When I asked her what she thought about Uncle Luigi's stories, Pei only said: "*Bu qing chu.*" It means "it's not clear to me" or "I don't know." I found young Chinese people often said this, not necessarily when they didn't have an opinion but when they weren't sure if their opinions mattered. In China, teachers, textbooks, and the mainstream media toe the party line and young people are taught not to question the stories shared by those who have authority to do so. Children learn history as they do their multiplication tables—by brute memorization—and teachers leave little room for debate or discussion during their lectures. That's not to say things in China aren't changing. Technology in the twenty-first century has provided a platform for free speech, and many young people are disseminating news among themselves. More than five hundred million Internet users in China are finding their voices with blogs, message boards, and Twitter-like programs, giving rise to a vibrant online community of online citizens who call themselves "netizens." Many of China's cyber citizens are now able to circumvent the country's Internet censors and scale the so-called great firewall. For Pei, physically leaving China was her way of leaping over that barrier.

Uncle Luigi liked to use an Italian phrase to describe himself: *mezza strada*. In the middle of the road. Neither here nor there. He vowed he would never return to China, but he had never considered applying for Italian citizenship either, despite living in Italy for more than two decades. "The Italians see me as Chinese. But the Chinese see me as a foreigner," he explained. It made Pei sad to hear that her uncle had no desire to go back "home" to China, but he didn't want her pity. "Go back to China? What for?" he scoffed. "Other than my parents, there is nothing for me there." Uncle Luigi insisted his heart was not bound to the land of his birth and that China was not his homeland. "I have no home," he said. But the name of his business—Bar Gru Gru—betrayed his sentimentality. "Gru" means crane in Italian and alluded to the name of Qingtian's largest municipality: Crane Town.

Luigi thought Pei a good worker who was willing to learn new things. He had previously hired a friend's son to help him, but the boy was lazy. Girls, Luigi said, were more obedient and well-behaved. In Solesino, Pei started off making just 500 euros a month. Uncle Luigi now offered her 800 euros (about $1100) a month for her work at the bar and he arranged and paid for her to live with the Jiangs—another Chinese family in town—since he had no home of his own. The Jiangs lived in an apartment close to the bar. Most of the 150 Chinese people living in Falconara worked in garment workshops—but there were a handful of families who had their own businesses. Uncle Luigi had the bar. A Chinese couple sold women's dresses down the street from the train station. Around the corner, a Chinese family opened a store that sold everyday housewares—anything from spoons and toilet paper to hair dryers and radios. The Jiangs had the most taxing job of all. They left their home in the early morning and sped along pitch-black highways to neighboring towns where they sold handbags, scarves, and accessories in the open-air markets. Pei shared a room with their sixteen-year-old daughter, Julia, who had high cheekbones and long black hair. She wore dark eyeliner and spoke even faster than Pei did.

It didn't take long for Pei to develop something she never had in Solesino: confidence. "I am the boss of me!" she said. "Sometimes, I don't feel like I am even at work. I feel like I haven't been working all day." Uncle Luigi instilled great trust in her. She handled cash, operated the till, and was even in charge of running the bar herself when Uncle Luigi retired to his broom closet for several hours in the early afternoon for his daily *riposo*. Like the other townspeople, he savored the rhythm of Italian time. After lunch, proprietors flipped their *aperto* signs to *chiuso* and went home for an afternoon nap. Just two businesses remained open during the mid-day slumber: Bar Gru Gru and a nearby Internet café run by a Pakistani man named Mukhtar, who had come to Italy nine years before as a migrant worker, leaving his wife and children behind. "The Chinese and the Pakistanis, we are friends, we are neighbors," he told me. "We work all the time. Too much. The Italians? They are sleeping."

In the broom closet behind the bar, Uncle Luigi slept alone. He was married once, having done what many immigrant men did—he went back to China to find a wife. His family searched for and found what they deemed an appropriate match, but the marriage was short-lived and they were divorced within a matter of months. That was three years ago and now at the age of forty-five, Luigi remained a bachelor. He didn't have many prospects when Pei arrived in Falconara, but he had gone on one date recently. He and a Chinese woman went out for dinner and all was going well until the end, when his date stopped at a street corner about a block or so away from her apartment and asked to say "good night." It was better, she said, that he didn't walk her to her doorstep. Luigi was insulted. "Are you embarrassed to be seen with me?" he asked. For weeks, he stayed prideful and angry, and though the woman tried to contact him again, he refused to speak with her. Eventually she stopped calling. He was still furious when he recalled the episode for Pei one night over dinner.

"Maybe you were being just a little sensitive?" Pei suggested.

"No," Luigi snapped. "I know what she was thinking. That I wasn't good enough for her!" Pei was embarrassed by her uncle's unexpected disclosure of his failed marriage and disastrous first date. The evening had begun rather cheerfully, with Luigi offering to cook dinner for his niece. He made pork chops, mashed potatoes, and a dish that had recently become Pei's favorite—a tossed green salad topped with tuna and drizzled in mayonnaise, olive oil, and vinegar. "I no longer have the urge to stir-fry my salad greens," she said. Uncle Luigi even opened a bottle of red wine he was saving for a special occasion. But the more he drank the gloomier he became. In Falconara, Pei chose a new name for herself—Lya—and at the bar, she listened to many depressing tales usually shared by someone who had had one drink too many.

By far, Pei's favorite customer was Paolo. At nearly six feet tall, he tottered into the bar for a drink in his Velcro sandals and blue socks, his pear-shaped belly leading the way. He had worked as an electrician for thirty years before he injured his foot and retired early on disability. Beneath his black baseball cap was a small, bespectacled face.

"Lya," he'd say warmly upon entering the bar.

"Paolo!" Pei would exclaim with a broad smile, showing way more than just eight teeth. "*Ciao!*"

Leaning over the bar, the Italian lessons would begin. Paolo pointed to a plastic rose in a dusty vase.

"*Rosa,*" he said.

"*Rrrroh-sah,*" Pei repeated.

Paolo pointed to sunflowers printed on the plastic tablecloths in the bar.

"*Girasole,*" he said.

"*Gee-ra-sole.*"

"*Questa qua lilium.*" These are lilies.

"*Lee-lee-um.*"

"Paolo," Pei said. "I teach you Chinese." Pointing to the *rosa* in the vase, she leaned forward and said loudly, "*Mei gwei hua.*"

"*Mei gwei hua,*" Paolo repeated. The two laughed and they carried on like that on a daily basis. They talked about the weather, about their cell phone plans, and most often about Italian pronunciation.

"*Plego,*" Paolo would tease. "You ate the 'r'."

"Ate?" Pei asked quizzically.

"Rrrrrr," Paolo said, demonstrating a roll.

"Rrrrr."

"You say it well," Paolo finally agreed. "*Bene.*"

But aside from the idle chitchat and vocabulary exchange, the men who came to the bar had a habit of sharing deeply personal stories with Pei. "I don't know if you can understand me at all . . . " they'd begin. If she understood, Pei would nod and say, "*Capito.*" If she didn't, she would blink and say, "*Non capisco.*" No matter her reply, the men continued to tell their long-winded tales, sometimes revealing very intimate details of their lives. It seemed easier for them to talk to a barista who did not fully realize the weight of their stories, the intensity of their pain. She would not ridicule them or pass judgment as others might. Pei was exactly the kind of listener they needed.

"*Tu lavoro?*" Pei asked Paolo one day. *You work?*

"I don't work anymore."

"*Prima?*" Pei asked. *Before?*

"I was an *elletricista.*" An electrician.

"*Elletricista.*"

"Yes, artisan and electrician."

"*Tu, moglie?*" Pei asked. *You, wife?*

"No."

"No?"

"They're all the same," Paolo said bitterly.

Pei pressed on with more questions. "You're not married before?"

"No," Paolo replied. "I used to live in Turin. I lived there thirty years."

"You born in Turin? Where you born?"

"I was born here, but I lived in Turin for thirty years. I lived with someone for seven years. One week before we were to marry, we had a fight. One week. *Una settimana.*"

"*Settimana,*" Pei repeated.

"*Una settimana. Sette giorni,*" Paolo said. "One week. Seven days. Before we got married we had a fight. I didn't get married. We had a fight right before.

Seven days before our wedding we had a fight." Paolo stared off in the distance as he spoke and Pei looked down and listened silently and patiently—the way she always did when she did not understand.

"My suit is still in my dresser," Paolo continued. "It doesn't fit me anymore, but I still hold onto it. Hand sewn, and it still hangs in my dresser. I should give it to Luigi; that way he'll get married."

Pei looked toward the broom closet where her uncle was taking his nap.

"*Tre anni,*" she said, looking at Paolo sadly. *Three years.*

"*Tre anni,*" Paolo nodded. "Divorced, I know." He heaved a sigh. "Those that marry for money get divorced. Maybe it's better not to get married?" Pei did not answer. She had not understood Paolo's story about his broken engagement, nor had she understood what he said about his hand-sewn suit that was still hanging in his closet. But she could see that Paolo was sad. Many of the men who came to the bar were that way—but it was the angry customers who were the worst.

There was one middle-aged man who liked to say "fuck" all the time. He had hazel skin, tawny eyes, and hair that was thick and knotted in curls. Once he picked up a chair and held it above his head, threatening to throw it at another customer. Uncle Luigi rushed out from behind the bar. "*Vattene via!*" he bellowed, pointing toward the door and ordering the man out. His voice boomed so loudly everyone in the bar had stopped to watch and Pei never imagined such a thunderous sound coming from her uncle. The man put the chair down and left, but he returned the next morning. This time Uncle Luigi was still asleep and Pei was running the bar on her own. The man ordered a cappuccino, then he lit a cigarette and blew a cloud of ash at Pei's face. She glowered at him but he stared right back. For a few seconds, Pei blinked and seemed to be contemplating her next move. Then she pointed at the door just as her Uncle Luigi had done the day before. "*Vattene! Vattene!*" she yelled. *Out! Out!* Surprised the young barista would dare to shout at him, the man reacted with a laugh. "Ha!" he roared, before taking a few steps back. He looked Pei straight in the eye and brought the cigarette up to his lips once again. The bar was still as people's eyes flitted nervously from Pei, who stood behind the bar, to the man smoking near the doorway. Pei wore a vicious scowl on her face as she glowered at the man for a few seconds more. Then she turned to face the coffee machine, picked up a white little cup, and prepared another cappuccino for her next customer.

If the men at the bar weren't aggressive, they were flirtatious. Some liked to ask if Pei was a virgin or if she had a boyfriend. Pei never knew how to answer. "Tell them you have a Chinese boyfriend who lives in a nearby town," Luigi advised. That seemed to stop most men from asking any further questions. But there was nothing Pei could do to stop them from touching her. There were men who liked to sneak up behind her, usually when she was clearing a table. By the time she felt the pinch, it was already too late: two strong fingers nipped her bottom and squeezed hard. Pei spun around, her face and her cheek burning with shame and anger. She wanted to scream. Instead she pushed her words down her throat and returned to clearing the table. "Before I left China, I had a lot of hopes because I heard everyone say how great Italians were and how cultured and mannered they are," Pei said. "But now that I am living abroad, I realize you can't generalize like that. Every country has good and bad people— even the Chinese."

During Easter celebrations in April, the townspeople erected a wooden cross in the main square where a priest led a small congregation in prayer. His voice echoed loudly into a microphone but could not compete with the raucous karaoke party raging in a nearby bar. The whooping applause that followed each Italian pop serenade reverberated through the town while the priest droned on in his ever-steady pace, never wavering from his prayers. It was a stormy Easter Sunday, with high winds and belligerent rain—too wet and too cold to be anywhere but in a church or in a bar, and many chose the latter. At Bar Gru Gru, the crowd grew so big the front doors had to stay open. Men clutched sweaty beer bottles in their hands and jostled to attract the young barista's attention.

"Lya!" one shouted, slamming down change. "*Vino!*"

"Lya," another bellowed. "Brandy!" Paper bills were pressed into her hands and Pei began to feel feverish.

"*Ni hao!*" a posse of young men chorused as they sauntered into the bar in their jackets and baseball caps.

"*Mei nu,*" said one, using the Chinese word for "beautiful girl."

"*Ni hao, chu nu!*" chimed another, using the Chinese word for "virgin."

"Albanians," Pei muttered under her breath as she flashed her eight-tooth smile at them. "*Buonasera,*" she said loudly. Her stomach rumbled, reminding her she hadn't eaten yet. Earlier in the evening, a drunk customer picked up the kebab she was saving for dinner and dropped it on the ground. Pei's face showed equal parts exhaustion, humiliation, and fury. At such moments her thoughts drifted back to China, to times when life was much simpler.

Pei settled into a routine at the bar, but it was in the heat of the summer when one phone call from her mother set in motion another wave of change. Pei's eighteenth birthday was fast approaching, and she needed to take an Italian-language test to be eligible for a residency permit. In 2013, there were 4.4 million foreigners officially living in Italy, compared to just 1.5 million in 2003. As immigrants continue to flow into the country, the government passed a law requiring all non-European immigrants to take the test. Some say it's only natural for newcomers to learn the language of their host nation so they can become contributing members of society. But some immigrant advocates worry the test, which was enacted in 2010, has become an instrument for intolerance rather than integration. Italy is just one of many countries demanding language skills in exchange for residency or in some cases citizenship. In Britain, those seeking citizenship or permanent residency must prove their "Britishness" by answering multiple-choice questions in English on British history, culture, and law. And in the United States, those seeking citizenship are asked ten questions about American history, geography, and government. The questions are not easy—What did the Declaration of Independence do? Why does the flag have fifty stars?—and at least six questions must be answered correctly and in English. Most of the Chinese immigrants I spoke to in Italy thought the test was a big pain, but Pei believed every opportunity to learn Italian was a good opportunity. She was grateful to her mother, who was keeping track of all the deadlines and prerequisites, and to her Uncle Luigi, who was kind enough to allow her some time off. Three days a week, she hopped on the train and traveled one hour north, back to the house with the peeling yellow paint. Her mother arranged private language classes with an Italian teacher to help her prepare for the test.

Lia Panelatti Santoro looked every bit a middle-aged schoolteacher, with her short brown hair and reading glasses that hung from a slender chain around her neck. She had a commanding yet caring voice that came with more than a decade of experience teaching Italian to Chinese immigrants. She spent a total of forty hours coaching Pei. "When she came to me, all she knew was cappuccino, Coca-Cola, and coffee. There weren't any other words," Lia said. Pei forced herself to memorize long lists of vocabulary and drilled dozens of new conjugations into her head. She bowed her head to listen as Lia read passages from a book. And her pen, which usually flowed across the page in a luscious Chinese script, now moved slowly as she traced square letters between the blue lines of her notebook. Lia charged Pei 13 euros ($18) a lesson and said she saw much potential in her despite Pei's limited vocabulary. "She was a promising young girl and instantly I told her that she should quit her job as a barista," Lia said. "I told her she should come work at the mushroom farm because here she could study Italian, because here she would have more opportunities."

In August, Pei arrived at a local school to take the test. Dry-mouthed and jittery, she sat in front of an administrator who played an audio recording of two brief conversations. The words flew past her ears and Pei closed her eyes so she could concentrate better. When she opened them, the administrator asked her a series of questions to make sure she understood the content. Pei answered as best as she could. Next, she was given two texts to read—a letter from a police station and instructions for using a washing machine. Pei lowered her nose close to the paper and quietly read aloud. The administrator waited for her to finish, and then drilled her with more questions to test her comprehension. Again, Pei did her best to answer. Finally, there was a writing test. Pei was asked to pen a letter in Italian to an imaginary friend.

When she held her newly minted residency card in her hand one week later, Pei felt a surge of pride. "So this little card is why I have worked so hard these last months," she said. "Today, I feel I have indeed stepped foot into Italian society for the very first time." Soon after the test, Pei left the bar in Falconara and moved back in with her mother at the house with the peeling yellow paint. On the advice of her teacher, Lia, she began working at the mushroom farm. A few months after that, she returned to the bar in Falconara for a visit, but none of the customers recognized her. "I was here too short a time," Pei said as she walked through the front doors she once opened every morning. Uncle Luigi stood behind the bar, in his dark slacks and navy top.

"Uncle Luigi, where is Paolo?" Pei asked.

"He's in the hospital," he said. "It does not look good. He won't be coming to the bar anymore."

Upon hearing the news, Pei was surprisingly unemotional. "He was just another customer," she remarked. "He was never my friend anyway."

SHIFTING TIDES

I left home as a youth and as an old man returned
My accent unchanged but my temples turned gray
The children see me but don't know who I am
Smiling, they ask: "Stranger, where do you come from?"

—Tang Dynasty poem "Returning Home"

Pei often dreamed about going home. Every migrant does. Sometimes, in the dream, they return to grand countryside estates where hearty soups, succulent dumplings, and fatty pork are laid out before them. Their loved ones gather around the table in welcome. Other times, the dream is a nightmare. They arrive in their villages and walk the dusty streets alone. Family members and old friends stroll by, but not one of them stops. They have become strangers in their own hometowns. Over time this nightmare may evolve. It's not only that friends and family don't recognize them. After so many years abroad, after so much upheaval and change, the migrants themselves can't recognize their villages. Living outside of China has changed them at the core.

"I am thinking of quitting school," Chen Junwei told his wife during one of their weekly long-distance phone calls from China to Italy. "I want to find a job." He was continuing his Italian lessons at Teacher Xu's school in Qingtian, but still there was no news on the visa front. Hearing her voice had always brought him closer to her. But that day she felt as distant as the bayberry *yangmei* harvest in the winter. "I sit in class every day in a room full of women. I am one of the few men there," Chen continued. "People will start talking. They'll say, 'His wife is out there working so hard for their family and he is in a classroom with no job!' This can't go on." Chen's wife knew her husband was an eternal optimist. This was simply a rare moment of weakness. She spoke patiently and once again stressed the importance of learning Italian. "You will be ahead of everyone else if you figure out the language," she said to him. "It is the single most important thing for a migrant."

More than half a year had passed since they had started the family reunification process. During that time, Chen watched many of his friends have their visas approved. He congratulated them personally, attended their farewell parties, and wished them happiness and prosperity on their new adventure. Meanwhile, his own passage to Italy remained elusive. Chen suspected a complicated family history had been slowing the process. A decade ago, his wife gave birth to their son while she was a migrant worker in French Guiana—a tiny country of pristine rainforests on the northeastern tip of South America. When their son was born, Chen was thousands of miles away in China. Because he wasn't there and because Chen and his wife were not yet legally married, the baby was registered under the mother's surname: Lin. Chen's wife had remained in French Guiana to work but had arranged for their son to be brought back to China when he was a year old. Chen remembers picking the toddler up at the airport and watching him sleep as they traveled back to Qingtian. "Poor kid," he thought at that time. "I'm going to be a good father to this boy." As Chen watched his son grow up without his mother, he spent a lot of time dreaming about the family he and his wife would one day raise together. Chen had even hoped to have another child. "A daughter will be better behaved," he said. "She would listen to her parents more." But now that dream seemed an impossibility. They had lived apart for nearly a decade; their son barely recognized his own mother. Was it all worth it? Chen heard himself uttering an ultimatum: "If I don't get my visa this year, you have to come back to China. Your son thinks of you as a stranger. We have been apart for nearly ten years. This is not the kind of life I want." He had never been so forceful. Over the years, he had tried to be supportive. He had strived to be a good father and a good husband. Most of all, he believed steadfastly in the sacrifice necessary to achieve the emigrant dream. But now he was losing hope. Chen wanted desperately for his wife to say she would come home to China to be with him and their son. When he finished speaking, she was silent for a moment. Then she said: "But I do not want to come back to China."

As the migrants continued to share their stories with me, I realized the terms *immigrant* and *emigrant* are misleading. They imply a one-off event, that people leave one place to settle permanently in another. In truth, an emigrant's life is a transient one. They uproot themselves again and again in search of opportunity.

Migration is temporary, repetitious, or circular. Migrants typically have their feet in two places, connecting China to the world and the world to China. Chen's wife may not have wanted to return to China, but the economic crisis in Europe was forcing out many migrants, willingly or not. Indeed, a reverse migration was under way. Restaurants weren't breaking even. Stores weren't selling enough stock. Real estate prices had tanked. The Eurozone crisis, which ballooned into a combined problem of banking, government debt, and competitive growth, was not entirely understood by the people in Qingtian. The grandmothers who gathered daily in front of the banks in town, eyes trained on the digital boards displaying foreign currency rates, spotted it first. They had organized an informal *bureau de change*, trading euros for yuan on the street, calling out like hawkers in front of a baseball stadium: *Euros, euros, want to change your euros?* When the red digits of the euro dipped but then seemed to recover, the women weren't sure what to make of it all. The clearest, surest sign that something was terribly wrong in Europe was when the migrants started returning home.

I arrived back at our apartment in Qingtian one day to find a man pacing in Grandmother's living room. He had friendly eyes and pursed lips and bore a striking resemblance to my father-in-law. From the living room I heard the clang of a spatula hitting the steel wok—Waipo was in the kitchen whipping up lunch for our guest. I soon learned the man in the living room was indeed related to the family. He was my father-in-law's cousin, and he had just arrived back from Portugal. In the complicated kinship system, there's a special relationship name for everyone you are related to, based on generation, maternal or paternal lineage, relative age, and gender. A mother's brother and a father's brother, for example, are different "uncles" and that name also changes depending on whether that brother is an older or younger brother. Your brothers-in-law are called different relationship names depending on if they are older or younger than your husband and which side of the family they're on. For simplicity's sake I called the man from Portugal, *Shushu*, which is a catch-all polite term that means "younger brother of my father."

"Business is terrible, just terrible," Shushu said, shaking his head. "Things in Portugal are very bad." He had been living in Portugal since 1990 and owned a Chinese restaurant in Lisbon for several years before moving south to Portimão, a town on the country's southern coast. There, he ran a wholesale store selling household goods made both in China and Portugal. Back in Qingtian, he was scouting business opportunities in the hopes he could move his family— a wife and three kids—back to China. "It's time we leave Portugal," he said. "There is nothing there for us anymore."

My cell phone rang the next morning. It was Shushu. "I am going fishing and will be at your place at a horse's speed," he said, using the Chinese phrase *"mashang"* which means "immediately." The Chinese use this term rather liberally, and for some reason, the stated immediacy is never quite fulfilled. I sprang out of bed, threw on some clothes, and then, of course, waited nearly an hour for Shushu to arrive. We drove to a rocky spot on the banks of the Ou River just outside of town where half a dozen men had planted modern fishing poles in the ground, their long lines floating in the gray-green waters rushing by. A white-hot sun beat down as we approached one of the men. He wore tall rubber boots and his bronze skin was crinkled like a paper bag. Shushu introduced him as his Shushu—and I respectfully called him by the same title. I opened up my pink umbrella and held it over my head as I sat down next to the two Shushus who stared out into the waters waiting for the fishing lines to move. Shushu from Portugal began to talk. He had left Qingtian when he was twenty years old, traveling north, past Beijing, to the province of Heilongjiang. From there, he took a boat to Russia and made his way to the Czech Republic, and with the help of smugglers, he scaled snow-capped mountains on foot crossing the border to Germany.

"Hold on," I said. "You had to climb over mountains to get to Germany? That's pretty incredible. Was it treacherous?"

"Treacherous? No, it was a lot of fun!" Shushu said. "I remember doing cartwheels on top of the mountain." From Germany, Shushu went to Holland where he worked as a cook in a Chinese restaurant. He learned how to make Chinese-Indonesian specialties including *nasi* (fried rice), *bami* (fried noodles), and *loempias* (spring rolls), and he spent hours carving carrots into intricate flower shapes that garnished every entrée. In Italy, he worked in a garment factory learning to stitch leather bags. The Chinese in Europe move restlessly from one country to another. At first, undocumented immigrants seeking legal residency flock to countries providing amnesties. In the last decade before the economic crisis, Spain and Italy were granting frequent amnesties. Later, they move again, this time in search of wealth and opportunity. "The Chinese see Europe as a chess board of opportunity," says sinologist Antonella Ceccagno. "European national boundaries present no barrier to them. The migrants move around fluidly and are connected through strong family networks, shared dialects, and places of origins." In Belgium, Shushu was thrown into jail when he was caught using a false passport en route to France.

"Jail?!"

"The bus was stopped for a passport check," Shushu explained. "I was traveling with a friend's passport. The officer looked at the photo and said, 'You don't look like the man on this passport.'"

Shushu played dumb. "No, officer, it really is me. Look again."

The officer gazed at the photo. "No," he said firmly. "It's not you."

Shushu knew he was in trouble then. "OK, OK," he said, his mind racing to coming up with another lie. "I found the passport on the floor of a public bathroom and just picked it up." Shushu laughed about it now. He was locked up in a detention center, but instead of talking about the fear and uncertainty that must have weighed down on him, Shushu told me how he spent his days playing poker with a Russian inmate. Detainees were given daily rations of butter so they could cook their own meals. With no access to money, cigarettes, or beer, the men gambled with sticks of butter and Shushu was proclaimed the "butter champion." After twenty-eight days in detention, he was set free.

"That must have been really tough, to be locked away for so long," I said.

"Nah," Shushu said. "Well . . . " He paused, appearing to change his mind. "It *was* pretty tough. The worst part was having to go without beer or cigarettes for a month. Now *that* was unbearable!"

After his release, Shushu made his way down to Lisbon where his sister had a Chinese restaurant. He worked for her as a cook before opening his own restaurant a year and a half later. As soon as he gained legal residency in Portugal, he sent for his wife and son in China, whom he hadn't seen in years.

"Why did you sell your restaurant in Lisbon?" I asked.

"I went down south and I thought, 'The weather is really nice here,'" Shushu said. "There were very few Chinese entrepreneurs in the area at the time. I thought a wholesale business might be a good opportunity."

I saw Shushu a few more times after that. He dropped off his catch after yet another afternoon of fishing, and he brought me to an isolated village nestled in the mountains to pick red bayberries during the summer *yangmei* harvest. During these outings, he mentioned several businesses opportunities he was looking into. Among them was opening a seafood restaurant and marketing a top-secret Chinese medicine elixir. He claimed only he and a handful of other men had the recipe.

"Would it be a difficult transition coming back to China?

"Not for me. This is my home," Shushu said.

"I mean for your family. Your wife and kids."

"Nah, we come back to China for vacation and my kids love it."

Shushu had literally scaled mountains, spent a month in jail, and worked a dozen different jobs across Europe. Now, he was willing to start over again. A month later Shushu stopped coming around. Waipo told me he had returned to Portugal. Half a year later, when I traveled to Portimão to see him, Shushu told me it was his wife and children who had summoned him back.

"My small son called and begged me to come home," he said, inviting me into his wholesale store where dozens of plastic Christmas trees—classic green ones, white frosted ones, and tinsel-blue ones—were displayed up near the front. Just one or two customers were browsing the store that afternoon. Shushu sighed. "There is no market. The Portuguese aren't spending!" He rang up an old woman's purchase—one plastic water gun and a few other small toys. "All these Christmas trees and decorations here. No one is buying them! I have hundreds of them in the back. Usually by this time of the year, I can sell everything." Shushu walked me up and down long, shiny aisles where his merchandise was stacked neatly on white shelves. "Take anything you like," he said. I picked a small black-and-red figurine of the rooster of Barcelos, a common emblem of Portugal. Generous as always, Shushu brought me out for lunch where he ordered clams dunked in a garlic and white wine broth and succulent jumbo prawns seasoned with nothing but sea salt. That day, his wife told me she preferred to stay in Portugal. Having lived abroad for so many years, she was unaccustomed to life in China. The children also felt the same way. They didn't mind visiting China for a week or two, she said, but didn't want to move back. And already Shushu had another destination in mind.

"I am thinking of going to Mozambique and getting into the seafood trade. They have lobsters THIS big!" he told me, extending his hands about half a meter long. "And I heard they sell for just one euro a pound!" Mozambique, a former Portuguese colony in southeast Africa, was just one of many African countries where Chinese entrepreneurs were establishing businesses. A new wave of migrants were taking advantage of China's increasing diplomatic and commercial clout on the continent. Chinese companies were striking giant mining deals, muscling into lucrative oil markets, and building infrastructure (railroads, highways, ports) across this new frontier. Shushu said it was his restless temperament that helped him stay healthy and energetic. "I will never stop searching for opportunities," he said. "It is my nature. It is what keeps me young."

As Shushu set his sights on Africa, some migrants attempted to reestablish themselves in China. On the same street as the four-star hotel in Qingtian where Ye Pei served as a waitress during her internship, the newly opened Barcelona Bar offered authentic Spanish coffee. The owner, Dong Xueli, had jammed her suitcases with as many coffee beans as she could when she left Barcelona and returned to Qingtian after more than a decade abroad. Although Dong was just thirty-seven years old, the deep creases in her face made her look much older. She had a husky voice and the thick hands of someone who had spent years working in a kitchen. Indeed she had worked so many places and so many jobs in her life that she had a hard time remembering where she had been. She was just a teenager when she left Qingtian and traveled to other parts of China to find work: first up the coast to Jiangsu province, then into the interior to Wuhan, and later to the cities of Hangzhou and Shanghai. At twenty-six years old she made her way overseas. She traveled to the former Yugoslavia on a tourist's visa. There she paid a smuggler to bring her to Austria via Hungary. They traveled by night and Dong recalled how she had huddled in a small boat with more than a dozen other emigrants, how her heart pounded when the boat swung to one side, almost capsizing, and how fast she had to run in order to make it across the border under a black sky. In Austria she got by washing dishes in the kitchen of a Chinese restaurant and babysitting the owner's children. Eventually, she made it to Spain where she applied for a residence permit and managed to save enough to buy a bar in Barcelona. In spite of its name, Tapas de Chinos sold nothing Chinese. It catered to Spaniards and served authentic local food like patatas bravas, bite-sized croquettes, and pickled anchovy fillets. Business, good for a few years, later slowed. Dong blamed the global economic recession and a new law banning smoking inside restaurants and bars. She sold her business in 2011 to another Chinese immigrant, a new arrival from Fujian province.

The only authentically Spanish item at Barcelona Bar in Qingtian was the *nong ka*, the Spanish espresso they served. The rest of the menu was Chinese, which appealed to returning migrants lounging in the bar's spacious booths. They slurped up noodles and snacked on potato pancakes, small latkes panfried with threads of pickled cabbage. It was a local delicacy the kitchen made especially well. Cigarette smoke rose from each and every booth, blanketing the restaurant in a foggy haze. Unlike in Spain, national smoking laws were not enforced here, as in the rest of China, and Dong was perfectly happy about that. But adjusting to life in the homeland wasn't as easy as she expected. Most of her friends had long migrated to Europe and she was lonely. Reestablishing all those important relationships necessary for running a business in China was difficult because Dong said all her *guan xi* was outdated. She was considering returning to Spain to open another bar in the southern city of Malaga. "I go where there is money to be made," she said.

In the past, returning home before you had "struck gold" was a loss of face. It meant you had failed to provide your family with a better future, that you were too weak to swallow the bitterness of a life overseas. But Qingtian's returnees, many of whom made a living selling Made in China products abroad, were now looking to capitalize on a market hungry for Made in Europe commodities. A new breed of wealthy Chinese consumers had become obsessed with brands and bling and were acquiring a taste for some of Europe's most famous delicacies. Across China, shops were selling Spanish olive oil, French wine, Italian cheese, and ice cream made from the milk of Dutch cows. Nearly every month, a new fancy restaurant opened with fanfare in Qingtian—some baking French baguettes, others serving Spanish *jamon* and brewing Italian espresso. Returning emigrants also invested in luxury hotels and karaoke clubs.

The young women wore high heels and *qipao*s, a body-hugging one-piece Chinese dress with a stand-up collar and high slits. They had perfect eight-teeth smiles, and I tried not to stare when they bowed as soon as the elevator doors slid open. I stepped out into a hallway overwhelmed with crystal and brass. The young women, called *xiaojie*, were numbered with gold tags pinned to their chests. Their official responsibilities were to pour drinks and make conversation with the guests, according to the job postings, but I often saw drunken *xiaojie* or "misses" outside karaoke bars late at night, clinging onto their customers like young girls who had fallen asleep on their father's shoulders. The four-star hotel's new karaoke club had only recently opened for business when I was invited to tour the facilities with one of the club's overseas investors. Wang Yucheng didn't look like a local. He wore glasses that were tinted purple, and he was light-skinned, a little pudgy, and taller than most of the other men around town. He ran several successful Chinese restaurants in Berlin. Wang told me he was just eighteen years old when he and his mother opened their first restaurant in Germany. "We couldn't even afford a fridge," he recalled. "We cut up the meat and put it outside. Thankfully the weather had already turned cold." Wang said business was so good that within one week of opening, he made enough money to properly equip his kitchen. Now, the teenager who at one time couldn't afford a refrigerator was a high-rolling businessman who shuttled back and forth from Europe to China. One night of karaoke could cost $500. VIPs, who reserved the finest rooms and booked the most expensive *xiaojie*s, sometimes paid as much as $1,000. Even more valuable was the priceless opportunity to show off.

Wang hollered for a server. Two busboys shuffled in, bowed to us as they took our orders, and then shuffled back out. Within minutes, they returned with bowls of fruit and platters stocked with chicken feet and marinated duck tongues. We were seated in a VIP room that looked more like an office, with a mahogany desk at the center of the room and several leather couches. A giant painting hung on the wall: a man in an enormous red cloak, gripping the reins of his steed with one hand, rearing the animal up on its hind legs and pointing his other hand dramatically up into the air. Like the copper statue that stood in Qingtian's riverside park, here was yet another rendition of the famous nineteenth century painting of Napoleon crossing the Alps.

We continued through several more gilded rooms. Marc's cousin, who came on the tour with us, stopped at one karaoke machine and punched in his favorite Chinese pop song. The flat-screen TV lit up with scenes from a melancholic music video. Leo Chen grabbed the microphone and began to sing. He was twenty-six years old and loved karaoke more than anyone else I knew. Leo had a bit of a nerdy look, with his pale skin, short black hair, and eyeglasses, but it was his mischievous grin that revealed just how clever and ambitious he was. He had always been a favorite cousin of mine because he was chatty, free-spirited, and generous. Though Leo lived in Italy for more than a decade, it was always been his dream to return to Qingtian and open a business of his own. Whenever he visited, he introduced us to his childhood haunts. He brought us down to a smoky basement pool hall where I learned to pocket 8-balls. He showed us a street-side stand where we huddled in between a leaning stack of bamboo steamers and devoured fluffy meat buns. Leo was the one who brought me to the coolest bar in town—J.J. Bar—where I got to know the owner who spoke English slang he learned from American movies. At night, we rarely saw him because that was when Leo was busy scouting out business opportunities. This usually involved smoking and consuming large amounts of *baijiu* rice wine in order to pound out those good relations and *guan xi* needed with potential partners and investors.

When his mother first went abroad, he was just a child and Leo says he was excited when she promised to send for him as soon as she could. But as the years passed and Leo grew into his teens, his excitement turned into dread. Leo often says he left China at the worst possible time—when he had many friends and when he was happiest. Leo was fifteen when he left for Italy, and though he desperately missed his friends in China, he was enchanted by the picturesque port town of Cesenatico where his parents had found work in a Chinese restaurant. The vibrant sails and beautifully painted hulls of old fishing vessels were moored in the town's canal, which, residents proudly point out, was surveyed by Leonardo da Vinci himself. Leo said he was grateful to the local school for assigning an Italian-language tutor to him. He was also indebted to an older cousin, who brought him to the *salon jockey* arcade, to the disco, and to the local Chinese school to scout out pretty girls. In the summer, they went swimming in the Adriatic Sea, suntanning on the beach, and hunting for oysters and mussels on local reefs in between the pounding surf.

Leo struggled to keep up in school and eventually dropped out to help his parents in the restaurant. He started off washing dishes and chopping vegetables and very quickly climbed his way up to become a chef. They opened their own takeaway and called it La Muraglia, the Great Wall. But Leo said the restaurant never really caught on with Italians, who seemed to prefer their own local cuisine. Leo says he understands why this was so. One of his favorite street-side snacks is the *dabing*—which literally means "big biscuit." It's a large pancake that is stuffed with a meat and vegetable filling. In Qingtian, one *dabing* costs just three yuan (less than fifty cents), and when the vendor angles it out from the depths of the oven, the dough is crispy on the outside while the insides are steamy and delightfully savory. "I know why the Italians prefer their own food," Leo said. "It's sort of like this: if there are two *dabing* street vendors and one is from Qingtian and the other from Wenzhou, then of course I would buy from the Qingtian vendor! I would do that, even if his *dabing* was inferior, just out of loyalty to my own home county!" La Muraglia's business plummeted in 2003 coinciding with the outbreak of SARS, the viral respiratory disease that claimed nearly 650 lives in Hong Kong and China. There were no reported cases or deaths in Italy, but Leo says Chinese enterprises, particularly restaurants, were stigmatized and suffered as a result. They sold the restaurant, and for a few years, Leo tried his hand as a retailer. He set up shop near the beach and sold women's fashions made in Prato. In my closet today, I still have the brown knit sweater Leo gave me just before he closed that store and left sunny Cesenatico for the western city of Turin, where he and his parents began a new venture—running a bar. The bar was beautifully renovated, with a smooth wooden bar and a lattice shelf extending across a wall displaying an impressive collection of wines. To prepare for his new gig as a bar owner, Leo watched YouTube videos that taught him how to mix drinks. Determined to keep loyal customers happy, he made sure peanut bowls were topped up and that bite-sized portions of bruschetta flowed from the kitchen to the bar counter. On the nights when Turin's local soccer league was playing, he projected the game on a big white screen for all to see. The bar was located in a rough part of town, however, and people were always running off without paying and many of the "loyal" customers kept long-running tabs that often went unpaid. Leo's mother was afraid to keep the bar open in the late evening hours. They struggled to keep the business afloat for two years, before Leo made another trip back to China to hunt around for more lucrative business opportunities in Asia. In the spring of 2014, he finally settled on a cafeteria in a Shanghai food court. He sold the bar in Turin and brought his mother and father back to China with him. At the cafeteria, they serve mostly Chinese food, but Leo also cooks up spaghetti and lasagna once in a while. Life in modern-day Shanghai is fast-paced and exciting, and Leo says he doesn't miss Italy one bit.

At the Longjin Road Foreign Languages Center where Chen Junwei was learning Italian, Teacher Xu let me use her classroom to give English lessons even though there weren't too many people interested in learning. There were migrants who had gone to the United States, the UK, and Canada, but it was difficult and expensive to apply for visas in those countries. Most of the migrants from southern Zhejiang had settled in continental Europe, and that was where the connections remained the strongest. Still, as soon as Teacher Xu posted ads all around the county advertising that "a foreigner" was teaching at her school, we received quite a few inquiries. Most of my students were either born in Europe to Chinese migrants or had migrated to Europe as children. They had come back to China for summer vacation and were looking for something to do during those long, hot days.

My first student was a sixteen-year-old boy named Jianyong Wu, who had spent half his life in China and the other half in Spain. Everything about Jianyong drooped. He had floppy cheeks, and he slouched like a sulky teenager; his eyes stayed trained on the floor as if he were searching for cockroaches in the old classroom. When he spoke, he breathed his words hesitantly and quietly as if he had a bad case of asthma. Jianyong was born in Qingtian, but left for Spain at the age of eight. The family settled in a city south of Barcelona, where his father built up a small empire: he owned five Chinese restaurants, and at the height of Spain's construction boom, he bought some land and built thirty-seven homes—homes he was not able to sell after the economic crisis hit Europe and Spain's construction bubble burst in 2008.

For the first few lessons, Jianyong refused to look up from his notebook. Despite my efforts to coax him out of his silence, he hunched over the little desk, eyes downcast and demure. His cursive script was barely legible, but it was clear he was more comfortable expressing himself on paper than with the spoken word. I had him fill out a "Tell Me About Yourself" form in English, where I learned, squinting at his scribbles, that his favorite subject in school was math, his favorite color was blue, and that he liked playing badminton and eating spaghetti. Over time, I learned more and more about him. I discovered that while he slouched and wore a blank expression on his face, he was, in fact, having fun. Most importantly, he was learning. Homework was usually done on time, and he remembered many of the new words and sentence structures we learned from week to week. A few months into our lessons, there was a homework assignment in which he had to write about the "Things I Like." Jianyong revealed that he "liked learning English."

On the hottest summer days, I waited for the sun to fall from the sky, dipping below the mountains and casting long shadows over the town. At last, some relief from the oppressive heat. All day, everyone had been trapped indoors, and when the mugginess finally lifted, people emerged from their homes in old plastic slippers and tank tops, fanning themselves in the streets. They set up lawn chairs on the pavement and sat with neighbors to enjoy the evening breeze. One night, I called Jianyong and told him to meet me in the town square to play some badminton. As soon as it grew dark, and the signs outside the karaoke bars and restaurants and coffee shops had flickered on, giant speakers in the square began to vibrate, the steady beat of old Chinese folk tunes reverberating through the town. The music drew hundreds of people—mostly older women—to the expansive cement park where they lined up under the glare of towering lamp posts and began to dance. Every step, every turn, every pivot and chassé followed a sequence and kept to the beat. Line dancing is a popular pastime in many parks and squares across China, and an aunt once tried to explain to me why she thought this was so: "We are a communal society," she said. "The Chinese like to do things altogether. As long as no one steps out of line, everything stays harmonious. No one feels isolated; no one is embarrassed."

On the other side of the square, a younger crowd volleyed feather birdies back and forth. And nearby, merchants set up little tables and chairs for children to paint. There were also inflatable pools filled with goldfish. Kids took little green nets and scooped the fish into blue buckets for fun. The first few times Jianyong came out to play, he kept a straight face as he lunged and returned shot after shot. I was a screamer, howling when I missed a good opportunity to smash the birdie and grunting as I raced across the pavement in pursuit of a falling shuttle. Night after night Jianyong remained emotionless until finally, one day, he broke. During our match, he smashed the birdie down hard and dropped sneaky shots at the net. A sweaty, panting Jianyong finally broke into a smile. We played round-robin tournaments that night until my legs trembled with exhaustion. Then we took a rest on nearby benches, sipping bottled water and watching the women twist into a grapevine and wave their arms in the air, swaying side to side in the moonlight.

Every class started off with a question in English: "How are you?" Jianyong loathed hearing this question. I had been teaching him English for months and he was learning quickly. He still struggled with pronouncing vowels correctly, but he had a decent understanding of the grammar and could read pretty smoothly. When it came to common greetings, however, Jianyong just couldn't do it. It wasn't so much a language problem but a shyness problem. Whenever we met for badminton, he never said "hello" to me. He would just show up and sit down on a nearby bench, eyes averted, waiting silently for his turn to play. One day he sat in class waiting for me, looking a little more sullen than usual.

"How are you?" I said, with a big smile. My student was silent.

"Jianyong," I repeated. "How are you . . . ?"

He took a shaky, short breath. "I am . . . I am . . . " There was a few seconds' pause, and my student switched to Chinese. "How do you say I'm feeling 'disorderly' in English?"

"Well, why don't you tell me what happened . . . "

Immediately, he began speaking in rapid-fire Mandarin. "My father called me today and said he is moving back to China. He's selling all his restaurants and bringing the entire family back to Qingtian."

Jianyong looked every bit like his father, only chubbier and lighter skinned. But their personalities could not be more different. Youliang Wu was outspoken, confident, and extremely chatty. He was twenty-five when he paid a smuggler $15,000 to get to Yugoslavia. From there, he joined a tour group to Pisa. He overstayed his tourist visa, moving to Milan, then to the eastern resort town of Rimini, and then onto Bologna. He got by working odd jobs, like sweeping the floors of a clothing factory run by Chinese emigrants. Sometimes he sold trinkets to tourists on the streets, something many other Chinese men did in those days, wandering from bar to bar trying to pressure young men into buying flowers for their female companions. For two years, he was on the move before he managed to get a residence permit in Spain. With an eye on the country's booming construction industry, he decided his goal was to one day build and sell homes. He started from the bottom, working as a construction worker for a Spanish company. Two years later, he became a contractor. Two years after that, he had saved up enough money to buy some land and begin building those thirty-seven homes he was later unable to sell. Jianyong's father once mentioned his plan to bring his two younger children, both born in Spain, back to China to receive a Chinese education while they were still young. But he never said anything about a permanent move. Now Jianyong was telling me that the decision to move the family back to China had already been made. The only question was: what was Jianyong going to do?

"I think the word you are looking for is *confused*," I said to him in Chinese and turning to the white board, I spelled out the English sentence for him: I AM CONFUSED. "You're not quite sure what to do. You have to make a decision and . . . it's rather complicated." Jianyong nodded and then began thinking aloud, speaking more than I had ever heard him say in one breath.

"I could go back to Spain by myself. I've been going to school there for eight years. It seems like a waste to drop out now. Our apartment isn't far from school. And we live near some aunts and relatives, so I could eat at their place . . . " He trailed off. "But then being there by myself I might be lonely." Jianyong's Chinese wasn't good enough to follow the high school curriculum in China. If he moved back to China with his family, he would probably have to find work. "I still don't know what kind of career I want," he said, his train of thought suddenly switching to the reality that he may never return to Spain, his home for the past eight years. "I would miss the peacefulness there. Here, the cars and the buses, they drive like crazy. The roads are a mess." At the end of the summer, Jianyong decided to head back to Spain while his family moved back to China. His father spent the rest of the year traveling back and forth between the two countries, after launching a new business importing red wine from Spain to China.

Jianyong wasn't the only one who was caught in the dizzying currents of modern-day migration. I tutored another young student named Carolina who was born in Portugal, moved to Spain as a teen, and had plans to go to North America for university. Carolina was just fifteen years old, with long black hair, big dark eyes, and a pale, moon-like face, but she seemed a lot older. She moved about with elegance and grace, and she was incredibly intelligent. I tutored her in essay writing, and she always turned in thoughtful and well-written pieces. In one of her homework assignments, she told me her father had recently relocated to Angola—China's second-largest African trade partner behind South Africa— to start a construction business. After the summer, Carolina said her mother planned to join him there. According to the Angolan government, more than one hundred thousand Chinese people have migrated to the country to operate cranes and bulldozers, work as railway technicians, or, like Carolina's parents, start a business. In 2012, in exchange for access to Africa's plentiful resources, then–Chinese president Hu Jintao offered $20 billion in cheap loans to African countries for three years. I asked Carolina how she felt about her parents moving so far away. "I'm used to everyone coming and going," she said to me in English. "That's why I have learned not to make any close friends. What's the point if I just end up leaving them anyway?" Today's migrants are more mobile than ever, responding quickly to changing economic conditions. They circulate around the globe, building bridges between countries through trade and commerce. But such a nomadic life can take its toll. Chen Junwei's son did not know his own mother, my restless Shushu from Portugal had his family to consider, and Boss Dong was having a hard time adjusting to life in the homeland despite the success of Barcelona Bar. Then there are children like Jianyong and Carolina—stuck in the middle of this back-and-forth migration and left to dangle in an intercontinental limbo. Would Ye Pei one day endure a similar fate? The young migrants I knew were neither here nor there. They straddled two countries and belonged to many worlds—and yet belonged nowhere.

THE FARM

Nothing can be gained with your fingers in the dirt.

Every time I planned to visit Ye Pei, I worried I wouldn't be able to find her. When I did find her, she was always in a new town, working a new job, and already thinking about her next move or imagining life someplace else. In between visits, we kept in touch mostly by long-distance phone. Each time I dialed her number and listened for the tones, ringing once, twice, a third time, I wondered if I would one day find her cell phone disconnected, her number changed, our close yet tenuous connection severed. Later, as Pei started to go online more often, we were able to send e-mails and instant messages. I could track Pei's life through her micro-blog. But like most of us who use social media, Pei only posted snippets of her life—her dinner at the local kebab store one evening, a meal she proudly cooked for her family, a new haircut. On the phone, Pei was often too exhausted to chat for too long. Late in 2012, more than a year after Pei first arrived in Italy, I found out she had moved back to her mother's house and started working on the mushroom farm. I was happy to hear she could finally rejoin her family again. But I wondered what happened to her goal of one day opening her own bar. Was working at the mushroom farm going to help her family become more financially stable? Would she continue to learn Italian? Was she happy?

I arrived in Rimini in the dead of winter. A thick fog rolled off the Adriatic Sea, shrouding the empty beachfront resorts and blanketing the hilly Romagna countryside in a spooky glow. Pei was meeting me in the evening, so that afternoon I made plans to visit an immigrant services group near the train station.

The association spokesperson, a fifty-six-year-old woman named Shio Mien, had came to Italy two decades ago as a student from Taiwan. She leaned back in her leather chair and pressed her fingers together as she spoke Chinese with an educated air. At the end of every sentence, she would smile and sprinkle Italian words as she spoke—*ecco, allora, bene*—in between sips of sweetened instant cappuccino. For a fee, the organization provided a number of essential services such as language classes, translation and notarization of documents, and counseling on workers' rights. Most of the immigrants that used their services worked either in garment factories scattered along the coast or on nearby farms. I perked up when Shio Mien said "farm." Did she know any of the Chinese workers on a nearby mushroom farm?

"Ye is the family name," I said.

"Ye," she repeated, looking upward in thought. "Ah, yes. Of course, they all work on the mushroom farm. A mother, father, and young girl, all members of our organization."

"Are there many Chinese people at the farm?" I asked.

"Oh, yes," Shio Mien said. "Without the Chinese, the farm would not have been able to survive."

It seemed odd to me that migrants left China to escape rural poverty only to end up on a farm. I knew other immigrant groups were working in the agricultural sector. Every year thousands of migrants from Africa and Eastern Europe flock to the fields and orchards of southern Italy to harvest tomatoes that are processed into pastes and purees and exported across Europe and around the world. In the parched countryside where temperatures can reach over 100 degrees Fahrenheit, they also pick grapes, lemons, olives, and oranges. They live in slums without electricity or running water and are paid less than $30 for ten- and twelve-hour workdays. Human rights campaigners call them "Europe's tomato slaves," but authorities continue to turn a blind eye. Without these migrant workers, Italy would be lacking in wine and tomato sauce. In the north, tens of thousands of Sikhs from India work in cheese farms in Parma, Reggio Emilia, Modena, Mantova, and Bologna, preserving the centuries-old tradition of Italian *fromaggio* that nearly collapsed in the late 1980s when young Italian dairy farmers left for white-collar jobs elsewhere. In desperation, the Italian government gave undocumented Sikhs wholesale amnesty. Making Parmesan cheese is a smelly, sweaty, and labor-intensive process, but these are conditions some Sikh immigrants are willing to endure.

"Obviously working in the countryside is not ideal. Most of these families came from China's countryside and the last thing they want is to be toiling in the soil," Shio Mien said, explaining how the Chinese turned to the farms after work at the garment factories slowed as a result of the economic crisis. "But the jobs on the farm were stable, at least more stable than factory jobs, and the Italian bosses followed the rules, at least much more than Chinese bosses usually do." Shio Mien showed little sympathy for immigrants who chose to work for abusive Chinese bosses. They "knowingly walk into a trap," she said. "Then they come to me asking for help, complaining about the long hours, and I say to them, 'It's your responsibility to get out of it.'" Shio Mien said immigrants had a duty to adapt to the lay of the land, to the Italian way of life. In order to do that properly, they had to learn the language. "Only then can you have a prosperous life." Shio Mien praised the mandatory language exam Pei and all non-European immigrants were forced to take in order to gain residency. "The government is paying for classes so you can learn their language. This is a privilege, not a millstone," she said. Shio Mien said she was good friends with the owner of the mushroom farm and had even taught Italian to the Chinese workers before the current teacher, Lia, took over. I asked if she could help me get in touch with the mushroom farm and act as a translator. Shio Mien said she could, for a fee. At the end of our interview, she offered to have someone drive me to Ye Pei's home. "Of course, you must cover the cost of the driver's gas. And it must be for his round trip," she said. I thanked her but declined. Then I made my way back to the train station to wait for Pei.

I waited for hours. To pass the time, I waded through the station's small bookstore and perused the panini selection at the station café. At one point, I noticed a surprising number of Chinese immigrants getting on and off trains. They wafted through the drafty station hall gripping flimsy plastic bags that stretched thinly over their fingers, ready to tear at any moment. I could see blocks of tofu resting at the bottom of those bags and the tips of leafy greens peeking out the top. Chinese grocery stores were still uncommon in these parts, but Rimini had a couple of places where immigrants could pick up familiar ingredients that helped them replicate the flavors of home. I sat on a steel bench and watched the clock. But as the sky turned dark and the temperatures dipped, my thighs turned icy cold. So I dragged my luggage to one corner of the station and paced back and forth, allowing my paranoia to resurface once again. What was taking Pei so long? Did she change her mind about meeting me this time around? In my experience, Chinese people don't like to say no to your face. It's considered rude and not very tactful. Instead, they often come up with a myriad of vague excuses, the most typical one I encountered was: *Wo you dian shi.* "Something's coming up." Maybe it's the journalist in me, but vague answers only compel me ask more questions, and I was always miffed when I heard, "*Wo you dian shi.*"

When Pei finally came through the front doors of the train station, I recognized her right away, but I also noticed how much she had changed. Relieved that she hadn't changed her mind about meeting me, we exchanged quick hugs. "I'm so sorry," she said. "I nearly got on the wrong bus, and when I finally found the right one, we were stuck in rush hour traffic all the way here." Pei's hair was now longer than her shoulders, and she had dyed it a lighter brown. She wore a pink skirt and knee-high suede boots. We left the station and immediately began walking toward the car rental office, Pei chattering away about the farm and about Li Jie. They were continuing their long-distance relationship with weekly phone calls and messages. We also talked about Shio Mien. "She offered to help you, right? For a price?" Pei asked. I nodded and we giggled. We talked about her time in Falconara and why she left the bar so suddenly after the residency exam. "I was losing my temper with the customers a lot," she said. "Uncle Luigi said I had a sour look on my face on many days."

"Well, it isn't your fault," I said, trying to console her. "It's hard to deal with drunks all day."

"Yes, but in the end, the customer is always right."

"Even when they pinch your bottom?" I challenged. Pei sighed.

I picked up my rental car—a compact Ford Focus that I paid double for because it was an automatic—and as I drove, Pei told me she was hoping to get her driver's license soon. She had enrolled in classroom sessions to prepare for a multiple-choice theory exam. If she passed the exam, which had to be completed in Italian, she could obtain a *foglio rosa*, a learner's permit. Then she could start taking road lessons. "That's one of the main reasons why I moved home," she said. "Life is so isolating without a car. In Italy, if you do not have a car, it's as if you don't have legs."

The rice cooker Pei brought in her luggage all the way from China was the first to stir in the still of the morning. A timer went off and steam began to rise from its vents as early as 4:30 a.m., signaling the start of another long day. Pei's cell phone alarm rang shortly afterward at 5 a.m. Most of the time her parents were already awake, shouting through the thin walls of the house to make sure both Pei and Mao were up. Mao needed to catch an early bus to school, so the entire family ate breakfast together, warming their cold hands against steaming rice bowls. To save money, the family did not turn on the radiators even when the temperatures outside dipped well below freezing. Many other migrants told me they did the same. In Pei's house, everyone was always bundled up in multiple layers including winter jackets. During those frigid winter months, the family huddled around the old cast-iron wood-burning stove in the kitchen—the only warm place in the entire house.

Pei, her mother, and her father were all working at the mushroom farm now. The three of them stepped into black rubber work boots and trundled down the cratered road with only moonlight guiding the way. During her first few days at the farm, Pei stayed close to her mother. Fen introduced her to a few co-workers in the central warehouse that hummed with the chatter of immigrants—a chorus of Chinese dialects, Turkish, Macedonian, and a little Italian. When the buzzer sounded, signaling the start of the workday, the immigrants scattered like birds. Shen went off with the men, pulling on gloves and putting on baseball caps as they headed outside to the greenhouses to harvest oyster mushrooms. Some women headed to the packaging area near the front of the central warehouse, and Pei followed her mother toward the back through enormous doors that looked like the entrance to an aircraft hangar. This was where they harvested white mushrooms.

Gigantic metal shelves were stacked six layers high and packed with a thick, chocolate-brown mix of straw and horse dung. These manure beds were filthy but very fecund: the perfect incubator for cultivating mushrooms. The air inside the enormous rooms smelled earthy and felt as though someone had just taken a long, hot shower. The chambers were kept at a balmy 60 to 68 degrees Fahrenheit when the grains of wheat inoculated with mushroom mycelium were sowed into the beds. Tiny mushrooms emerged within two weeks, doubling in size every twenty-four hours. Within three days, they were fully grown and ready for harvesting. Fen showed Pei how to stoop low in between manure beds to pick the creamy tops emerging from the soil. They had to be careful not to remove the roots, which can sprout new mushrooms every three to five days for about three weeks after the first harvest. The medium- to large-sized mushrooms needed to be collected while the small ones were left so they could continue to grow. If they were picking brown mushrooms, Fen reminded Pei to leave a few large ones in the soil. These would eventually grow into portobello mushrooms. It was also important to arrange the mushrooms caps facing up in Styrofoam containers. The oddly shaped mushrooms went on the bottom and acted as a podium for the round and unblemished mushrooms on top.

Fen was one of the fastest pickers on the farm. She could pick a hundred mushrooms in the same time it took Pei to pick thirty. But it annoyed Fen when co-workers and farm managers commented on this disparity. "They should stop comparing us," Fen said. "It's not fair. Pei is so young; she's only a child." Pei worked slowly, stopping to scratch her head, stretch her neck, or gasp and shake out her bare arms whenever leggy insects crawled up them. Meanwhile Fen's hands darted from soil to Styrofoam container like a pendulum. Nothing distracted her from her tasks. Fen was considered one of the most efficient workers on the farm not only because of her lightning-fast hands but because of her reserved disposition. Workers were generally discouraged from talking with one another while they were working, but idle chitchat was often exchanged when supervisors had stepped away. Fen rarely stopped to chat with others. Even at lunch, when workers crowded in big groups around the lunchroom tables, Fen usually preferred eating with her uncle (the one who introduced her to the farm) or even alone. She kept her distance not because she was anti-social. Rather, Fen believed silence was a source of great strength. The lunchroom was reminiscent of a high school cafeteria. The Turks sat with the Turks, the Macedonians with the Macedonians, the Chinese with the Chinese.

"Don't talk too much," Fen advised her daughter. "Just concentrate on your work. Do a good job."

Pei believed her mother had grown taciturn after spending the past five years alone in Italy. "During that time, she learned to keep things in her stomach," said Pei, using a Chinese idiom. "Sometimes it can be hard to really know her." Fen was quiet not only at work but also at home. When Pei and Mao were bickering or horsing around with their father, she always sat back and preferred to listen and watch. Fen may have seemed removed and detached from her family, but it was after dinner one night, when I asked Fen to recount her own migration story for me, when I discovered how much she cherished them. Fen spoke to me about the shock of getting her work visa to Italy approved, about the restaurateur who was late picking her up at the airport, and about her frantic search for a garment factory job. Then she came to the part of her story when she was waiting at the Milan airport for her husband and two children. That's when Fen's voice cracked, and I looked up to see her small face awash with tears, her pale cheeks blotchy and damp. Pei was sitting across the kitchen table from her mother, staring hard at the empty dinner plates when suddenly her shoulders collapsed. The tears were swift and sudden, racing down her face and dripping off her chin before she had time to wipe them away. Shen got up from his chair to sit next to his wife. He put one arm around her small frame as it trembled with each sob. Gently, I asked Fen if she was crying because she was sad.

"No," she croaked, her voice barely audible between her sniffles. "I cry because I am so happy we are together again."

For Pei, the warmth and humidity of the chambers were a nice change from the loud and raucous bar scene. Italian pop songs played softly on the radio and Pei enjoyed humming along. She couldn't make out all the words, but she understood *amore* and *solitudina*, the themes of love and loneliness resonating in her teenage heart. Pei felt she could relax at the mushroom farm. No one snuck up behind her to pinch her bottom, and she relished the reality that the little ivory heads before her did not drink, smoke, or curse. They waited obediently in their bed of soil, and Pei was never asked to make conversation with them. In Solesino, she took on the name Alessia. In Falconara, she became Lya. At the farm, everyone called her Pei, and at least for a short while, she felt like she was herself again.

A family of mice had moved in with the Ye family, and when Pei, Mao, and their parents gathered in the kitchen for dinner, the pesky little things zipped across the floor and over the countertops. I gave a frightful scream whenever I saw them, but the rest of the family found the rodents more of a nuisance than anything else. "*Fan si le,*" Shen said, stomping his feet to send the tiny fur balls bolting behind the cabinets. *How annoying!* Pei was equally fearless, even when mice managed to sneak between the space under the door and into her bedroom. A number of times, I awoke to the sound of bags rustling and jumped out of bed, turned on the lights, and screamed, "*Laoshu! Laoshu!*" Mouse! Mouse! Pei, always the heavy sleeper, simply groaned and pulled the blankets over her head. When I told Pei that the mouse had jumped into a paper bag where I kept my laundry, she swung her feet out of bed and took the bag to the kitchen where she opened the window and held the bag upside down. The mouse dropped from the second-floor window to the ground. Then she climbed back into bed and immediately fell asleep. Another time, we absentmindedly left a half-finished package of biscuits on the dresser table. In the middle of the night, I awoke to the unmistakable sound of crunching and reacted much in the same way as I had the night before. I threw off the covers in a panic, lunged at the light switch by the door, and screamed, "*Laoshu! Laoshu!*" Poor Pei had gone to sleep well before 10 p.m., trying to get as much rest as she could before her 5 a.m. wakeup call. She cracked her eyes open and saw the gray little mouse had buried its head in our box of biscuits. She reached for a pillow and threw it across the room toward the dresser. I screamed and the mouse looked up, its beady little eyes narrowed to slits. Then it leaped from the dresser onto the floor and scurried toward the door, squeezing under the gap back into the hallway. The worst was when the mice got into the bag of rice in the kitchen. Fen had to spend the evenings sifting through the grains by hand and picking out dark little lumps before she could wash the rice and set the timer to cook for the next morning.

There was a good reason why Fen told Pei not to talk too much when she was at the farm. Their fellow workers, especially the Chinese women, had long ears that stretched to every corner of the farm, clinging onto every little thing that was said and not said. There was gossip about a skirt that was too short, a face that wore too much makeup, or the newest worker who was too friendly with the foreigners. In the lunchroom the racial cliques were obvious, but not so apparent to an outsider was how fragmented the Chinese themselves were. There were three factions: those from Zhejiang province felt a certain allegiance to one another; migrants from China's northern provinces, who had only recently begun migrating to Italy, preferred speaking pristine Mandarin to each other; and the Fujianese, who came from southern China, stuck together. Pei preferred socializing with the foreigners. There were many young workers on the farm who were in their early twenties, but Pei was the youngest at eighteen. There was Fatima from Turkey, a pretty blonde named Marita from Albania, and Afrona and Mendim from Macedonia. Pei called Marita *amore* and Afrona her *sorella*, her "sister." They spoke in halting Italian to one another, and because less was said, they made an effort to make each word count. Pei felt most of those words were sincere. As winter approached, the sun fell quickly from the sky as she climbed the steep hill toward home. Many of her Chinese co-workers had cars, but they rolled by without stopping, the cool wind slapping Pei's cheeks red. When Mendim or Afrona drove past, they often offered her a ride.

I didn't fully understand the importance of Pei getting her driver's license until I visited her that winter. I realized that while you could see the farm from their home, the commute to and from work was a bit of an ordeal, especially if you spent the entire day on your feet picking mushrooms. Getting to the grocery store, which was a half-hour bike ride away, was a half-day affair. It could only be done on weekends and only if you had the guts to traverse that death-defying hill on bike and then have the strength to make the uphill trek back home. The family rarely had the chance to visit the Chinese supermarkets, which were usually located well inside the city centers and closer to the train stations. Without a car, Pei and her family were tied to their jobs and to that house with the peeling yellow paint. They could not actively look for work elsewhere, nor could they scout for new places to live.

To get her driver's license, Pei had to first pass a theory exam consisting of ten main subjects, each one with three true or false questions, for a total of thirty questions. Four wrong answers was an automatic fail. If she failed the exam twice in a row, she would have to register again and pay another $110 fee. After dinner every night, Pei opened up her laptop and went through practice exams for hours with her frayed Chinese-Italian dictionary by her side, but sometimes Pei couldn't understand the questions. The wording was tricky, sometimes nuanced. A couple times a week, she took the afternoon off to attend a class in the nearby city of Riccione. Skipping out meant she wouldn't be paid for the hours she missed at the farm, but she was grateful her bosses allowed her to do it. In a Chinese factory, coming and going as she pleased would have been difficult. Pei took forty minutes to ride into the city, leaning forward on her handle bars and pedaling hard. Her secondhand bicycle wheels were bent out of shape, so she inched along dusty industrial roads as trucks and cars rumbled by, breathing in dirt, before she finally arrived at the school sweaty and short of breath. If she was early she sat down in front of one of the free computers to scroll through practice questions before the teacher, a tall Italian man with graying hair, came in to signal the beginning of class.

"*Buongiorno*," he said, promptly dimming the lights. A projector flickered on and illuminated a white screen above his head. A circle outlined in red appeared. Inside the circle, the number 50. "For anyone in Italy, this is the maximum speed that one has to respect, not just Italians, but everyone," the teacher said. "*Massimo*. What does that mean? It means maximum. The maximum speed in a city is 50, but in a bigger city the speed limit can go up to a maximum of 70. But you must always follow the sign postings." The slide changed. The red and white circle remained, but inside, the number changed to 110. "Outside of the city it's 90 for the first three years," the teacher continued. "However, having driven with a license for more than three years, I can go 110 on the main highway. However, *you* have to drive at . . . ?

There was a pause. Collectively, the class murmured: "100."

"No," the teacher said, "90."

"90," the students repeated.

"90, *va bene*," the teacher repeated. "So how fast can *I* go on the highway?" The teacher pointed to a student sitting in front of Pei.

"90?" the student guessed.

"No, no. You can go at 90," he said, pointing at the student. "And me," he pointed at himself, "110. OK?" A few students nodded, Pei took notes, and the teacher carried onto the next slide, whether they understood or not.

At the farm, Fen continued to coach Pei on her mushroom picking. "You need to position yourself properly so you can reach deep into the beds," Fen said. "Look. Like this." Pei watched her mother tilt her head and stick both arms over the manure mound so she could pluck even the farthest mushrooms from their loamy berth. "You can even grab a few mushrooms at a time in just one hand. This will speed things up," she said, nabbing four heads at once.

"I can't help it if I am slow," Pei mumbled, rolling her eyes.

"Can't help it?" Fen's voice rose a decibel. "Of course you can! Just watch me."

"I am watching!" Pei shot back, a little too loudly. Fen looked at her daughter, waved her hand with a sigh, and continued working in silence. Pei turned away and dug her hands into the mud in a huff. "When people who aren't that close to you teach you, it's no problem. It's up to you whether you want to take their advice," Pei said to me later. "But if it's your own mother, and she gives me instructions with a certain tone of voice . . . " she sighed. "The first time is OK, but by the second time or the third time she might raise her voice, and then I really can't accept that. That is when I just *have* to say something back." Pei was getting to know Fen for the very first time, not just as a mother but also as a co-worker. The bickering usually lasted only a few minutes and mostly they argued about nothing at all. They quarreled mostly when they were tired and tempers flared, and Pei realized it was a sign that she and her mother were growing closer. She wondered if things were better when they were strangers. "When we had distance between us, we kept things in," she said. "Now we say what's on our minds. We don't hold anything back."

While Pei was slow at picking mushrooms, she was quick to pick up Italian. The farm owners had made learning Italian mandatory for all immigrant workers, and Lia, the Italian teacher who helped Pei pass her residency exam, came by regularly to teach them. Classes were held in a second-floor classroom on the farm complete with a whiteboard, a map of Italy, and a projector Lia used to play Italian movies. Pei looked forward to class, skipping into the room with her Italian-language textbooks under her arm and giving the woman a big hug. "I've always felt close to Lia, because she is the one who helped me pass my residency test," Pei said. "It's because of her that I speak Italian the way I do." Pei sat in the front row and opened up her books. The pages of her dictionary, which was held together by pieces of yellowing tape, were marked up with scribbles written in Chinese and Italian.

"What do you eat for breakfast?" Lia asked her students one weekday afternoon at the mushroom farm.

"*Riso*," the students answered. Rice.

"And for lunch?"

"*Riso*," the students answered again.

"And dinner?"

The students shifted in their seats. "*Riso*."

"Breakfast, lunch, and dinner, always rice?" The class nodded.

"How much rice?" asked Mendim, who came from Macedonia and who was the only non-Chinese worker in the class.

"*Mezzo kilo*," Pei said. Half a kilo.

"Half a kilo . . . . in a day," Lia confirmed. Pei nodded.

"*Mamma Mia!*" Mendim exclaimed.

"Never a cappuccino, a baked good?" Lia asked, taking off her reading glasses and placing them on the desk.

"Ah, but we eat rice when I hungry," Pei said in halting Italian. "Need to eat rice."

"Need?"

Pei tried her best to explain why Chinese workers at the farm "needed" to eat rice every day. Rice was filling, and it gave them enough energy to get through a long workday, Pei said. A croissant wasn't enough fuel for the morning.

"But couldn't you eat, I don't know . . . a brioche, a panino with prosciutto?" Lia tried again.

"No, Chinese never," Pei said. "In China, yes. In China, one drinks milk."

"So why not in Italy?"

"Because need to work."

"Ah, OK. I understand," Lia said. "But for example, here in Italy, one goes to work at seven and eats mid-day. Italians eat a panino, a brioche, a cappuccino. An Italian has fruit juice for breakfast. Lots of things! Yogurt!"

"*Ah yoghurt molto mi piace*," Pei said. *Ah yogurt, I like a lot.*

"But not rice! You guys always have rice, even in the morning!" The students nodded. Lia, unconvinced, tried again. "How about yogurt, panini, croissant . . . or an apple?"

"*Ma non va bene*," said a Chinese worker in the back row. *No, it doesn't work.*

"*Una banana?*" Lia said.

"No," the students repeated.

"If one has to work a long day, one might eat a panini with prosciutto, a glass of orange juice, or a banana and a croissant. A nice croissant. But not rice. Oh, *Mamma Mia*! Three times a day you eat rice!" Lia exclaimed. "I just have a coffee. A coffee! That's it."

When the Magnanis and the Simonis, the two families running the mushroom farm, began hiring more and more immigrant workers, they realized how difficult it was to communicate with their own employees. At first, they hired teachers and paid them out of pocket. Later, farm owners were able to continue their language program with the help of grants. Lia started teaching at the mushroom farm in 2008. Every employee was obliged to attend her classes, and they were split up into different levels according to language ability. Pei was put in the highest level. "The biggest problem for all of them, Pei included, is that they don't use their Italian," Lia told me minutes before the workers, many of them still wearing their green work uniforms, trailed into the classroom reeking of soil and sweat. "Most of them, once they reach the minimum level they need for the residency exam, stop studying. However, Pei and others, because they are young and also because of their personalities, are full of ambition and passion. They go beyond the minimum of what the state asks of them. But the others, they suffer through it because the farm owners have made learning Italian mandatory."

Lia's Italian lessons reminded me of the migrants I met in Teacher Xu's classroom in Qingtian. Two years had passed since I last saw them in China. I tried keeping in touch with them as they arrived in Europe one by one. A handful of wives had been reunited with their husbands, and within a couple months, many announced their pregnancies by posting photos online as they caressed their rounded bellies. I was eager to see many of them again, but it seemed none of them were able to meet with me. They all gave plausible explanations: they were working long hours and had no time; they weren't allowed to bring visitors into the factories where they hemmed clothes; and some said they didn't know exactly where they lived and therefore couldn't give me an address. Pei said the same thing to me when I first tried to track her down in Solesino. I had to push and prod to have her ask Ayi for the correct spelling of "Solesino" so I could look it up on the map.

Chen Junwei was one of the last migrants I knew who had finally made it to Italy. Chen was the man who was diligently learning Italian at Teacher Xu's school, the man who was losing patience as he waited for more than a year for his visa to be approved, the man who had raised his son alone while he and his wife endured a decade of separation. Chen arrived in Italy around the time Pei started working at the farm, and when I sent a message to him saying I was coming to Italy, I wasn't sure what kind of response I would receive, if any. A couple days later, I received a reply. "Teacher Ma," he wrote, continuing to refer to me as he did when I was teaching at Teacher Xu's school. "I would love to see you. But it is not convenient for you to come to where I am. It is very hard to get to." Determined, I pressed him to give me an address. He said he didn't know his address, but he knew the name of the town where he and his family now lived: Serra de' Conti. I searched for it online and found very little information: "Serra de' Conti is a *comune* (municipality) in the Province of Ancona in the Italian region of Marche, located about 40 km west of Ancona," an article on Wikipedia read. A few Italian websites described a town encircled by a high, medieval wall. Within those walls, charming narrow streets brought visitors to the town's central *palazzi* and past impressive towers and ancient monasteries. Google Maps told me it would take a little more than an hour to drive there from Pei's home. I set out on a late Saturday morning. Pei climbed into the passenger seat with an armful of snacks and a stack of my maps. She insisted on coming with me in case I got lost. "At least I can ask for directions," she said. She had finally realized that my English skills weren't any use in these parts of Italy. In large cities like Rome and Venice, English is widely used to cater to tourists. But here in the Romagna countryside, most people spoke only Italian. We took the *autostrada* for as long as we could, then turned off at the coastal city of Senigalia and tried to follow the maps and the signs toward Serra de' Conti. The landscape was more striking than Romagna, because the mountains were higher and the fortified towns built upon them more beautiful. We traversed narrow country roads that rose and fell as quickly and steeply as a roller coaster. Pei saw panoramic views of the region, but I hardly had the chance to look for fear of taking my eyes off the road. When we finally arrived nearly three hours later, we found a town that seemed completely void of people on a Sunday afternoon. A minute or so before anyone appeared, I could hear the pitter-patter of footsteps—someone was approaching. It was Chen's eleven-year-old son who was the first to come bounding up a nearby staircase. Chen followed seconds later. He was wearing a puffy, down-filled navy jacket that dwarfed his small but sturdy frame, and he had the same tan, though it was lighter now since he spent most of his time indoors working at a shoe factory. His eyes still flickered with the charm and enthusiasm I remembered, and he smiled broadly, extending his hand toward me. "Teacher Ma!" he exclaimed. "How strange to see you here!" I was so happy to see him, I pushed his hand out of the way and, even though it was not the Chinese way, I gave him a hug. Images of Chen and his friends packed into that little classroom in Qingtian flooded my mind. I could hear their voices, struggling with those tongue-twisting words. "I am so happy to see you," I said. Chen suggested we find a café inside the old city.

At the bar, Chen hung back shyly and waited for the barista to lift her head. Then he stammered: "*Tre cappuccino.*" He rarely interacted with Italians. He was always in the shoe factory and always surrounded by other Chinese workers. Remembering his enthusiasm for spaghetti, I asked if he had had the chance to sample any of the local cuisine. He shook his head. "No, not really. The coffee is much too strong here. I need milk to soften it," he said. "I also can't eat any prosciutto. Raw foods don't agree with my stomach." I agreed about the coffee but said it was a shame he couldn't enjoy prosciutto. Just as we were sitting down, a Chinese woman walked into the café. She had a sweet, plump face and the sing-song voice of a young girl—not at all what I expected Chen's wife to look like. We spent the rest of the day hanging out at a local park, catching up as their son played on the swings, the slides, and the monkey bars. He called his mother *lao ma*, which literally means "old mother." It can be considered an endearment, but to Chen's wife it showed the disconnect between them. "I told him to call me Mama, but he refuses," she said. "I think we have just been apart for so long, it is difficult for him to feel close to me." Their son was aware of the family's complicated history. Chen had spent many nights in China explaining why their family lived apart. Now that dialogue continued in the playful banter exchanged between father and son.

"Baba, where was I born?" the boy asked him a teasing tone.

"Guiana," Chen said.

"And where were you?"

"I was in China with my other girlfriends."

"How many girlfriends, Baba?" The two erupted in raucous laughter, and Chen's wife watched from the park bench as Chen chased their son around the swing set. As the sun began to dip below the horizon, I insisted that Pei and I had to be getting home. But Chen was making it difficult. He apologized for not taking me out for dinner or inviting me back to his home for tea. He and his family stayed in a single room provided by their factory boss and bringing guests there was not a good idea, he said. I told him it wasn't a problem and expressed how happy I was that we were able to meet in Italy. Chen remained conflicted. For months after our meeting, he left me messages apologizing again and again for what he considered his inhospitality. In China, when I had visited Chen in his home village, he had booked a room in one of the most beautiful farm-to-table restaurants in the area. He ordered the most expensive items on the menu: steamed river shrimps, a whole free-range chicken, and *tianyu*, Qingtian's famous fish that were raised in the area's flooded rice paddies. Chen had added several plates of vegetables, a special green tofu dish, and several bottles of beer, and then took me to the mountains where we plucked bright-red *yangmei* fruit from family-owned trees. In Italy, Chen felt he had lost face by not offering the same kind of hospitality. "Next time you visit me," he promised, "things will be different."

"You cannot learn a language if you do not want to." Lia often said this to her students, especially when their faces went limp with apathy, sweaty brows pained by boredom.

The oldest workers on the farm, many of whom had grown up in rural China and barely attended elementary school, were some of the hardest students Lia had to work with. Lia had the painstaking task of teaching them how to properly grip a pencil and how to write their ABCs.

"We are too old to learn," they lamented.

"You are never too old!" Lia insisted. But she saw how they "suffered" through her class—yawning, sighing, eyes wandering to the wall where the clock was ticking.

These older students, in the introductory language class, were indeed difficult to deal with. But it was one particular student in the advanced class who really tried Lia's patience.

Mendim spoke Italian fairly well but could not read or write and was not interested to learn. He never brought his books to class and didn't take any notes. Instead, he fraternized with Pei and doodled on the one piece of paper she ripped out from her own notebook to give to him. It was during a grammar exercise one afternoon when a normally patient Lia lost her composure. She was attempting to explain the difference between two verbs: "obligated," *io devo*, and "want," *io voglio*, when Mendim proudly said aloud: "I am obligated to come to your class." Lia sighed, touched the palm of her hand to her forehead, and launched into a tirade.

"Next year, if we are still doing Italian lessons, I will only invite those who want to come. I can't force people who don't have the desire to be here," she said in rapid-fire Italian. "Let's leave Mendim at home and we'll just have his wife come. She is very intelligent and we'll put her with Pei next year because she needs to move forward . . . "

"I can understand what you're saying," Mendim interrupted.

Lia turned to look at Mendim, but she only rattled on. "It's not that you don't understand. It's that you don't have any drive! It's more than just understanding; you don't have the desire to learn! No, next year I won't teach Italian under these conditions . . . "

"So I salute you and I'm off!" Mendim said, raising his hand to his head.

"Exactly, go be a waiter!" Lia shot back.

"Ah, but you have to remember to tip!" he quipped. Exasperated, Lia threw her hands up. She spent so much of her time teaching immigrants Italian. Next to her responsibilities at the mushroom farm, her local Catholic church organized a number of programs for immigrants, and Lia took part by tutoring children and helping adults obtain their high school diplomas in Italy. Through the church, she even housed immigrants in her own home when they were in between jobs or looking for work.

Lia's church was perched atop a steep precipice overlooking a gorgeous landscape of green farms. When I arrived, the nuns rushed out to greet me, their chocolate-colored veils fluttering in the mysterious morning fog. They grabbed my hands in theirs, and instead of saying *buongiorno*, they spoke to me in Chinese. "*Ni hao*," they said. "Welcome to our home!" And what a beautiful home it was. Monte Tauro, as the church was called, means "the tower at the top of the hill." The tower and the church itself were constructed in the thirteenth century out of beautiful ocher-colored brick. The surrounding buildings, where the nuns and brothers live, eat, and pray, had pale walls, green shutters, and citrus rooftops. Nearby, the church gardens were lined with vineyards and leafy olive trees. The nuns and brothers of Monte Tauro lived at the church all year round and functioned much like social workers do. Some were skilled in physiotherapy and cared for mentally and physically disabled individuals who lived at the church with the sisters and brothers. They organized youth groups and went out into the community to provide tutoring and counseling services. On Saturdays, the church's dining room was used as a classroom where dozens of people, mostly Chinese immigrants, gathered weekly for a free Italian-language class. Many of the volunteer teachers were Italian students or young professionals who had spent some time in China or had studied Chinese in school. The immigrants sat awkwardly at large wooden tables waiting for instructions. Most were preparing to take the mandatory language test required for the long-term residency permit. But once they had their permits in hand, they usually stopped coming to class. There were always a few people, a small minority, who felt the pull of the congregation and the power of the collective. These people usually wanted to know more about the church. "When I first came to Italy, I had no friends," one Chinese parishioner told me. "My Italian didn't improve because I was always surrounded by other immigrants. But here at Monte Tauro, I felt encouraged to learn. Here, I met so many friends and learning Italian came quite naturally." Another woman told me she had been a Buddhist in China but converted to Catholicism after migrating to Italy. When I asked why, she quoted a Chinese maxim: *Ru jing sui su*—a Chinese saying that means "enter a village, follow the customs" and is often translated with the English saying, "when in Rome, do as the Romans do." For many migrants, their faith began with a desire to belong rather than a yearning to proselytize. In the past decade nearly fifty Chinese immigrants had been baptized at Monte Tauro.

Pei and her family were wary of taking part in any church-organized events because they considered themselves Buddhist, though they had only occasionally gone to temple when they were in China. Pei's mother, Fen, attended classes at Monte Tauro when she was preparing to apply for residency, but after she received her permit, she stopped coming. Pei's brother, Mao, had done the same. Shen, Pei's father, was the only one in the family yet to take the test. He had been in Italy nearly a year, but he could only manage a few words and he had a terrible accent. It was imperative he start learning Italian as soon as possible, but he often couldn't make it to the free lesson because the family had no way of getting him to the church. Walking or cycling were not viable options since the hills were especially steep in and around Monte Tauro. The only time Shen could make it was when a friend offered to drive him. That didn't happen regularly, and Shen preferred not to ask for favors. On Saturdays, if she didn't have to work, Fen usually stayed at home to rest and Mao was almost always too busy playing video games on his laptop. It was Pei and her father who tried to get to the church whenever they had the chance.

Before the start of every lesson, the nuns invited a bespectacled Chinese man with a short and spiky haircut to the front of the room to say a prayer in Mandarin. He was in his forties, tall, and light-skinned, and his smooth hands clutched a Bible. When I looked a little closer, I noticed a black-and-white collar tucked underneath his sweater. Father Giuseppe Tong came from the Chinese city of Xi'an. He had been in Italy for nearly six years. At Monte Tauro, he acted as a liaison with the Chinese community. He tutored the nuns and brothers at the convent to help them improve their Chinese, met with young Chinese immigrants to help them with their homework, and helped organize events at the church's Chinese-Italian Cultural Center. Father Tong spoke impeccable Italian, having studied the language as a young priest in China, and the church eventually posted him abroad. When he spoke Chinese, Father Tong had a distinct and sonorous voice that immediately told me he had come from Xi'an, an ancient city nestled in China's central northwest region with more than three thousand years of history. It is considered the epicenter of early Chinese civilization, the starting point of the Silk Road and where Emperor Qin Shi Huang's army of terra-cotta soldiers was unearthed.

"I tell the immigrants I hope they will stay after they have completed their residency exams," Father Tong said. "This is all for their benefit. Italians are always saying the Chinese aren't learning the language and the Chinese people aren't integrating into Italian society. This is our chance to prove them wrong."

Today, China's government officially recognizes five religions: Protestantism, Catholicism, Buddhism, Islam, and Taoism. Christianity ranks among the fastest-growing religions in the country, but for China's more than twelve million Catholics, worshipping has been a complicated affair. When Beijing cut ties with the Vatican in 1951, it began ordaining some bishops without the approval of the pope. As a result, some people worship in "underground" churches loyal to the Vatican while others attend mass in government-sanctioned Catholic churches. When I was living in Beijing in 2007, attending Catholic mass had become a craze. I stood in line for more than an hour in order to secure entrance tickets for Christmas Eve mass at the city's oldest Catholic church. Locals told me the church had become a popular venue for young people who wanted to impress their dates. On Christmas Eve the church was jam-packed like a rock concert. By the time I arrived, it was standing room only and all I saw was the back of people's heads.

Three decades ago, religion was banned in China. During the Cultural Revolution, churches, temples, and mosques were closed down and converted for secular uses. Today, the situation is vastly different: one in three people in China describe themselves as religious, according to official surveys. Most of the Chinese migrants I met in Italy weren't Christians. They often told me the only thing they had faith in was the euro. Now, with the crisis, even that was failing them. "It's OK if you believe in the euro," Father Tong would say. "You don't need to let go of that belief. Money is important. But money cannot make you entirely happy nor can it completely satisfy you. Besides keeping your bellies full, people still have many other needs." Father Tong often spoke about having faith in something bigger than all of us, but he admitted that kind of discourse often fell on deaf ears. Another way he and the sisters and brothers of Monte Tauro reached out to the immigrants was first by satisfying their immediate needs. "They say, 'I don't know the language,' so we teach them. They say they don't have work; we help them find it. They say, 'We can't find someone to rent us a house because the Italians think Chinese immigrants are dirty,'" Father Tong said. "So we help them find a home." I remembered how one migrant called her own home an "eyesore" compared to her Italian neighbors, how many immigrants grew vegetables in their lawns instead of flowers, and how smoky and pungent the Chinese kitchen can be compared to an Italian one.

Father Tong told me the church was also a place of refuge. The very first time a Chinese immigrant came to the church was a little more than a decade ago. Maria Chiara, a nun at Monte Tauro who had kind brown eyes, remembers the day when a twenty-three-year-old man showed up at the church. His hollow black eyes seemed to be searching for something. Was it food? Clothing? Shelter? Maybe even faith? Words fumbled out of his mouth, and the nuns couldn't tell if it was because he was in shock or because he could barely speak Italian. Slowly, Maria Chiara and the sisters of Monte Tauro learned of his plight: the man had come to Italy with the help of a snakehead. Enslaved in a garment workshop, he worked endless hours to repay his $15,000 debt. But the snakeheads continued to hound him for cash. Calls and visits turned into threats. With nowhere to turn and fearing for his safety, he came to the church. Maria Chiara was just twenty years old at the time, and she remembers forming an instant connection with the young man, despite not being able to speak Chinese and him not being able to speak Italian. She recalled how easy it was for her to start learning Chinese simply by conversing with the man every day. "It was my friend's language, so I was motivated to learn it," she said. Maria Chiara continued her studies with a Chinese tutor and now spoke Chinese more fluently than I did. She exercised her language skills by spearheading outreach into the local Chinese community. The nuns of Monte Tauro worked tirelessly, visiting schools, jails, and hospitals—wherever translators were needed—and many soon realized a trend among the migrants. Both the men and women worked long hours, much longer hours than Italians, and many Chinese families had either left their children in China or were sending their Italian-born children back to China to be raised by relatives. These kids were known as China's "left-behind" children. The nuns decided to organize a series of after-school programs. They helped the children of immigrants with their homework and tutored them in Italian. When it later became apparent how important heritage languages were, they organized Chinese lessons for the children, too. The nuns hoped their efforts would help stem the number of "left-behind" children in China and convince immigrant parents that raising their children in Italy was indeed a viable option.

One Sunday, I noticed a young Chinese woman in her early twenties helping to sweep the floors of the church kitchen. It seemed she was always at Monte Tauro, and I wondered what her story was. I walked up to her and asked how long she had been a parishioner at the church. "I live here," she said to me, hardly taking her eyes off her broom. "The church, the nuns, they took me and my mother in." I asked Father Tong about the girl later. Who was her mother? Father Tong reminded me of a woman who had joined us for lunch earlier in the week. The one that stared off into space? Who spoke loudly and abruptly at times? Like so many Chinese migrants, she had come to Italy and worked in the garment factories, Father Tong said. "She worked so hard that she lost her mind. That's when the church took them in."

"What does Father Tong do all day?" Ye Pei's family asked me. "Surely he must have another job?"

I told Pei and her family Father Tong's job was to be a Catholic priest.

"But how does he support himself?"

"The church supports him and his work," I said.

"What does he do all day?"

"He helps people."

It was hard for them to believe that someone's full-time job was to help others. Chinese migrants, especially those from Qingtian, relied heavily on each other. Money was lent to friends with no questions asked, but these acts came with the understanding that the loan would be repaid as quickly as possible and that the favor would soon be returned. So the question was: what did the church and Father Tong want in return? I was baptized a Catholic but have drifted from the Church for a number of personal and political reasons. At first I liked to joke about it, telling people, "Jesus and I are on a break." Now, more than a decade later, my "break" has turned into an extended separation. At Monte Tauro, I was impressed with the clergy's unfailing dedication and tireless commitment to help others. It was my first time hanging around a Catholic church in many years, and it seemed to me that Father Tong, Maria Chiara, and the nuns and brothers at Monte Tauro were asking for nothing in return.

It was already dark outside by the time Pei arrived home from her driver's test. The multiple-choice theory exam had taken nearly an hour, and she had already telephoned home to tell her parents the results. Now they were preparing dinner in time for her return. Her father heated up the wok and watched the flames lick the black iron before he dropped in slices of ginger and garlic and a few chili peppers. The family liked to eat spicy. As the ingredients sizzled, the entire kitchen flooded with fragrance and flavor. He added a whole fish to the wok, searing it on both sides before pouring a brown sauce in the pan and covering it with a lid so the fish simmered in its juices. Then we heard the front door creak open. Face flushed and breathing heavily after the long trek uphill, Pei was still reeling from the day's results. She pushed open the kitchen door and everyone looked up. Even Ye Mao took his eyes off his computer screen to look at his sister. Pei pulled off her thick winter jacket, unraveled her scarf, and threw it on the countertop. Seven errors; three mistakes too many. Her heart was hammering in her chest as she held the piece of paper that told her the results. She became groggy and thick-tongued when she realized she would not be getting her driver's permit anytime soon. The family sat down to eat, and Pei spoke in a loud and loose voice, drunk on disappointment. She did not talk about the test; instead she launched into a diatribe, complaining about work on the mushroom farm, about the gossiping Aunties, and about a particular worker at the farm, Yanzhi, whom Pei considered a good friend.

"She has a boyfriend now, you know?" Pei huffed. "She posted a bunch of photos online. She didn't even bother to tell me herself." Apparently the Aunties on the farm already knew about Yanzhi's new man and Pei was the last one to find out. "Aren't friends supposed to share this kind of news with each other?" she asked glumly. I didn't understand why Pei felt so slighted by news of her friend's new boyfriend until I realized that Valentine's Day was fast approaching. Pei was feeling as lonely as ever. She rarely heard from her boyfriend, Li Jie, who remained in Qingtian and expressed little interest in coming abroad. When she called him, he often seemed too busy for her and brushed her off. The next day, if he called back to apologize, Pei said there was nothing to talk about. At times, she thought about Li Jie a lot. She liked to talk about his height and reminisce about their carefree nights in Qingtian. More than once she showed off an expensive handbag or cell phone he had given to her as a present in Qingtian. Other times she forgot about him completely. Li Jie made sure to call on her birthday every year, but Pei usually forgot about his.

"It doesn't matter anyway," Pei moaned. "I need more Italian friends, not Chinese ones. I will never pass this test if I am speaking Chinese every day! That's what I do at the farm, you know. I speak Chinese every single day!" Her parents looked at each other, and Pei continued. "And wow, guess what I'm doing for the next two weeks?" Too slow at picking mushrooms, her supervisor had reassigned her to cleaning duty. "I'm washing the toilets! That's what I have come to Europe to do: WASH TOILET BOWLS!" Pei was yelling now. On any other day, Fen or Shen would have told their daughter to lower her voice. They would have been stern with her and reminded her to be grateful for the work. But today, they were tactfully silent. Pei ate more quickly than anyone else, shoveling the last bit of rice into her mouth, and then stood up abruptly to announce she was going to wash up.

Mao's mouth hung open as he watched his sister leave the room. As soon as Pei had gone, Fen spoke up quietly. "Maybe there is just too much pressure," she said. "Her temper has been so bad these weeks." In bed, Pei continued to brood. Normally, she fell asleep within minutes of turning off the lights, her body heavy with fatigue. But that night she was weighed down by a force so strong, she felt a choking sensation in her throat. "I can't stand being treated like a child," she said. Her words escaped from her lips in small bursts of fog that drifted out into the cold room. "Everyone just dismisses my concerns. They call me a child, but this is a designation I cannot accept." Pei's parents had not called her a child that night, at least not in my presence. But her failure that day provoked a rare display of indignation that had long been swelling inside of her. What galled her the most, Pei told me, was not being treated like an adult despite the immense responsibilities imposed on her. She was the one who went to work at the bar, the one learning Italian, the one learning to drive.

Then she told me something I thought I'd never hear her say: "I regret coming to the mushroom farm," Pei said. "Lia said working at the farm would help improve my Italian, but it has actually gotten worse. In the farm, I am blocked off from the rest of the world. It is very isolating. I feel . . . as if I was tricked into coming," she sighed. "Nothing can be gained with your fingers in the dirt." She wanted to share these feelings with her parents, but she didn't know how. With the Chinese Lunar New Year fast approaching, Pei was hoping for a lucky break. In China, the New Year is more commonly known as the Spring Festival. It is a time of renewal and celebration, a time when families gather together to usher in good fortune into their homes. They wish family and friends happiness and luck, and they pray to the god of wealth for prosperity in the coming year. Pei pulled the pink covers up to her chin and lay back, trying to sleep. This was a bitterness that had become too hard for her swallow. For the first time in a long time, she felt as helpless as that barista I met in Solesino all those months ago.

A NEW YEAR

There is nothing either good or bad, but thinking makes it so.

—*Hamlet*, Act 2, Scene 2

A fine white powder coated the hands and faces of everyone crowded into the church kitchen that Saturday afternoon. Women fastened aprons around their waists, rolled up their sleeves, and stood shoulder to shoulder along the counter, kneading sticky mounds of dough. Thin blue veins bulged in their pale arms as they plunged into the gooey heaps with the heels of their hands, pushing and prodding and reshaping it. When they were satisfied, the women nipped off small bits, which they flattened with long wooden pins, rocking back and forth as they chattered to one another.

Pei and Mao stood a few feet away next to a metal cart where several glass bowls were filled with ground pork mixed with minced garlic and chopped bok choy and seasoned with soya sauce and Chinese rice wine. They joined a group of younger volunteers who spooned dollops of meat onto small doughy circles rolled out by the assembly line. Pei expertly folded the sides together in the shape of a crescent moon, crimping the dough to seal the contents inside. She and everyone else in the church's kitchen were dumpling connoisseurs. In one afternoon they wrapped a total of two thousand dumplings, called *jiaozi* in Chinese. The *jiaozi* were then placed on long, rectangular steel trays and stored in a large freezer. They would be pan-fried and served at the church's annual Chinese New Year dinner the following week.

In China, all families, from the youngest to the oldest family member, sit around the dinner table and wrap dumplings for the New Year. Dumplings are typically filled with ground meat and vegetables and are wrapped in the shape of ancient Chinese silver and gold ingots, which symbolize wealth. One tradition is to put a gold coin in one dumpling. The person who gets that dumpling is said to have good luck in the coming year. Pei and Mao grew up with these customs. Faces dusted white, hands crusted with dough, the juices of freshly smashed garlic on their fingertips—these were the flavors of a traditional Spring Festival.

I could have sworn we were back in China when I saw how many Chinese people were crammed into the kitchen that day. I was brought back to reality when Maria Chiara, the nun with the kind brown eyes, breezed into the kitchen and rolled up her coffee-colored sleeves. She stood next to Pei, picked up a dumpling wrapper, and placed it on her open palm.

"Show me how to do this," she said in Chinese.

"Maria Chiara, watch me," offered a young volunteer who spooned some meat filling onto the dough and deftly pinched the ends together. The nun observed for less than a minute before trying it herself. When she presented her creation, a round ball of dough pleated like a drawstring purse, the volunteers marveled at her fine work.

"Maria Chiara, you are a natural!" they exclaimed.

"I may look Italian," she said in Chinese. "But it's not what is on the outside but what is inside that counts, am I right? I must have a Chinese heart." Maria Chiara giggled. The group continued to chitchat as they wrapped more dumplings, and Pei listened to the conversation as it flowed effortlessly between Italian and Chinese, hoping she could one day do the same.

Chinese holidays and festivals usually bring on homesickness. Within China, no matter how far migrants wander from their homes, they always make an effort to go back at least once a year. It is considered the largest annual human migration in the world. More than three billion trips are made within China during the forty-day period surrounding the holiday, according to the Chinese government. The Chinese pack onto trains and buses and travel in suffocating discomfort for days just to be with their families for the Spring Festival. During this time, children receive "lucky" money in red envelopes. Windows and doors are decorated with red paper couplets blessing the house with good fortune. Families spend days preparing a feast. Sticky glutinous rice cakes symbolize a cohesive family. Long and pliable noodles signify a long life. Peanuts represent health, and fruits like peaches stand for immortality. There is always fish on the dinner table—a pun for abundance in the new year. The loud crackle and boom of fireworks are believed to ward off evil spirits. In Pei's hometown, people spend a small fortune on fireworks, lighting up the skies and blanketing the streets in a smoky haze. Thunderous explosions send shockwaves through town, setting off car alarms and making babies cry. Ash drifts down from the sky like hot snow. Alas, this is not how Chinese New Year is celebrated in Italy. Pei and Mao lamented how they would be getting no red pocket money, no family feast with relatives and friends back home, and Pei grumbled about having to work on New Year's Day, something even workaholic migrants in China didn't do. Despite their complaints, this was the first time in more than seven years the family would be together for the Spring Festival. Even though they had immigrated to Italy the previous year, they had spent the holiday apart because Pei had been working at the bar in Solesino and her father was cooking for factory workers in another town.

It took some convincing to get the Ye family to attend the church's Chinese New Year party, which was scheduled for a Saturday night.

"My mother and I have to work," Pei muttered.

"Heavens, you have to work on Chinese New Year?" Father Tong said. "What time do you get off?"

"It's not always the same time," Pei said. "Usually by noon."

"That's no problem." Father Tong smiled. "I'll come pick you up in the early afternoon!"

"We also have to work the next day," Pei griped.

"Chinese New Year comes but once a year!" Father Tong insisted. That Saturday, Fen and Pei worked a morning at the farm, then rushed home to shower and change. Pei stood in front of the mirror drawing sparkly liner across her eyes and dusting her lids with a light blue shadow before going to her mother's room to help Fen get ready. She powdered her mother's face and then brushed out her thick hair, gathering a few strands above her ears and pulling them back into a loose ponytail. As a finishing touch, she clipped her mother's jeweled brooch—the one Fen often wore on her days off—in an elegant half up-do. A few days earlier, Pei had her own hair dyed a deep cerise and now she combed her shiny locks back into a stylish bun. When they heard the crunch of Father Tong's car tires on the gravel driveway, mother and daughter pulled out matching white coats, each with a fur trim collar. The last time Pei wore her coat was the day she visited Venice.

The nuns and a crew of young volunteers had hung red lanterns and strung red streamers across the gymnasium of the Chinese-Italian Center, where the church ran their after-school programs for the children of Chinese immigrants. For more than a decade, the church had organized a Chinese New Year dinner and show for the community. Cafeteria tables were covered with red tablecloths and the paper plates and napkins came in red too. In Chinese culture, red is the color of prosperity and joy. More than one hundred people packed into the hall, most of them Chinese church parishioners. Everyone bowed their heads when Father Tong walked to the front of the room, cleared his throat, and began to sing a hymn in Chinese. His voice carried across the room, and many people joined Father Tong in song. Pei and her family shifted uncomfortably in their seats. Even though the hymn was sung in Chinese, not one of them had ever attended a Catholic mass before and this form of prayer was very foreign to them. When the people around them murmured, "Amen," young volunteers burst into the gymnasium balancing large platters of food. The dishes cooled quickly in the drafty space, and Pei and her family picked at soggy spring rolls, limp noodles, sticky spare ribs, and pan-fried dumplings that were lukewarm by the time they arrived at the table. By nine o'clock, the hall was emptying out. Pei and her family followed the revelers who walked toward a nearby theater for a special New Year performance.

The heat was on full blast inside the Teatro Moderno. Pei and her family settled into plush red seats near the back just as the lights were dimming. Pei yawned and sunk low in her chair. Not used to the heat, she fluttered her eyes and rolled her head back. Then the voices of children filled the auditorium. She sat up in her chair just as the little ones moseyed on stage in pink tutus, waving their arms in unison to Chinese folk music. Next, a group of teens performed a peppy dance sequence to a frenzied techno beat. Their act was followed by an older Chinese woman who sang classic songs from the homeland. A guest from Myanmar brandished a guitar and strummed melodies he had composed in his native Burmese. Later, a Chinese artist from Turin performed tai chi, and a young Chinese student from Parma plucked the four strings of a pear-shaped instrument called the *pipa*, a kind of Chinese lute. For the grand finale, all of the performers gathered on stage and held their heads high as they sang a song called "Big China." Soon, those in the audience joined in, too:

We have a home, and China is its name
We have lots of brothers and sisters there
The scenery is beautiful
Our big China; our big home
Bless you, China
You are forever in my heart

In the dark theater, I leaned forward in my seat to see Fen's and Shen's faces illuminated by the glow of the stage lights. Their lips were moving ever so slightly as they mouthed the words to the song: *Bless you, China, you are forever in my heart* . . . As the finale came to an end, people rose to give the performers hearty applause, and when the theater lights came back on, people were already streaming out the doors. We heard a hiss and a crackle—the unmistakable sound of fireworks.

"The fireworks won't wait for us!" Pei shrieked, grabbing my hand and hurrying outside where a crowd had already assembled in the town square. Every head was raised expectantly to the sky. A flare sizzled and exploded, and Pei hooted as it sprayed the sky with color and light. The last time she had seen fireworks was more than two years ago while she was still living in China. "Happy New Year!" she exclaimed, her face softening for the first time in weeks until it wore a look of wonder and innocence. The last time I had seen that face was the day Pei visited Venice. A flicker of orange lit up the skies. Never did she imagine she would be celebrating the Spring Festival in a *piazza* so far away from home.

Almost as soon as the last sparkle fizzled out, heavy, wet snowflakes poured from the night sky. Father Tong's car skidded and stalled on the icy roads all the way back to Pei's home. Exhausted from all the excitement, Pei fell asleep in the backseat. Fen leaned forward and made small talk with Father Tong, as he switched on the car's emergency blinkers, gripped the steering wheel, and inched along the slick pavement. By the time we arrived home that night, it was too late and too cold to take a shower. Pei climbed into bed at 1 a.m. and set her alarm. In less than five hours, she and her mother were getting up to start another workday.

In the moonlight, the two women slogged down the rutted road toward the farm. The women typically had Sundays off, but their schedules were sometimes hard to predict because work hours were ultimately determined by how many mushrooms were ready to be harvested. That weekend, the mushroom harvest was in full swing. It seemed like only a few minutes had passed after Pei's heavy head sunk into her pillow when her cell phone called her awake that morning, vibrating and lighting up in the dark room. She instinctively reached over, fumbling to snooze the alarm. It was her mother's voice from the other side of the wall that roused her. "Ah Bai," Fen called, using Pei's nickname in Qingtian dialect. "Time to get up." While the two women were at work, Shen lay in bed as he made his weekly long-distance calls to China, shouting greetings into his phone until the sun crept over the horizon. He then spent the entire day at home in the kitchen. Shen was a savvy chef who relished preparing his mother's recipes for the family to feast upon. An intoxicating smell of food flooded the entire house as he pickled daikon radishes, braised beef tendons in a spicy broth, and prepared *po*—a classic Qingtian braised pork dish eaten only during the New Year. *Po* is similar to pulled pork, except it is marinated in a sweet soy sauce and steamed for hours until the meat stews in its own juices and fat. That evening, the family sat down for its first New Year's dinner together in seven years, and everyone agreed the food was far more delicious when cooked and eaten at home.

2013 was the year of the snake according to the Chinese zodiac and Pei's horoscope was telling: *Your impatience may hinder your studies. Your income is directly proportional to your authority. Without authority, your income will be flat. When dealing with people, beware of your temper and forcefulness. If you are single, consider marriage.* A few months after the family's New Year dinner, Pei took another run at the theory exam for her driver's license. When the results came back, she couldn't believe her eyes. She had failed again. The excitement of the Chinese New Year had long worn off, and Pei fell into another bout of gloom. Living away from home and working at the bars taught her to hide her emotions behind an eight-tooth smile. Now that she was living with her parents, she let her emotions pour out like a summer rainstorm.

"*Gao bu dong!*" she exclaimed in frustration one night, slamming her laptop closed. *I just don't understand!* She considered giving up and told me she intended to move to Venice to find work in a bar. "That has been my dream for so long, maybe I should just go for it," Pei said. But she was torn between chasing her own dreams and taking care of her family. Since she first set out to work at the bar in Solesino, Pei had found strength knowing her exertions were helping her parents pay the bills and move toward financial stability. She took it upon herself to do right by Fen and Shen and to support them in every possible way so they could return to China and escape the bitterness of the emigrant life. "I usually try not to say too much to my parents," Pei said. "Perhaps my bitterness isn't nearly as bitter as theirs. Perhaps," she continued, "life is neither good nor bad, but thinking makes it so."

"What do you mean by that?" I asked.

"I mean maybe I think too much, that's all," Pei said.

Rooting herself in thoughts of filial devotion, she pushed aside her Venetian dreams and enrolled for another round of driver-theory classes, determined to succeed on her third and final attempt. In August of 2013, she took the exam and, to her surprise, passed. "I did it!!" she howled, throwing her hands up in the air as her cheeks flushed bright red. Four months later she took a road test. Pei's *autoscuola* instructor rode shotgun while the examiner sat in the back. She drove straight, turned, went through a roundabout, made a three-point turn, performed a parallel park. When she pulled into the test center's parking lot, she was given her Italian driver's permit right away. Pei wept tears of joy and relief.

Days before Christmas she purchased a secondhand two-door Chevy coupe. She polished the car until it shone brightly in the sun and posed next it, dressed in her green work suit, in the mushroom farm's parking lot. She proudly posted the photos on her micro-blog and wrote: "The fruits of my year-long effort."

In Pei's new car, Shen was able to make it to the church every week for the free Italian-language classes at Monte Tauro. The grocery store was no longer a thirty-minute bicycle ride away, and they could buy water and toilet paper, and even a case of wine, whenever they wanted to. The car brought the family to neighboring cities where they could start looking for a new house and even scout out new jobs and business opportunities. For Pei, the car let her experience a new kind of freedom. She bought gelato at the nearby mall and shopped for new clothes. She drove into the city with her brother, Mao, and gorged at a Chinese buffet. She partied at a disco for the first time in her life. Under the powerful strobe lights, Pei bobbed her head, swayed her hips to the music, and even danced with a few strangers.

※

The first time I saw Ye Pei in Italy was at the bus stop in Solesino. I remember getting up from my seat and bracing myself as the bus driver slammed on the brakes. I had already spotted her from a distance. Outside, the street lamps lit up her cherubic face. She was the only Chinese person waiting at the stop, and she was stretching her neck to look for me as the bus lurched to a halt in front of the town's blue steeple. The doors flapped open, and I tumbled out onto the sidewalk into the cold night air.

I glimpsed her swollen and blistered hands, pink as raw salmon. I took them in mine. Some parts of her skin were tender and wrinkled like an over-ripe tomato, other parts fibrous like a piece of ginger root.

"What happened to your hands?" I gasped.

"Oh, it's nothing," Pei said. "I'm just not used to working at the bar." I turned them over and brought my nose to her skin, inspecting her hands. Embarrassed, she pulled them back. "Jie," she said, using the Chinese word for older sister. "Don't worry about it. Really, I am fine." Pei was just seventeen years old. I tried to think what I was stressing about when I was her age. A daunting math exam? Who I was going to bring to the prom? It was nothing compared to the challenges Pei wrestled with as a migrant worker.

The habits of migration and its momentous effects are as old as humanity itself, since humans departed from Africa some fifty or sixty thousand years ago. Every one of us has migrant blood pumping through our veins. Migrants journey long distances in search of safety and economic opportunity, and like all human beings they seek acceptance and tolerance in their new homes. Not all of them find what they are looking for. Almost all the migrants I know are optimists. They are determined to improve their situations and driven to become something more than what they are. They often move about in a frantic pace, believing that if they linger too long in one place, an opportunity elsewhere might disappear or get snatched up by someone else. The migrants I know are open to trying new things. They are curious about other people and other worlds, and that's why I think they chose to talk to me—not only to share their lives but to find out about mine.

I can't say if Pei is typical of all immigrants, but her story is emblematic of all migrant tales, which, at the core, are stories about leaving home, enduring hardship, and starting a new life. Migrants tend to be more dynamic than the people they leave behind. They have no choice but to become familiar with at least two different cultures and therefore see opportunities where others might not. Migrants are clever and learn to think outside of the box: acquiring new languages and adapting to new environments and new ways of thinking. They create networks and bring those new ideas with them wherever they go. Once migrants have gained legal residency in a country, there is a strong tendency to put down roots. Many raise their children in their adopted homes with the hopes that they will have the chance to go to school, master the local language, and never taste the bitterness of a migrant's life.

On one of my last evenings with Pei, I trudged up the hill with her toward her home. The orange sun was already nudging the horizon when suddenly she spoke. It took a moment before I realized she was telling me a story:

A monkey was headed home when he passed by a peach tree. Looking up, he saw fruit so pink and plump, they looked just like the longevity buns he ate every year on his birthday. He scrambled up the trunk, swung himself up onto the branches, and plucked the ripest peach he could find. Then he continued on his way home. Sometime later, the monkey passed by a field of watermelons. The melons were even bigger and rounder than the peach he held in his hand and the monkey thought, "Look at those delicious watermelons!" With that, he dropped his peach and trudged through the dirty field. He hoisted the largest watermelon he could find up onto his shoulder and then continued on his way home. Down the road, he was passing by a cornfield and the monkey found he had grown tired of carrying the heavy watermelon. Looking at the ears of corn, standing so tall in the late afternoon sun, he dropped the melon on the ground and went to gather a few stalks of golden corn. Then, he continued on his way. Soon, the monkey passed through a forest and saw a white rabbit foraging in the woods. He thought to himself: "A rabbit is better than this corn!" So he tossed the corn to the side and ran into the forest, chasing after the rabbit. But the white rabbit was too fast for the monkey, and like a ghost, it dodged out of his grasp and disappeared into the woods. And the monkey returned home, empty-handed.

"Do you understand?" Pei asked. She feared her nomadic lifestyle would one day leave her unfulfilled. She worried about taking the wrong job, making the wrong decisions, and never quite finding the satisfaction her restless soul sought. In early 2014, a year after our last meeting, Pei's father, Shen, moved 130 miles away to a city east of Verona where he stocked shelves and helped customers find products on the floor of a Chinese-run store. Pei had found the job for him through an Internet posting. She said his Italian was steadily improving because he was interacting with Italians every day, but she also hadn't seen him for months because he worked seven days a week without a day off. That year, Shen didn't even have time to come home for a Chinese New Year dinner.

Pei quit the mushroom farm in early 2014 and enrolled in a series of night courses to learn about workplace safety, food safety, and hygiene. Five days a week she drove forty minutes to the city of Rimini to attend the classes, which Pei said were necessary for her to apply for a business license. Was she planning to open a bar? Maybe run a restaurant? "Not right away," she said. "We need to save a lot more money to do that." Pei now knew how to temper her expectations. While she attended night classes, she found a job as a waitress clearing stacks of dirty dishes at a nearby Chinese buffet. The owner of the buffet, a Chinese man, offered to house her in his apartment, which was just a ten-minute walk from the restaurant. Six other restaurant workers lived there too. Pei decided staying there would spare her the daily forty-minute commute. When I first met Pei in Italy, she was making 500 euros a month and living with her mean-spirited Ayi in a small town outside of Venice. Two and a half years later, she was working as a waitress at a Chinese buffet and she was back to her "five-hand" salary. She made just 500 euros a month, less than $7 an hour—but something within her had changed.

"I feel very free here," she said, and it wasn't because her boss granted her any particular freedoms. Pei recognized that she was working toward something bigger. The waitressing job was holding her over until she completed her night courses, which she hoped would bring her to the next milestone: getting a business license. She was keeping the big picture in mind and she wasn't letting herself get bogged down with how daunting it all could be. She realized that while success didn't always come when she wanted it to, success did eventually come. It was only a matter of time. "I wasn't very happy when I first left China. I was young and I had so much pressure," she said. "Now I have confidence. I believe that if I work hard and try my best, I will be satisfied with myself."

"Was it worth it in the end, coming to Europe?" I asked.

Pei took some time to think before answering. "Here in Europe, our minds are very active. We can think more clearly than the people back home," she said. "We are forced to learn a new language, pick up new skills. The wheels of our brains turn faster." She never did answer my question—whether or not it was worth coming to Europe. Many migrants were returning home to China, but Pei and her family chose to persevere in Italy. Her 500 euro salary was half of what she had earned at the mushroom farm, but it was still more than she could ever make if she returned to China.

"I may not make a lot of money," Pei said. "But I am very happy."

EPILOGUE

One year after my last meeting with Pei in Italy, I came across a quote from Shakespeare's Hamlet: "There is nothing either good or bad, but thinking makes it so." It brought me back to the house with the peeling yellow paint, when Pei was struggling to pass her driver's exam. She was frustrated with her circumstances, angry even, but she managed to calm herself down, put things in perspective, and unintentionally quote the bard himself.

Pei's migration journey from China to Italy, with all its surprises and disappointments, brought her many highs and many lows. Through it all, Pei realized how important it was to keep the bigger picture in mind. Was her Ayi in Solesino really cruel and uncaring? Pei told me not to judge. Maybe, she said, this Ayi was more kind and giving than many of the other Chinese bosses out there. In Falconara, the men pinched her bottom but she also learned how to make a cappuccino. At the mushroom farm, there *were* things to be gained with her fingers in the dirt. Every job, every move, and every decision was part of the journey. Pei taught me that.

She spent the first few months of 2014 studying hard for her business license, all the while complaining she couldn't understand a word the teacher was saying during her weekly classes. Her books, which were all in Italian, covered topics ranging from workplace safety and sanitation to commercial law and tax management. Many of the Chinese immigrants I knew didn't bother taking the test themselves—they spent a few thousand euros to buy the licenses from somebody else. When I asked Pei whether she had considered buying the license, she said: "First of all, I don't have that kind of spare change. And second of all, isn't it better to learn these things for yourself?"

Pei passed her exams in April 2014. Then she began scouting out local shops—bars, restaurants, stores—for business opportunities. It was also in April when she finally broke it off with Li Jie, her boyfriend in China. They had not seen each other for two and a half years, since Pei left China in the fall of 2011. They broke up over the telephone, when Pei finally worked up the courage to ask Li Jie a question that had long been on her mind:

"When are you planning to come to Italy?"

Li Jie was frank. "I don't want to leave China," he said. "I'll wait for you to return." Pei told him she wasn't planning on going back to China and that she couldn't return—not until she was running her own business in Italy. Once she achieved that, she would have to work even harder to keep the business afloat. The responsibilities would be endless. The worst part about the breakup, Pei said, was how Li Jie forced her to end it. "I was the one who said it," she said. "He wouldn't agree to it. I didn't want to break up. But I'm tired of working so hard at something that has no clear resolution."

One month later, Pei told me she had met someone new: a Chinese boy from Sicily. They had yet to meet in person but had started communicating through text messages and a few phone calls. They were introduced by a customer at the Chinese buffet where Pei was still a waitress. The boy was also a Qingtian emigrant who had been living in Italy for six years, and he was looking for a girlfriend. He sent Pei a few photos of himself, and as they loaded on her cell phone, Pei couldn't help but notice how much the young man resembled Li Jie: tall and skinny, with big brown hair permed and carefully gelled upward. In some photos, he looked away from the camera sporting shiny aviator sunglasses. Over the next two months, the young man visited Pei twice, each time taking a five-hour flight from Sicily and spending about a week with her. At the end of May, he visited Pei again, this time meeting with Fen and Shen. Pei said her parents approved of her new boyfriend, who then asked if she would consider getting engaged to him sometime during the summer. They had known each other just two months, and Pei had spent just a little more than ten days with him in person. "Things are moving too quickly," she told him. "I need more time to get to know you." Her boyfriend was disappointed, but agreed to give Pei some more time.

In July, Pei told me she and her new boyfriend were moving in together. They weren't going to get engaged just yet, but they had decided to join forces and open a business together. They rented a room in the city of Rimini. Pei continued to work as a waitress at the Chinese buffet while her boyfriend spent his days visiting bars and shops, scouting for a business venture. "When I come home from work, he cooks for me and prepares a lot of my favorite snacks," Pei told me. "He gives me a sense of security and I like that." One month later, Pei and her boyfriend successfully negotiated the purchase of a bar in a small city outside of Verona. They opened their new business on August 8; an auspicious day since the number 8 in Chinese, *ba*, rhymes with the word *fa*, which means develop and prosper. Pei was just nineteen years old, and she was already her own boss. I don't know if she will ever strike it rich, and if she or her parents will ever be able to retire in China "dressed in silken robes." I only know that Pei's adventure is just beginning.

August 2014
Vancouver, Canada

SOURCES

I learned about Qingtian and the world of Chinese immigrants mostly through first-hand observation and personal interviews. I used real names throughout the book, with the exception of three minor characters who asked for anonymity. There are also books and articles that I have relied on for context, statistics, and background. Below is a summary of the resources that were the most useful to me.

CHAPTER 1: THE BAR

The exchange rates used throughout the book reflect the rates at the time of events. In 2014, the euro-dollar exchange rate was 1.38:1 and the yuan-dollar exchange rate was 6.2:1.

For background on Chinese migrants in Italy:

Ceccagno, Antonella. "New Chinese Migrants in Italy." *International Migration* 41, no. 3 (2003): 187–213.
Ma, Suzanne. "Chinese Migrants Step Out of Factory Shadows in Italy." *Deutsche-Welle*, May 27, 2013. http://dw.de/p/18dbT.

For background on how immigrants are portrayed in Italian-language media:

Taylor, Charlotte. "Working Paper: The Representation of Immigrants in the Italian Press." *Centre for the Study of Political Change* 21 (2009).

Zhang, Gaoheng. "Contemporary Italian Novels on Chinese Immigration to Italy." *California Italian Studies* 4, no. 2 (2013).

For official population numbers in Italy:

I used the Italian National Institute of Statistics: http://www.istat.it/en/.

CHAPTER 2: LEAVING CHINA

For more about Zheng He:

Kahn, Joseph. "China Has an Ancient Mariner To Tell You About." *New York Times*, July 20, 2005. http://www.nytimes.com/2005/07/20/international/asia/20letter.html ?pagewanted=all.

For background on Qingtian:

Qingtian huaqiaoshi. [Qingtian Overseas History]. Hangzhou: Zhejiang renmin chubanshe [Zhejiang People's Publishing House], 2011.

Wu, Dezheng, et al. *Qingtian, xiudingpian*. [Qingtian, revised edition]. Beijing: Zhongguo huaqiao chubanshe [Overseas Chinese Press], 2010.

Zhang, Xiuming. "Remittances, Donations and Investments in Qingtian County since 1978." In *Beyond Chinatown: New Chinese Migration and the Global Expansion of China*, edited by Mette Thuno, 67–78. Copenhagen: Nordic Institute of Asian Studies Press and University of Hawaii Press, 2007.

For background on the Chinese in Europe:

Christiansen, Flemming. *Chinatown, Europe: An Exploration of Overseas Chinese Identity in the 1990s*. London: RoutledgeCurzon, 2003.

Gregor, Benton. "The Chinese in Europe: Origins and Transformations" *Religions & Christianity in Today's China* 1 (2011): 62–70.

Li, Minghuan. *Ouzhou Huaqiao Huaren Shi* [History of the Overseas Chinese in Europe]. Beijing: Zhongguo huaqiao chubanshe [China Overseas Press], 2002.

——. "'To Get Rich Quickly in Europe!'—Reflections on Migration Motivations in Wenzhou." In *Internal and International Migration: Chinese Perspectives*, edited by Frank N. Pieke and Hein Mallee, 181–98. Richmond, Surrey: Curzon Press. 1999.

Thuno, Mette. "Moving Stones from China to Europe: The Dynamics of Emigration from Zhejiang to Europe." In *Internal and International Migration: Chinese Perspectives*, edited by Frank N. Pieke and Hein Mallee, 159–80. Richmond, Surrey: Curzon Press. 1999.

For the history of the overseas Chinese:

Pan, Lynn. *The Encyclopedia of the Chinese Overseas*. Richmond, Surrey, England: Curzon, 1999.
——. *Sons of the Yellow Emperor: The Story of the Overseas Chinese*. London: Mandarin Paperbacks, 1991.

For more about Wenzhou and southern Zhejiang:

Hessler, Peter. *Country Driving: A Chinese Roadtrip*. New York: Harper Perennial, 2011, 280–415.
Wu, Bin, and Valter Zanin. "Exploring Links between International Migration and Wenzhou's Development." Paper presented at the Community Research Networking Conference, Prato, Italy, November 5–7, 2007.

CHAPTER 3: EAST MEETS WEST

Ceccagno, Antonella. "The Chinese in Italy at a Crossroads: The Economic Crisis." In *Beyond Chinatown: New Chinese Migration and the Global Expansion of China*, edited by Mette Thuno. Copenhagen: Nordic Institute of Asian Studies Press and University of Hawaii Press, 2007.
Wu, Bin, and Valter Zanin. "Healthcare Needs of Chinese Migrant Workers in Italy: A Survey Report on Chinese-Owned Workshops in Veneto." Paper presented at the International Forum for Contemporary Chinese Studies Inaugural Conference, Nottingham University, UK, November 2008.

CHAPTER 4: CHINATOWN

For more about the Chinese in Prato:

French, Rebecca, Graeme Johanson, and Russell Smyth, eds. *Living Outside the Walls: The Chinese in Prato*. Newcastle upon Tyne, UK: Cambridge Scholars Publishing, 2009.

For more about the fire at Teresa Moda:

Aloisi, Silvia. "Italy's Chinese Garment Workshops Boom as Workers Suffer." Reuters, December 29, 2013. http://reut.rs/1hOwLIx.
Montanari, Laura, and Massimo Mugnaini. "I parenti delle vittime del rogo a Chinatown 'Aiutateci, fateci lavorare qui a Prato'" ["Relatives of the Chinatown Fire Victims:

'Help us, let us work here in Prato'"]. *la Repubblica*, January 12, 2014. http://firenze
.repubblica.it/cronaca/2014/01/12/news/i_parenti_delle_vittime_del_rogo_fateci_
lavorare_al_posto_loro-75691038/.
Povoledo, Elisabetta. "Deadly Factory Fire Bares Racial Tensions in Italy." *New York
Times*, December 8, 2013, A8.

For more about Lampedusa:

"More than 1,100 Migrants Rescued Off Italy in One Day." *BBC News*, February 6,
2014. http://www.bbc.com/news/world-europe-26064697.
Sunderland, Judith. "Lampedusa, a National Shame for Italy." *Human Rights Watch*,
December 18, 2013. http://www.hrw.org/news/2013/12/18/dispatches-lampedusa
-national-shame-italy.

For more about organized crime in Italy:

Saviano, Roberto. *Gomorrah: A Personal Journey into the Violent International Empire
of Naples' Organized Crime System*, translated by Virginia Jewiss. London: Picador,
2008.

For more about Cecile Kyenge:

"Italy's Cecile Kyenge Calls for Action on Rising Racism." *BBC News*, January 15,
2014. http://www.bbc.com/news/world-europe-25748943.
Kington, Tom. "Italy's First Black Minister: 'I had bananas thrown at me but I'm here to
stay.'" *The Guardian*, September 8, 2013. http://gu.com/p/3tt42/tw.
Ma, Suzanne. "The African Woman Changing Immigration in Italy." Huffington Post,
May 8, 2013. http://huff.to/12VkY1t.

For more on the Northern League:

Salucci, Lapo. "Migration and Political Reaction in Italy: The Fortunes of the Northern
League." Paper presented at the Midwest Political Science Conference, Chicago,
April 2–5, 2009.

About the Belleville Chinatown riot:

Baïetto, Thomas. "A Belleville, les Chinois critiquent l'inaction de la police" ["In Belleville, the Chinese Criticize Police Inaction"]. *Le Monde*, June 23, 2010. http://www
.lemonde.fr/societe/article/2011/06/22/a-belleville-la-communaute chinoise-exprime
-son-mecontentement_1539077_3224.html.

"Chinese Protest in Paris Ends in Tear Gas." *China Daily*, June 22, 2010. http://www
.chinadaily.com.cn/world/2010-06/22/content_10000029.htm.

"Les Chinois de Belleville en ont ras le bol de l'insécurité" ["The Chinese of Belleville Are
Fed Up with Insecurity"]. *France 24*, June 21, 2010. http://observers.france24.com/
fr/content/20100621-chinois-belleville-veulent-denoncer-insecurite-manifestations
-echauffourees-chine-racisme.

Guangjin, Cheng. "Chinese Protest in the Streets of Paris." *China Daily*, June 21, 2010.
http://www.chinadaily.com.cn/cndy/2010-06/21/content_9994654.htm.

For more on the Chinese Labor Corps:

Xu, Guoqi. *Strangers on the Western Front: Chinese Workers in the Great War*. Cambridge, MA: Harvard University Press, 2011.

For more about migration and migrant communities:

Guest, Robert. *Borderless Economics: Chinese Sea Turtles, Indian Fridges and the New
Fruits of Global Capitalism*. New York: Palgrave Macmillan, 2011.

Saunders, Doug. *Arrival City: The Final Migration and Our Next World*. Toronto:
Vintage Canada, 2011.

CHAPTER 5: LA DOLCE VITA

To read Marco Polo's *Il Milione*:

Polo, Marco. *The Travels of Marco Polo, The Venetian*, translated by William Marsden;
edited by Thomas Wright. London: Henry Bohn, 1854, 314–15. https://archive.org/
details/travelsmarcopol00marsgoog.

For more on China's civil society:

Brown, Kerry. *Struggling Giant: China in the 21st Century*. London: Anthem. 2007.

For more about Chinese tourists in Europe:

Bryan, Victoria, and Clare Kane. "Chinese Overtake Germans as Biggest Spending
Tourists." Reuters, April 4, 2013. http://reut.rs/17fgjg4.

Osnos, Evan. "The Grand Tour: Europe on Fifteen Hundred Yuan a Day." *New Yorker*,
April 18, 2011. http://www.newyorker.com/reporting/2011/04/18/110418fa_fact
_osnos?currentPage=all.

"Rapporto Annuale della Fondazione Italia Cina 2013" ["Italy-China Foundation 2013 Annual Report"]. http://issuu.com/fondazione/docs/rapporto_2013_edizione _git?e=1348265/5967938.

CHAPTER 6: SHIFTING TIDES

For more about undocumented immigrants:

Yun, Gao, ed. *Concealed Chains: Labour Exploitation and Chinese Migrants in Europe.* Geneva: International Labour Office, 2010.

For more about China and Angola:

"China Pledged $20bn in Credit for Africa at Summit." *BBC News*, July 19, 2012. http://www.bbc.com/news/world-asia-china-18897451.
"Chinese Chamber of Commerce in Angola Sets Up Service Center." *Xinhua*, March 11, 2014. http://english.peopledaily.com.cn/90883/8561690.html.

CHAPTER 7: THE FARM

For more about migrants in the south of Italy:

Aloisi, Silvia. "Modern Slave Migrants Toil in Italy's Tomato Fields." Reuters, September 29, 2009. http://www.reuters.com/article/2009/09/28/us-italy-immigrants -tomatoes-idUSTRE58R1TW20090928.
Wasley, Andrew. "Scandal of the 'Tomato Slaves' Harvesting Crop Exported to UK." *The Ecologist*, September, 1, 2011. http://www.theecologist.org/News/news _analysis/1033179/scandal_of_the_tomato_slaves_harvesting_crop_exported_to _uk.html.

For more about Sikh migrants in Italy:

Gualazzini, Marco. "Parmesan Goes Indian." *Caravan Magazine*, May 1, 2012. http:// caravanmagazine.in/photo-essay/parmesan-goes-indian#sthash.u8VjX8Fq.dpuf.
Povoledo, Elisabetta. "In Italian Heartland, Indians Keep the Cheese Coming." *International Herald Tribune*, September 8, 2011. http://www.nytimes.com/2011/09/08/ world/europe/08iht-italy08.html?pagewanted=all.

For more about religion in China:

Lousia, Lim. "New Believers: A Religious Revolution in China." NPR Series, July 2010. http://www.npr.org/series/128644059/new-believers-a-religious-revolution -in-china.

CHAPTER 8: A NEW YEAR

About the largest annual human migration in the world:

Century, Adam. "Lunar New Year Ushers in Greatest Human Migration." *National Geographic*, January 31, 2014. http://on.natgeo.com/1mms3Un.

ACKNOWLEDGMENTS

I poured my heart into writing this book. But this book would not be possible without the opening of many hearts and many doors.

I want to first thank all the migrants who shared their stories with me, especially Ye Pei and her family, who invited me into their home and their lives. Pei, thank you for your honesty and trust. Your strength and resolve are an inspiration to me and many others—thank you for allowing me to be a part of your incredible journey. To my agent, Elizabeth Evans, for having faith in a first-time author with big dreams. To Susan McEachern, Carolyn Broadwell-Tkach, Flannery Scott, Alden Perkins, Kimberly Smith, and the team at Rowman & Littlefield: thank you for championing untold stories and independent thinking.

In China, I was especially grateful for the help of Marc's uncle, Sun Jianzhong, and Marc's grandmother, Guo Huixing, especially for putting up with my inability to speak Qingtianese. Thanks also to migrant Chen Junwei, Teacher Xu Mengqiu, and Michelle Sun, who gathered research materials, arranged interviews, and showed us around town.

In Europe, Marc's family was incredibly supportive, especially my in-laws, Tuful Kuo and Qiaomei Sun. Across the continent, we relied on the kindness of so many friends, family, and strangers—apologies if I've forgotten any of you. In Holland, special thanks to Jolanda Kuo, Adam Diels, and Carianne van Dorst. Big thanks to Philip Valhaelsmeerch, for enlightening us during a whirlwind day trip around Ypres, and to Leilei Ji and her husband, Xiaogang, for sharing stories with us on their day off. We were delighted to have met Zhu Renlai and Ji Jianfen.

In Spain, thanks to Haohua Sun, Dan Rodríguez García, Carles Brasó, Miguel Armillas, Jianyong Wu and Youliang Wu, Yan Zuhao, Sun Jiane, Chen Deng and Katia Wu, and Carolina Lin Chen. In Italy, I relied heavily on the connections of Chen Kecheng and Sun Qiaojie. Without them, this book would be missing many chapters. I'm also very grateful to have spent quality time with Sun Wenlong and Dino Giovannini in Bologna. Thanks also to Valter Zanin, Agnese Morganti, and Courtney Clinton, who helped a great deal with translations. To Father Giuseppe Tong, Maria Chiara, Alessandro Centanni, and all the brothers and sisters at La Piccolo Famiglia in Monte Tauro for their hospitality and for renewing my faith in the Church.

My research was funded with the help of a Pulitzer Traveling Fellowship in 2009 from the Columbia University Graduate School of Journalism. Friends, family, and a few strangers also sent generous checks and supported my Kickstarter campaign. Thanks to Melissa Chan, Yam Ki Chan and Tianne Wu, Josh Chia, Jeanie Chin, Danny Chen and the Chatham Towers' Board of Directors, Dr. Joseph Du and Jeannine Du, Linda and Jon Kanitz, Chen Shen, Eddie and Julia Hui, Guy Chen and Ana Liao, Dean and Jill Lin, Patrick and Thalia Ma, Ann Lin, Desmond Lim, Hoori Chitilian, Gina Huang, Violet and Dirk Narinx, Andrew Ho, June Lee, Jim Scott, Gene and TinhVan Lin, Kevin Fung, Insiyah Saeed, Changhoon Sung, Wendy Li, Shan Hu, Wi Jie Kuo, Gayathri Vaidyanathan, Entzu Anne Lin, Stephanie Wells, Melissa Ng, Syzmon Buhajczuk, and Nicole Breskin. Special thanks to Gerry McCaughey for his generosity. I'm also very grateful for the friendship and support of friends Merhdad Rezaei and Sanaz Vosough Ghanbari, who illustrated the beautiful maps at the beginning of this book.

To my dear proofreaders, Stephanie Wells and Jill Lin, for spending hours upon hours on my manuscript, poring over early drafts, and providing invaluable, detailed feedback. To Ann Lin, for early advice and direction; Nick Chow for reading through it all; and to my dear brother, Patrick Ma, and lovely sis-in-law Thalia, for reading, liking, supporting, and being the best siblings ever. To Leslie T. Chang and Peter Hessler for their advice and for writing great books that inspired me to be an author. To my professors at Columbia, especially Howard French, who taught me about going off the beaten path for a story worth telling. To Jan Wong, who went through the manuscript with a fine-tooth comb and helped smooth out the writing—thank you for being a wonderful mentor and a good friend, and pushing me to fight the good fight!

I am eternally grateful to my amazing parents: Mark and Anita Ma. I have been able to achieve all that I have because of your love, hard work, and sacrifice. Thank you for supporting my work and my dreams, and for giving me a huge head start in life.

Finally, thank you to my loving husband, Marc Kuo, who has been by my side for this long and storied adventure. Thank you for showing me all the wonders in life. I dedicate each and every day to glorious new possibilities with you.

ABOUT THE AUTHOR

The work of award-winning journalist **Suzanne Ma** has appeared in numerous publications including the *Wall Street Journal*, *Bloomberg Businessweek*, the Associated Press, the Huffington Post, and Salon, among others. She has crisscrossed the globe, filing stories from cities across Europe, Canada, China, and the United States, where she was a reporter in New York City for the Associated Press and DNAinfo, a digital news start-up. A graduate of Columbia University's Graduate School of Journalism, Suzanne was awarded the Pulitzer Traveling Fellowship, which helped fund her fieldwork in China for *Meet Me in Venice*. Suzanne and her husband live in Vancouver, Canada.